Third Edition

Dynamics of Strength Training and Conditioning

Gary T. Moran Ph.D., M.A., FACSM

President, Biomechanical Analysis and Research

University of San Francisco

George McGlynn Ed.D., M.A.

Professor Emeritus

University of San Francisco

Boston Burr Ridge, IL Dubuque, IA Madison, WI New York San Francisco St. Louis
Bangkok Bogotá Caracas Lisbon London Madrid
Mexico City Milan New Delhi Seoul Singapore Sydney Taipei Toronto

McGraw-Hill Higher Education

A Division of The **McGraw-Hill** Companies

DYNAMICS OF STRENGTH TRAINING AND CONDITIONING
THIRD EDITION

Published by McGraw-Hill, an imprint of The McGraw-Hill Companies, Inc., 1221 Avenue of the Americas, New York, NY 10020. Copyright © 2001, 1997, 1990 by The McGraw-Hill Companies, Inc. All rights reserved. No part of this publication may be reproduced or distributed in any form or by any means, or stored in a database or retrieval system, without the prior written consent of The McGraw-Hill Companies, Inc., including, but not limited to, in any network or other electronic storage or transmission, or broadcast for distance learning.

Some ancillaries, including electronic and print components, may not be available to customers outside the United States.

This book is printed on recycled, acid-free paper containing 10% postconsumer waste.

2 3 4 5 6 7 8 9 0 QPD/QPD 0 9 8 7 6 5 4 3 2 1 0

ISBN 0–697–29577–X

Vice president and editor-in-chief: *Kevin T. Kane*
Executive editor: *Vicki Malinee*
Senior developmental editor: *Michelle Turenne*
Senior marketing manager: *Pamela S. Cooper*
Project manager: *Jill R. Peter*
Production supervisor: *Laura Fuller*
Coordinator of freelance design: *Rick D. Noel*
Cover designer: *Joshua Van Drake*
Interior designer: *Sheilah Barrett*
Cover images: *©Corbis Images,* Volume 180 *"Woman lifting weights"*;
©PhotoDisc Inc., Volume 67 *"Close-up view of dumbbells," "Man doing sit-up," "Man lifting dumbbell," "Close-up of barbells"*
Senior photo research coordinator: *Lori Hancock*
Compositor: *Interactive Composition Corporation*
Typeface: *10/12 Garamond Light*
Printer: *Quebecor Printing Book Group/Dubuque, IA*

The credits section for this book begins on page 181 and is considered an extension of the copyright page.

Library of Congress Cataloging-in-Publication Data

Moran, Gary T., 1944–
    Dynamics of strength training and conditioning / Gary Moran, George McGlynn — 3rd ed.
        p.   cm.
    Includes bibliographical references and index.
    ISBN 0–697–29577–X
    1. Weight training.   I. McGlynn, George.   II. Title.

GV546 .M56   2001
796.41—dc21   00–036157
                                                                           CIP

www.mhhe.com

Dynamics of Strength Training and Conditioning

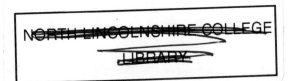

about the authors

ary Moran, Ph.D., M.A., FACSM, is the president of Biomechanical Analysis and Research, the Director of Sports Medicine with Biosports, Inc., Research Associate at Ralph K. Davies Medical Center in San Francisco, former visiting professor at the University of California, Berkeley, and a professor at the University of San Francisco. Dr. Moran has an M.A. in Exercise Physiology from San Diego State University and a Ph.D. in Anatomy and Kinesiology (Biomechanics) from the University of Oregon. Dr. Moran has done extensive research in the sports medicine field and has worked with athletes and teams at the university, post-graduate, Olympic, and professional levels. He was the Director of Research at the Nike Shoe Company and Associate Director of Biomechanics at Shriners Hospital for Crippled Children. Dr. Moran is considered an authority on physical fitness, weight training, and the biomechanics of running, cycling, and the triathlon.

Dr. George McGlynn is professor Emeritus of Exercise physiology. He was formally professor and chairperson of the Department of Exercise and Sports Science at the University of San Francisco. He received his A.B. and M.A. at Syracuse University and his doctorate at the University of California at Berkeley. He is the author of numerous articles and received the Liberal Arts' College Merit Award for outstanding teaching and research. In addition, he is the author of the highly successful text *Dynamics of Fitness.* He has served as a fitness consultant for a number of federal and state agencies and helped to plan and supervise the first cardiac rehabilitation program in the San Francisco Bay area.

To my wife, Ingeborg, and my son, George.

George McGlynn

To my sister, Deborah Denise Brown, and in memory of my grandmother, May Sheehan, for their unconditional love.

Gary Moran

brief contents

1 Introduction 1

2 Elements of Fitness 9

3 Fundamentals of Weight Training 15

4 General Programs 29

5 Motivation and Mental Conditioning 35

6 Evaluation and Self-Assessment 41

7 Muscles 55

8 Training Concepts 63

9 Advanced Training 71

10 Exercises 79

11 Women and Weight Training 107

12 Cardiorespiratory Fitness 113

13 Flexibility 123

14 Injuries 133

15 Nutrition 139

16 Drugs 147

17 Equipment 155

contents

Preface xi

1   Introduction   1

  Importance of Strength Training   1
  Misconceptions   1
  Muscle Strength, Endurance, Power,
    and Conditioning   2
  Why Do People Lift?   2
  Benefits of Strength Training   2
  Body Building   3
  Adaptation   4
  Age and Exercise   5
  Youth and Exercise   6
  Glossary   6

2   Elements of Fitness   9

  Strength (Skeletal-Muscular Strength)   9
  Endurance (Skeletal-Muscular
    Endurance)   10
  Cardiorespiratory Endurance   10
  Flexibility   10
  Body Composition   11
  Muscle Power   11
  Glossary   12

**3   Fundamentals of Weight
     Training   15**

  Principles   16
  Setting Up a Program   16
    Strength Training   16
    Muscular Endurance Training   16
    Bodybuilding   17
    Sport Training   17
    Selecting the Amount of Weight   19
    Strength-Testing Protocol for
      Repetition Maximum   20
    How Often Should You Lift?   21
    How Many Sets?   21
    Overload   21
    Progressive Resistance Exercise   22
    Specificity   22

  Application of Force   22
  Recommendations for the Aged   22
  Breathing   23
  Youth Guidelines   23
  Order of Exercises and Recovery   23
    Combination of Exercises and
      Balance   23
    Warm-Up and Cooldown   24
    Flexibility and Range of Motion   24
    Breathing   24
    Positioning   24
    Back   25
    Head   25
    Safety   25
  Equipment   26
    Belts   26
    Gloves   26
    Shoes   26
  Cheating   26
  Glossary   27

4   General Programs   29

  Sport and Fitness Conditioning
    Programs   29
  Strength Development Program   30
  Muscular Endurance Development
    Program   30
  Bodybuilding   30

**5   Motivation and Mental
     Conditioning   35**

  Why We Drop Out   35
  A Few Tips for Staying Committed   36
  Changing Behavior   36
    Setting Goals   36
    Some Important Aspects of Goal
      Setting   37
  Why Do People Lift?   37
  Mental Preparation   37
  Attention, Focus, and Concentration 38
  Visualization and Imagery   38
  Positive Self-Thoughts   39

Guidelines 39

Glossary **39**

6 Evaluation and Self-Assessment 41

Muscle Strength Test 41

Muscular Endurance 41

Precaution Regarding the One RM
  Maximum Strength Test 42

Strength Evaluation 45

Push-Ups 45

Head-and-Shoulder Raise 46

Modified Sit-and-Reach Test 47

Determine Your Cardiorespiratory
  Endurance Level 48

1.5 Mile Run 48

Walking Test 48

Test for Body Composition 51

Body Mass Index 54

Glossary **54**

7 Muscles 55

Structure of Skeletal Muscle 55

Agonist and Antagonist 58

Tendons 59

Ligaments 59

Atrophy 59

Slow–and Fast–Twitch Muscle Fibers 59

Hypertrophy 59

Hyperplasia 60

Muscle Soreness 60

Glossary **61**

8 Training Concepts 63

Strength, Power, and Speed 63

Strength 64

Neuromuscular Facilitation 64

Force Potential 64

Nerve Impulses and Strength 64

Muscle Cross Section 65

Muscle Length 65

Weight-Resistance Methods 65

Muscle Contraction 65

Isotonic Exercise 65

Eccentric Loading 65

Isometric Exercise 65

Isokinetic Exercise 66

Advantages and Disadvantages of
  Weight-Resistance Programs 66

Isotonic Exercise 67

Eccentric Exercise 67

Isometric Exercise 67

Isokinetic Exercise 67

Glossary **68**

9 Advanced Training 71

Pyramid System 71

Single Set Systems 72

Multi-Poundage System 72

Super Pump System 72

Super Sets 72

Burnouts 72

Partial Repetitions 72

Forced Repetition 72

Negative Work 73

Split-Routine 73

Power and Speed Exercises 73

Plyometrics 73

Definitions of Plyometric Exercises 74

Periodization 75

Strength and Power 76

Glossary **77**

10 Exercises 79

Chest, Upper Back, and Shoulder Exercises 79

Arm Exercises 88

Lower Back and Abdominal Exercises 92

Lower Body Exercises 96

11 Women and Weight Training 107

Physiology 107

Physical Differences 108

Percentage of Body Fat 108

Menstruation 109

Exercise Guidelines for Pregnancy 109

Exercise After Childbirth 109

Osteoporosis 110

Female Athlete Triad 110

Eating Disorders' Warning Signs 110

Glossary **111**

12 Cardiorespiratory Fitness 113

Maximum Oxygen Uptake 113

Cardiorespiratory Endurance 114

Aerobic-Anaerobic 114

Energy Systems 115

Intensity 115

Training Effect 115

Duration 117

Frequency 117

Cooling Down 118

Circuit Training 119

Pre-Exercise Screening 119

Exercise Prescription 120

Exercise Precautions 121

Glossary **121**

13 Flexibility **123**

Flexibility 123

Static Stretching 124

Ballistic Stretching 124

Proprioceptive Neuromuscular
Facilitation (PNF) 124

Stretching and Warm-Up Principles 124

Glossary **131**

14 Injuries **133**

Common Injuries 134

Tendinitis 134

Runner's Knee 134

Strains and Sprains 134

Bursitis 135

Dislocation and Fractures 135

Healing 136

Rest 136

Compression 136

Elevation 136

Other Remedies 136

Glossary **137**

15 Nutrition **139**

Nutritional Concepts 139

Nutritional Requirements 139

Carbohydrates 139

Proteins 140

Fats 140

Vitamins 140

Minerals 140

Water 140

Energy for Muscle
Contraction 141

Diets 141

Diet Rating 141

Fraudulent Claims 142

"Super-Protein" Diets 142

Vitamin and Mineral Supplemented Diets 142

Fad Diets 144

Basic Nutritional Recommendations 144

How to Gain Weight 144

How to Lose Weight 144

Glossary **145**

16 Drugs **147**

Anabolic Steroids 147

The American College of Sports
Medicine Position Statement on
Anabolic-Androgenic Steroids in
Sports 148

Amphetamines 149

Caffeine 149

Growth Hormones 149

Cocaine 150

Erythropoietin 150

Steroid Replacers 150

Substances Currently Banned by the
International Olympic Committee 150

Supplements 150

Androstenedione 151

DHEA 151

Creatine 151

Beta-Adrenergic Agonist 152

HMB 152

Chromium and Vanadium 152

Carnitine 152

Glossary **152**

17 Equipment **155**

Equipment 155

Resistance Machines 155

Free Weights 156

Strength and Muscle Endurance
Equipment 156

Isokinetic Machines 156

Universal Machine 157

Nautilus 157

CAM II 157

Hydra Fitness 157

Polaris 157

Power Exercise Equipment 157

Appendix A Weight Training Activities for
   Various Sports 160
Appendix B Weight Training Standards for
   College-Age Males 161
Appendix C Universal Super Circuit 169
Appendix D Aerobic Running Program 171
Appendix E Sample of a Racquet Sport
   Mesocycle 173
Appendix F Major Vitamins and
   Minerals 174

Appendix G Detailed Training Cycle for One
   Year (Volleyball) 176
Appendix H Web Sites 179
Appendix I ACSM Position Statement 180

Credits 181
Index 182

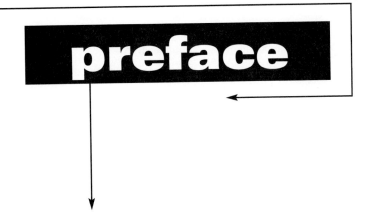

preface

Since the completion of the second edition, there have been a number of advances and refinements in the area of muscle strength and endurance. As with the second edition, the purpose of the third edition is to give clarity to this new information by providing a simple, logical, and individualized approach to strength and endurance training. Further, our intent is to enable the reader to distinguish between what is valid and safe from what is false and potentially dangerous. The book also is intended to be a practical guide for understanding the physiological basis for muscle strength and endurance and the most efficient and effective strength-training techniques. The information presented here represents a consensus of presently available scientific evidence.

The text is intended primarily for college classes in physical fitness, conditioning, strength and weight training, circuit training, and bodybuilding as well as for the average person who wishes to increase her or his strength and endurance. The information presented reflects the latest research while helping readers to avoid useless products and dangerous practices.

Approach and Features

The goal of this book is to bridge the gap between scientific knowledge and the application of that knowledge and also to provide you with the most efficient and up-to-date methods of strength training to insure that your body's adaptations from the training are beneficial and safe. The book also answers basic questions about how to select and prepare for physical training and how this training affects you physically over both short and long periods of exercise.

• *An individualized approach.* A sequence of simple tests enables you to evaluate not only your present muscle strength and endurance, but also your cardiorespiratory endurance, body density, and flexibility. The first part of the book describes the benefits of strength training, basic fundamentals and exercises, motivational and mental concentration techniques, and muscle training procedures.

• *Currentness.* Other important areas covered are cardiorespiratory endurance; strength training for women, the aged, and the young; injuries; nutrition; drugs; flexibility; and an analysis of various strength-training equipment.

New to this Edition

The third edition has been updated to integrate the latest guidelines from the American Heart Association (AHA), the American College of Sports Medicine (ACSM), and the American Academy of Pediatrics (AAP) to provide readers with the most current information available.

• Chapter 1, *Introduction,* now includes new coverage of the distinctions between acute and chronic adaptations to strength training, and introduces the SAID principle. Additionally, the section on *Age and Exercise* has been expanded to include the effects of strength training on adolescents, as well as the benefits to older adults.

• Chapter 3, *Fundamentals of Weight Training,* contains new information on strength-testing protocol for repetition maximum, ACSM weight training recommendations for the aged, and recommendations for proper breathing during weight lifting.

- Chapter 6, *Evaluation and Self-Assessment,* includes a new section on strength evaluation which addresses the reasons for monitoring strength.
- Chapter 9, *Advanced Training,* includes new coverage of power and speed exercises. The plyometrics section now includes an explanation of the term "stretch-shortening cycle."
- Chapter 10, *Exercises,* has been organized by body regions (i.e., chest, upper back, and shoulder exercises; arm exercises; lower back and abdominal exercises; and lower body exercises), and now includes new anatomical illustrations to show the muscles affected.
- Chapter 11, *Women and Weight Training,* now includes a new section of the Female Athlete Triad, including warning signs of eating disorders. Also, the discussion of the physiological differences between women and men as they relate to weight training has been expanded.
- Chapter 14, *Injuries,* now includes runner's knee and suggestions on how to prevent it.
- Chapter 16, *Drugs,* contains a new list of supplements banned by the International Olympic Committee. New coverage of dietary supplements, androstenedione, DHEA, creatine phosphate, and HMB have been added to this chapter. Their side and after effects are also discussed.
- Chapter 17, *Equipment,* expands its coverage of resistance machines, including free weights and isokinetic machines.
- New Appendix H provides web site addresses for selected chapters as a resource for further information.
- New Appendix I provides the ACSM position statement for cardiorespiratory and muscular fitness, and flexibility in healthy adults.
- A new detachable Weight Training Record Card for personal recordkeeping is located inside the back cover of the text.
- Critical Thinking exercises provide brief scenarios of actual situations in selected chapters that challenge the reader to apply the content studied to resolve the problem identified. Possible resolutions are provided at the end of those chapters.
- New Review Questions conclude selected chapters and help to reinforce the content learned.

Pedagogy

Each chapter begins with chapter objectives. Critical thinking exercises and resolutions, glossaries, and references are presented in selected chapters to reinforce content and provide additional resources.

Acknowledgements

We would like to express our gratitude to the following reviewers for the input they provided in the development of this third edition:

Carrie Bradley
Tusculum College (TN)

John Cissik
Texas A & M University

Justin Garner
Idaho State University

Mary Meier
Iowa State University

Alan E. Mikesky
Indiana University

David D. Pascoe
Auburn University

Stafford Rorke
Oakland University (MI)

Ryan Taylor
Idaho State University

chapter 1

introduction

Objectives

After studying this chapter you should be able to

1. Describe some of the misconceptions concerning strength training.
2. Describe the physiological benefits of strength training.
3. Describe the psychological benefits of strength training.
4. Describe the body's adaptation to strength training.
5. Describe the benefits of strength training for the aged.
6. Describe growth changes during youth.
7. Define body building.
8. Define muscle endurance.
9. Define muscle power.
10. Define muscle strength.
11. Define conditioning.
12. Define weight lifting.
13. Define power lifting.
14. Define weight training.
15. Define the SAID principle.

IMPORTANCE OF STRENGTH TRAINING

Little doubt remains today as to the importance of muscular strength and endurance in competitive sports and in the demands of everyday physical activities. Whether you are an athlete looking for increased performance, a sedentary individual dissatisfied with your present lifestyle, or just someone in search of a healthful and satisfying exercise experience, strength training can play a major part in meeting your needs. All that you need is a willingness and determination to take on a new and exciting challenge.

MISCONCEPTIONS

Muscle strength training for many years had been associated with physical fitness. The individual who spent hours in the gym lifting weights had always been considered the model of fitness. We know today, however, that strength training, though essential, is only one aspect of total body fitness. In the past many competitive athletes generally avoided strength training because they thought such training exercises were detrimental to the development and maintenance of certain sports skills. Fears that strength training would bring muscle-boundness, loss of flexibility, and reduced coordination were generally accepted. Current research, however, tells us these concepts are erroneous. Strength training is essential for competitive athletes and also plays a role in determining one's physical fitness level. It is not unusual to see weight lifters engaged in long-distance running and competitive long-distance runners spending more time in weight training. In addition, we now know that resistance training not only leads to increased strength and power but also increases flexibility. The latter benefit puts to rest outdated fears of muscle-boundness.

MUSCLE STRENGTH, ENDURANCE, POWER, AND CONDITIONING

The terms strength, muscle endurance, and power are sometimes used interchangeably. However, each of these terms has its own definition. Muscle strength is the amount of force that can be exerted by a muscle group for one movement or repetition. Muscle endurance is the ability of the muscle group to maintain a continuous contraction or repetition over a period of time. Power is simply the product of strength and speed and the ability of the muscle to produce high levels of force in a short period of time. Conditioning is the development of high levels of skeletal muscle strength and endurance, and a high level of cardiorespiratory endurance. This enables one to perform at a high work level for prolonged periods. The muscle system is the foundation of all physical exercise. No matter what activity you participate in, your muscle strength, endurance, and power determine your exercise limits.

In addition, there are other terms that are commonly misused; therefore it seems appropriate to define them before any further discussion.

Weight Lifting is a competitive sport where an individual is judged on the amount of weight that can be lifted relative to weight classification. The clean and jerk and snatch are the two standardized Olympic events in this competition.

Power Lifting is a competitive sport where the goal is to lift the greatest amount of weight from three exercises (bench press, squat, and dead lift).

Weight Training is an exercise program where free or stationary weights are used for the purposes of increasing strength, endurance, flexibility, skill, and power.

Bodybuilding is an exercise program utilizing free or stationary weights to change body shape and form.

WHY DO PEOPLE LIFT?

The reasons people lift weights are as varied and numerous as the people who lift. The weight room may be the most democratic of settings in all of sports and society. People of both sexes, and all ethnic, socioeconomic, and age groups lift weights. The reasons may be to improve sport performance, improve physical appearance, improve fitness level, enjoyment of the physical activity, or a combination of the preceding.

BENEFITS OF STRENGTH TRAINING

Properly designed resistance programs' benefits are many and have practical implications for many populations. The ability of the human body to generate force is also highly related to performance in most sports and a variety of everyday physically demanding activities.

The main attributes developed by strength training are muscular strength and endurance, power, flexibility, and body composition. Certain weight training programs can also lead to development in cardiorespiratory endurance. These basic elements of fitness are discussed in detail in chapter 3.

Strength is essential to a variety of everyday physical activities. Even though strength is a relative factor related to the demands of the activity, all individuals need a minimum level of strength. Those with low levels of strength run a greater risk of injury in lifting or while engaging in other physical activity. Performance in recreational sports and athletics is enhanced by high levels of strength. Strong abdominal muscles provide important protection against lower back problems. Strength training is also an essential part of physical rehabilitation. Common sports injuries such as tennis elbow, rotator cuff, ligament and tendon strains respond well to muscle strength programs. Better posture accompanied by more aesthetic appearance are also benefits from strength training.

> **Critical Thinking 1-1**
>
> A student baseball player has decided not to participate in a strength-training program. He has heard that strength training will have a detrimental effect on his skill and coordination.
>
> What could you tell him that will allay his fears?

BODY BUILDING

Many individuals lift weights to improve body shape and form and have little interest in athletic performance. Muscle size and definition take priority over strength and endurance gains. Body building refers to the body's morphology or form and structure that depend mainly on inherited or genetic factors. While your body type or build can be altered only slightly, substantial changes can take place in body composition by decreasing body fat and adding muscle mass. When you exercise you burn more calories than when you are sedentary; therefore you start to lose weight, provided your food intake remains the same. A strength and endurance program results in an increase of muscle tissue with a decrease in stored fat. Your body dimensions will change, resulting in a slimmer waist, trimmer hips and thighs, and improved overall appearance.

Table 1.1 lists in more detail the benefits that you may experience as a result of weight training.

Table 1.1

Benefits of Weight Training
Increase in
Muscle strength
Muscle endurance
Strength of bones and ligaments
Thickness of cartilage
Capillary density in the muscle
Muscle mass (hypertrophy)
Longer duration of effort before exhaustion—stamina
Increased flexibility
Speed and power
Blood volume and hemoglobin
Muscle enzyme levels
Skill
Maximal work capacity
Equalization of muscle development
Decrease in
Body fat
Stress and tension
Resting heart rate
Additional benefits may
Help prevent injuries
Help rehabilitate injuries
Improve function of cardiorespiratory system
Alter metabolism to improve caloric utilization
Facilitate quicker recovery from workouts or competitions
Increase self-image and confidence
Improve appearance
Increase feeling of well-being
Naturally induce fatigue and relaxation

ADAPTATION

The human body has an amazing capacity to adjust to and benefit from the many physical demands placed upon it. For example, the body is capable of adapting to many kinds of stress and even increasing its efficiency as a result of stressful stimuli. In the case of fitness training, research indicates that repeated physical stress (intensive training) will lead to increases in our functional capacity (strength and endurance). The main purpose in strength training therefore is to stress the body through a variety of exercises so that beneficial adaptations will occur. Strength training is only beneficial as long as it causes the body to adapt to the physical efforts. If the stress is limited, adaptation will not occur. If there is too much stress, then injury and deterioration will result. An important point to remember is that your physical fitness is largely a reflection of the level of your training. When you work hard, your fitness will be high. However, when you interrupt the intensity of the training, your fitness will decline. Further, individuals with low levels of strength and endurance can look forward to substantial gains in muscular strength and endurance after only a few months of rigorous exercise.

Resistance training programs are highly specific to the types of adaptations that occur. The activities of specific patterns of motor units in training will determine what tissue and what physiological systems will be affected. Resistance training therefore should be specific to one's goals.

Both acute and chronic physiological changes occur with resistance training. Acute changes are immediate responses such as increases in heart rate and breathing. Chronic changes respond to training over a period of time. Examples are enlargement of muscles (hypertrophy) and gradual increases in the number and size of myofibrils. Increases in the size of ligaments, tendons, and bones occur, as skeletal muscles become stronger. These tissues adapt in order to support increased forces. Changes in neural activation resulting from different resistance systems can produce varied types of adaptation such as increases in strength with little change in muscle size. Adaptation may also result in reduced inhibition of the central nervous system, which may be responsible for greater recruitment of muscle fibers. Cardiovascular adaptations result in cardiac wall thickness and lower blood pressure.

Resistance training has positive effects on bone, muscle and associated connective tissue. The entire muscle and skeletal systems undergo a coordinated adaptation to strength exercises. The changes in force-generating capabilities of the muscle also result in a coordinated and proportional increase in the load bearing capacity of bone and other connective tissue. The changes that occur in the property of muscle fibers are specific to the metabolic and force requirements of the resistance-training program.

It is important to remember that each person will respond differently to a strength-training program. The amount of change will depend on the muscle capacity to adapt to the training regimen. Important here is the SAID principle (specific adaptation to imposed demand). Because the type of demand placed on the body will determine the type of adaptation that will occur, the training program should be specific to the individual's ultimate goals. For example, training for peak athletic performance requires higher levels of intensity and volume than training for general health and fitness. Also training for high-speed events requires a training program that activates as many motor units as possible in the shortest period of time.

The unique thing about your strength-training program is that you are completely in charge. You make all the decisions, set your own goals, and decide when and how to exercise. Your goals in strength training are very clear and measurable, with few ambiguities confronting you. Further, you are in a no-lose situation; failure is impossible. There are no records to break, no complex skills to learn; success is there for the asking. There is an immediate payoff; you will be visibly improved by your physical activity. Improved muscle efficiency will produce feelings of increased energy, health, and overall well-being. The benefits of training will be especially noticeable if you are in a poor level of physical condition when you begin your program.

AGE AND EXERCISE

Exercise for older persons is a comparatively recent phenomenon brought about by a change in social mores and a new perception of the role of exercise in life. Exercise programs for older persons should consist of flexibility exercises, weight training, calisthenics, and continuous fast walking or jogging. Sudden rigorous bursts of exhaustive exercise such as sprinting or lifting very heavy weights should be avoided. Older people should concentrate mainly on endurance activities that are moderate and rhythmic in nature such as jogging, walking, swimming, bicycling, and light weight lifting.

Maximum strength of men and women is generally achieved between the ages of twenty and thirty-five, and significantly high strength levels can be maintained well into advanced age. Normally a progressive decline of muscle strength takes place with age due to a reduced muscle mass brought about primarily by inactivity. Physical training, however, can significantly modify the strength decrement with aging. Older persons can expect improvements when they begin to train in later life no less than younger counterparts.

Resistance training appears to be a safe and potentially beneficial form of exercise for the great majority of the adult population, even including patients with heart disease and neuromuscular disorders. There is still a need, however, for more information on the clinical population. Aging is a very complex process, which involves a number of interacting variables. However, regular physical activity may cut across all of these variables and contribute to the physical and psychological well-being that defines healthy aging.

Strength training is important to older adults for a variety of reasons. Loss of muscle mass begins at age 30 and is accompanied by decreased muscle density and increased intramuscular fat. Muscle atrophy may result from loss of muscle fibers and is directly proportional to age-related decreases in strength. From age 65 to 84 the average decline in strength is approximately 1.5 percent per year. In addition, one in three adults over age 65 falls at least once a year. Of those aged individuals who suffer hip fractures, 50 percent will die within a year and a half. Resistance training may minimize or reverse the syndrome of physical frailty, which is prevalent among the most elderly and puts them at a greater risk for falls.

Bone mass also decreases with age. Bone mass and density is regulated by loading. Loading conditions can lead to hypertrophic response in bone resorption. Strength training also enhances and preserves the durability, solidity, and wear resistance of joint tissue.

The age-related decline in bone density could be significantly impacted by strength training. In addition, resistance training will result in increased energy requirements, which can cause a decrease in the fat mass in the maintenance of lean body mass. High intensity strength training may also be safe in selected patients with well-controlled rheumatoid arthritis. Resistance training has also been found to lower systolic pressure in men and diastolic in women.

Old age causes a decline in most aspects of physical performance, including muscle strength. Resistance training can be initiated at any age and can result in improvement over pre-training levels. Strength training can prevent or reverse muscle loss along with increases in muscle strength, power and endurance, making one more mobile, active, and energetic than before. Obviously previous skill and physical activity in addition to posture, body size, and individual biomechanical differences will affect capabilities.

🎯 Critical Thinking 1-2

A senior individual said that he was afraid of engaging in strength training because it would put him at risk for high blood pressure.

How could you convince him that he should not be concerned?

The National Institute of Aging studying 6,000 adults over a twenty-five-year period found those with the lowest third of strength were nearly three times as likely to develop difficulties in walking and more than twice as likely to become disabled as those in the higher third. If a middle-aged individual cannot hold a standard twelve quart bucket full of water with her or his arm down at her or his side for at least three minutes, the National Institute on Aging recommends strength training for that individual.

YOUTH AND EXERCISE

Adolescents begin pubertal growth at varying ages. The onset of puberty can vary between ages 8 to 13 in girls and ages 9 to 15 in boys. After the onset of puberty a period of growth for boys and girls extends from one to four and one-half years. Once puberty begins, changes in body composition occur. The bigger, early-maturing children will have an advantage in absolute strength over late-maturing children because of the greater amount of muscle tissue. In boys, maximum strength occurs about nine months to a year after the peak velocity of growth in height and weight, with body weight the best indication. During adolescence, growth spurts increase first in mass and then in the ability to express strength. In girls, maximum strength occurs after a peak velocity of growth in height. The gains in height and body weight in both boys and girls are related to gains in strength and power performance. Therefore strength-training programs must be adjusted to individual differences, especially physiological age, which will determine the functional capabilities and performance and should be considered in developing resistance programs.

The American Academy of Pediatrics has recognized that a properly supervised and prescribed program may increase muscle strength and local muscle endurance, decrease injuries in sports and recreational activities, and improve performance capacity in sports and recreational activities.

Finally, if you follow the individualized exercises and guidelines presented in this book, you will be following procedures based upon sound scientific principles, which will benefit your health, and also be a source of continued satisfaction and enjoyment to you.

Glossary

Bodybuilding   Exercise program that utilizes free and stationary weights to change body shape and form.
Conditioning   The development of high levels of muscular strength and endurance and high levels of cardiorespiratory endurance.
Muscle Endurance   The ability of a muscle group to maintain a continuous contraction or repetition over a period of time.
Muscle Power   The product of strength and speed (force and velocity).
Muscle Strength   The amount of force that can be exerted by a muscle group for one movement or repetition.
Power Lifting   A competitive event where the goal is to lift the greatest amount of weight for three different exercises (bench press, dead lift, and squat). Explosive power is important in this event.
Weight Lifting   A competitive event where the goal is to lift the greatest amount of weight for two exercises (clean/press and snatch). Skill, speed, and strength are important.
Weight Training   Exercise program using free or stationary weights for the purpose of increasing strength, endurance, power, skill, and flexibility.

Solutions to Critical Thinking

1-1. There is substantial research that strength training is not detrimental to a learned skill if exercises are performed properly. In addition, resistance training will increase the student baseball player's speed and power, which will increase his hitting and throwing performance.

1-2. You would first acquaint this older individual with the ACSM Guidelines for the Aged. In addition, indicate to him that properly prescribed resistance training will not dangerously elevate his blood pressure, but in fact may significantly reduce it.

Review Questions

1. What are the physical benefits of strength training for the aged?
2. Discuss the American Academy of Pediatrics' position concerning strength training for children.
3. Discuss the physiological adaptations of skeletal muscle to resistance training.

References

Beunen, G., and R. M. Malina. Growth and physical performance related to the timing of adolescent growth spurt. In: K. B. Pandolf, ed. *Exercise and sports sciences reviews.* Vol. 16, pages 503–540. Macmillan, New York, 1988.

Braith, R. W., J. E. Graves, and M. L. Pollock. 1989. Comparison of two versus three days per week of variable resistance training during 10 and 18 week programs. *International Journal of Sports Medicine* 10:450–459.

Carter, D. R., D. P. Fyhrie, and R. T. Whalen. 1987. Trabecular bone density and loading history. Regulation of connective tissue biology by mechanical injury. *Journal of Biomechanics* 20:785–94.

Clarke, D. H. Adaptations in strength and muscular endurance resulting from exercise. In J. H. Wilmore, ed. *Exercise and sports sciences reviews.* Vol. 1. Academic Press, New York, 1973.

Evans, William J. 1999. Exercise training guidelines for the elderly, *Medicine and Science In Sports and Exercise* 31-1:12–17.

Feigenbaum, Matthew S., and Michael L. Pollock. 1999. Prescription of resistance training for health and disease. *Medicine and Science in Sports and Exercise* 31-1:38–45.

Fiatarone, M. A., E. C. Marks, N. D. Ryan, C. N. Meridith, L. A. Lipsits, and W. J. Ebans. 1990. High intensity strength training in nonagenarians, effects on skeletal muscle. *Journal of the American Medical Association* 263:3029–34.

Frontera, W. R., C. N. Meridith, K. P. O'Reilly, H. G. Knutgen, and W. J. Ebans. 1988. Strength conditioning in older men, skeletal muscle hypertrophy and improved function. *Journal of Applied Physiology* 64:1038–44.

Graves, J. E., M. L. Pollock, S. H. Leggett, R. W. Braith, D. M. Carpenter, and L. E. Bishop. 1988. Effects of reduced frequency on muscular strength. *International Journal Sports Medicine* 9:316–19.

Hagberg, J. M. 1985. A hemodynamic comparison of young and old endurance athletes during exercise. *Journal of Applied Physiology* 58:2041–2046.

Hakkinen, K. 1988. Neuromuscular and hormonal adaptations in athletes to strength training in two years. *Journal of Applied Physiology* 65:2406. Tesch, P. A. 1988. Skeletal muscle adaptations consequent to long-term heavy resistance exercise. *Medicine and Science in Sports and Exercise* 20:S132.

Heath, G. W., J. M. Hagberg, A. A. Ehsani, and J. O. Holloszy. 1981. A physiological comparison of young and older endurance athletes. *Journal of Applied Physiology* 51:634–640.

Kraemer, W. J., and S. J. Flack. *Strength training for young athletes.* Human Kinetics, Champaign, IL, 1993.

Larsson, L. 1982. Physical training effects on muscle morphology in sedentary males at different ages. *Medicine and Science in Sports and Exercise* 14:203–206.

McCarthy, N. A., L. Hicks, J. Martin, and C. E. Webber. 1995. Long-term resistance training in the elderly: Effects on dynamic strength, exercise capacity, muscle, and bone. *Journal Gerontology: Biological Science* 50:B97–104.

Meredith, C. N., M. J. Zackin, W. R. Frontera, and W. J. Evans. 1987. Body composition and aerobic capacity in young and middle-aged endurance-trained men. *Medicine and Science in Sports and Exercise* 19:557–563.

Paffenbarger, P. S., R. T. Hyde, and A. L. Wing. 1986. Physical activity, all-cause mortality, and longevity of college alumni. *New England Journal of Medicine* 314:605–613.

Sale, D. G. 1988. Neural adaptation to resistance training. *Medicine and Science in Sports and Exercise* 20:135.

Shephard, R. J. Nutrition and the physiology of aging. In: E. A. Young, ed. *Nutrition, aging, and health*. Alan R. Liss, New York, 1986.

Snow-Harter, C., and R. Marcus. Exercise, bone mineral density, and osteoporosis. In: J. O. Holloszy, ed. *Exercise and sports sciences reviews*. Vol. 19. Williams & Wilkins, Baltimore, MD, 1991.

Stamford, B. A. 1988. Exercise and the elderly. *Exercise and Sports Sciences Reviews* 16:341–379.

Willoughby, D. S. 1993. The effects of mesocycle-length weight training programs involving equated volumes on upper and lower body strength. *Journal of Strength and Conditioning Research* 7:2–8.

chapter 2

elements of fitness

Objectives

After studying this chapter you should be able to

1. Describe the importance of strength training.
2. Describe the basic elements of physical fitness.
3. Define muscle strength.
4. Define muscle endurance.
5. Define cardiorespiratory endurance.
6. Define flexibility.
7. Define body composition.

Our misconceptions about fitness are legend. Many people still find it surprising that professional athletes such as baseball players or golfers may have poor cardiorespiratory fitness. Others feel that vibrating and whirlpooling their muscles in a health club will insure fitness, or that by taking a short walk once a week, fitness will automatically be conferred upon them. Misconceptions stem partly from two different concepts of fitness: performance-related fitness and health-related fitness. Performance-related fitness refers to many of the tests you may have taken that measure your level of strength, skill, power, endurance, and agility in specific sports. These performance-related tests measure only limited aspects of fitness. Health-related fitness concerns those aspects of our physiological and psychological functioning that afford us some protection against coronary heart disease, problems associated with being overweight, various muscular and skeletal disorders, and the physiological complications of our response to stress. The President's Council on Physical Fitness and Sports defines health-related fitness as the ability to carry out daily tasks with vigor, without undue fatigue, and with ample energy to enjoy leisure-time pursuits and to meet unforeseen injuries. This definition means fitness is a relative term relating to your everyday activities. Some of us need higher levels of fitness than others (physical laborer or competitive athlete). However, all individuals must meet a minimum level of fitness to lead a healthy and productive life.

There are five major elements to physical fitness, and the training program you choose should be geared toward the development of these elements. They are muscular strength, muscular endurance, cardiorespiratory endurance, flexibility, and body composition.

STRENGTH (SKELETAL-MUSCULAR STRENGTH)

🎯 Critical Thinking 2-1

A long-distance runner is concerned that engaging in a strength-training program will negatively affect her aerobic capacity.

What advice would you give her?

Strength is the ability of a muscle to produce a maximum amount of force. It is measured by the ability to perform one repetition of an exercise at maximum resistance (1 RM). An example of maximum strength would be the greatest amount of weight one can lift in the bench press exercise.

Strength is of major significance in many sports and sport skills. Strength is a significant factor in one's ability to put the shot, throw the javelin, have a high velocity tennis serve, throw a fastball in baseball and softball, and many other sport skills. Strength is also important in sport skills that require a large amount of force to be applied to an opponent, such as wrestling and football.

ENDURANCE (SKELETAL-MUSCULAR ENDURANCE)

Endurance is the ability of a muscle to produce force continually over a period of time. It is measured by the number of repetitions of the movement or skill. If a person can perform thirty-five push-ups, then push-ups are for him or her an endurance skill. If, however, a person can do only one push-up, then for him or her the push-up is a strength skill. The key here is that endurance is the ability to apply force repeatedly or for a prolonged amount of time. Examples of sports requiring endurance are rowing, wrestling, hurdling, sprinting, sprint swimming, and sprint bicycling.

An athlete can continue to produce muscular force for only a short period of time before the energy stored in the muscle is depleted. In movements that require maximum force (strength), this occurs very quickly (one or two repetitions). If less force is required (less than maximal), then the movement can continue for a longer period (endurance).

If the amount of force required of a particular muscle or muscle group is low and the movement is cyclic, allowing a brief rest period (during which another muscle group is producing the movement), then the blood stream can bring nutrients to the muscle cells, and the movement can be prolonged for long periods. Examples of such movement are distance running, swimming, and bicycling. The ability to supply the necessary nutrients to the muscle cells in this fashion is a function of cardiorespiratory endurance.

CARDIORESPIRATORY ENDURANCE

Cardiorespiratory endurance refers to the ability of the respiratory system (lungs and associated blood vessels) and the circulatory system (heart, arteries, capillaries, and veins) to supply oxygen and nutrients to the muscle cells so that muscular activity can be continued for prolonged periods of time.

Endurance events such as distance running, cross-country skiing, bicycling, swimming, crew, and triathlons are excellent activities for improving cardiorespiratory endurance.

The importance of cardiorespiratory endurance, aside from its role in sport success, is that it can significantly improve your cardiac risk profile.

Aerobic exercises such as running and bicycling are recognized by sport medicine specialists as important in the prevention of heart disease. Heart disease is the number one cause of death in this country, and we should all take steps to improve our risk profile. You should strongly consider including some type of cardiorespiratory endurance exercise in your program. See chapter 12 for more details.

While some sport skills rely more heavily on one aspect of fitness, most athletes need some measure of each of the three components of fitness mentioned (strength, endurance, and cardiorespiratory endurance) as well as flexibility.

FLEXIBILITY

Along with strength and endurance, flexibility is an important component of muscular performance. There are two kinds of flexibility, static and dynamic. Dynamic flexibility is defined as the opposition or resistance of a joint to motion. In other words, it is concerned with the forces that oppose movement over any range rather than the range itself. This type of flexibility is difficult to measure and has received little attention in exercise programs and competitive sports.

THE FAR SIDE   By GARY LARSON

The Vikings, of course, knew the importance of stretching before an attack.

Static flexibility is defined as the range of motion that can occur at a joint. As a general rule you need enough flexibility to be able to go through the range of motion required for your sport or exercise without any restriction in the movement.

Stretching exercises can increase the range of motion of the joint. Weight lifting, if performed through the full range of motion, can also enhance flexibility. Flexibility exercises are often performed as part of a general warm-up prior to weight lifting. A general warm-up that includes flexibility exercises is recommended, particularly if you are stiff or sore from a previous workout or if the temperature is cold. A stretching program for weight lifting is included in chapter 13.

BODY COMPOSITION

Body composition refers to the proportion of body fat and lean body tissue to total body weight. The relative balance of these components is a better gauge of your fitness level than ordinary body weight. A recommended proportion of body fat for a man in his early twenties is approximately 12 to 17 percent. For a woman in the same age group, about 19 to 24 percent is recommended. Obesity is one of the most serious health problems confronting Americans today. Approximately 30 percent of all men and 40 percent of all women weigh 15 to 20 percent more than they should. Not only will obesity have a negative effect on physical performance, it also has important health ramifications. Being overweight is one of the major risk factors in heart disease. In addition, diabetes and high blood pressure generally accompany obesity. Physical exercise may reduce obesity and directly affect these two common problems. Obesity is also associated with gallbladder dysfunction, joint disease, and complications during surgery.

MUSCLE POWER

🌀 Critical Thinking 2-2

A sedentary individual wants to be begin a resistance-training program to build upper body strength. However, he is not sure how much resistance he should begin with using free weights.

Explain to him the proper procedures for individuals beginning a resistance program.

Power, which was discussed in chapter 1, is the ability of the muscles to produce high levels of force in a short time (explosive strength). Power can be increased by strength training and is basic to a number of daily activities and competitive sports. There is also a need for coordination and agility, especially if the need for the execution of power is in a particular sports skill such as rebounding in basketball or a lateral movement by a football lineman.

At this point you should think about the requirements of your sport or specific needs and also your strengths and weaknesses in that sport. Most people tend to work on their strengths, as this is easier and more self-satisfying. Working harder on your weaknesses, however, usually produces greater overall improvements.

Chapter 6 contains information to help you determine in which areas you are strong and in which areas of fitness you may require more attention.

Glossary

Aerobic (with Oxygen)   Refers to an activity in which demands of the muscles for oxygen are met by the circulation of oxygen in the blood.

Anaerobic   The process of energy production in which the oxygen supply cannot keep pace with tissue demands.

Body Composition   The proportion of body fat to lean body tissue.

Cardiorespiratory Endurance   The ability of the heart to deliver oxygen and nutrients to vital organs of the body.

Flexibility   The extent and range of motion around a joint.

Muscle Endurance   The ability of a muscle to produce force continually over a period of time.

Muscle Power   The ability of the muscle to produce high levels of force in a short time (strength and speed).

Strength   The ability of a muscle to produce a maximum amount of force.

Solutions to Critical Thinking

2-1. A proper prescription of resistance training included in her overall program will not affect her aerobic capacity as long as she maintains her regular aerobic schedule. In addition, resistance training will aid in increasing the strength and endurance of her running muscles and reduce the risk of injury.

2-2. He should begin his program with weights that he can successfully lift ten to twelve times without fatiguing. He should only complete one set of exercises for each muscle group. If he wants to increase strength he will have to use heavier weights. Weights that he can only successfully lift four to six times. However, he should not attempt this load until after eight to ten weeks when he has successfully developed skill in lifting.

Review Questions

1. What is the definition of muscle power?
2. Why is aerobic exercise a vital aspect of a sound physical fitness program?
3. What is the recommended percentage of body fat for men and women in their twenties?

References

Abernethy, P., J. Jurimae, P. Logan, A. Taylor, and R. Thayer. 1994. Acute and chronic response of skeletal muscle to resistance exercise. *Sports Medicine* 22–28.

Allsen, Phillip E., Joyce M. Harrison, and Barbara Vance. *Fitness for life*. 6th ed. McGraw-Hill, Dubuque, IA, 1997.

Anspaugh, D. J., M. H. Hamrick, and F. D. Rosato. *Wellness: Concepts and applications*. 4th ed. McGraw-Hill, Dubuque, IA, 2000.

Arnheim, D. D., and W. E. Prentice. *Principles of athletic training*. 10th ed. McGraw-Hill, Dubuque, IA, 2000.

Cooper, Kenneth. *Aerobics program for total well being*. Evans, New York, 1982.

Corbin, C. B., R. Lindsey, and G. Welk. *Concepts of fitness and wellness*. 3rd ed. McGraw-Hill, Dubuque, IA, 2000.

Corbin, C. B., R. Lindsey, and G. Welk. *Concepts of physical fitness: Active lifestyles for wellness*. 10th ed. McGraw-Hill, Dubuque, IA, 2000.

Costill, D., and A. Richardson. *Handbook of sports medicine: Swimming*. Blackwell Publishing, London, 1991.

Coyle, E., W. Martin, D. Sinacore, M. Joyner, J. Hagberg, and J. Holloszy. 1984. Time course of loss of adaptations after stopping prolonged intense endurance training. *Journal of Applied Physiology* 57:1857–1864.

DeVries, H., and T. Housh. *Exercise physiology*. 5th ed. Brown & Benchmark, Dubuque, IA, 1994.

Di Gennaro, Joseph. *The new physical fitness: Exercise for every body*. Morton, Englewood, CO, 1983.

Dintiman, George B., Stephan E. Stone, Jude C. Pennington, and Robert G. Davis. *Discovering lifetime fitness*. West, St. Paul, MN, 1984.

Falls, Arnold B., Ann M. Baylor, and Rud K. Dishman. *Essentials of fitness*. Saunders, Philadelphia, 1980.

Getchell, Bud. *Physical fitness, a way of life*. Prentice Hall, Englewood Cliffs, NJ, 1998.

Hockey, R. *Physical fitness: The pathway to healthful living*. 8th ed. Mosby-Year Book, St. Louis, 1996.

Lamb, D., and M. Williams. *Ergogenics: Enhancement of performance in exercise and sport.* Vol. 4. Brown & Benchmark, Madison, WI, 1991.

Margen, S., et. al., eds. *The wellness encyclopedia.* Houghton Mifflin, Boston, 1991.

Marley, William. *Health and physical fitness.* Saunders, Philadelphia, 1982.

McGlynn, G. *Dynamics of fitness: A practical approach.* 5th ed. McGraw-Hill, Dubuque, IA, 1999.

Paffenbarger, R., J. Kampert, I-Min Lee, R. Hyde, R. Leung, and A. Wing. 1994. Changes in physical activity and other lifeway patterns influencing longevity. *Medicine and Science in Sports and Exercise* 26:857–865.

Pollock, Michael, Jack H. Wilmore, and Samuel M. Fox. *Exercise in health and disease.* Saunders, Philadelphia, 1984.

Powell, K., and S. Blair. 1994. The public health burdens of sedentary living habits: Theoretical but realistic estimates. *Medicine and Science in Sports and Exercise* 26:851–856.

Powers, S., D. Criswell, J. Lawler, L. Ji, D. Martin, R. Herb, and G. Dudley. 1994. Influence of exercise and fiber type on antioxidant enzyme activity in rat skeletal muscle. *American Journal of Physiology* 266:R375–R380.

Prentice, W. E. *Fitness and wellness for life.* 6th ed. McGraw-Hill, Dubuque, IA, 1999.

Prentice, W. E. *Get fit, Stay fit.* Mosby-Year Book, St. Louis, 1996.

Robbins, G., D. Powers, and S. Burgess. *A wellness way of life.* 4th ed. McGraw-Hill, Dubuque, IA, 1999.

Rosensweig, S. *Sports fitness for women.* Harper & Row, New York, 1982.

Williams, M. *Lifetime fitness and wellness.* Wm C. Brown, Dubuque, IA, 1996.

Wilmore, Jack. *Sensible fitness.* Leisure Press, New York, 1986.

chapter 3

fundamentals of weight training

Objectives

After studying this chapter you should be able to

1. Describe the training goals in strength training.
2. Describe and define the basic principles in a strength-training program.
3. Describe the sports training continuum.
4. Describe the process of selecting intensity of training.
5. Define progressive resistance.
6. Define specificity.
7. Define application of force.
8. Describe safety procedures.
9. Define cheating.
10. Define overload.
11. Define repetitions.
12. Define duration.
13. Define frequency.
14. Define intensity.
15. Describe recommendations for the aged.

The muscle system is the foundation of all physical exercise. No matter what activity you participate in, your muscle strength and endurance will significantly affect your exercise limits. It is also important to remember that your muscles are not independent from the rest of the body systems, and conditioning is not limited to the muscles. Your muscles' ability to do work is dependent upon the efficiency of the heart, blood vessels, and lungs in providing energy and waste product elimination. Muscles, the heart, blood vessels, and the lungs are simultaneously conditioned because of their interdependence.

More specifically, weight training goals may be directed toward increases in strength and power, in muscular endurance, or in a combination of strength and endurance. Strength and power training are important for power lifters, weight lifters, football linemen, and weight throwers in field events. Muscular endurance training is vital in order to increase the aerobic capacity of the muscles, which is required for activities such as cycling, swimming, and rowing. Finally, general conditioning exercises that aim to increase both muscle strength and endurance are vital for success in a number of sports activities. In addition, general conditioning prepares the muscle system to meet the everyday demands of individuals who are not involved in competitive sports. A large number of individuals also participate in weight training programs simply to increase the size and strength of their muscles for personal and aesthetic reasons. Regardless of your goals, a weight training program should incorporate the basic principles outlined in this chapter in order to derive the maximum strength and endurance gains in an efficient and safe manner.

Certain physiological principles need to be understood in order to develop a program that will turn your efforts into maximum gains.

Training is stress, and what we try to do while training is to apply stress in the correct amount with the correct frequency to achieve the maximum result. If we apply too much stress or apply the stress too frequently, with insufficient rest, then improvement will not be maximized. Improvement may even be hampered, and detraining (loss of gains) and injury can occur.

1. **All-or-None.** When stimulated by the nervous system, a muscle fiber contracts fully, or it does not contract at all. This means that an individual fiber, once stimulated, contracts with all its force. We graduate the amount of force we produce by regulating the number of fibers we innervate or stimulate by the nervous system. To increase strength, you try to innervate as many fibers as possible at one time, thus lifting heavy loads with few repetitions. To increase endurance, lighter loads are used and fibers alternate their contractions to allow a rest and recovery period and, thus, a greater number of repetitions.

2. **Overload.** In order for the muscle to increase its capability, a greater load than normal must be applied. In order for the adaptation to occur, a progressive increase in the amount of work must be performed. Increases in strength require an increase in resistance. Increases in endurance require an increase in repetitions and/or resistance. As an adaption to this increased stress occurs, a greater stress must be imposed for further increases.

3. **Specificity of Training.** The gains that occur from training will be specific to the type of stress imposed upon the systems. A lot of long-distance running will improve your cardiorespiratory endurance but will do little to improve skeletal-muscular strength. The opposite is also true, in that strength training yields little improvement in cardiorespiratory endurance.

4. **Use and Disuse.** As a muscle is trained, it increases in size and functional ability; it is said to hypertrophy. If training ceases, the muscle begins to detrain, decrease in size, and lose its newly gained capacity; in other words it will atrophy.

5. **Individuality.** Individuals often respond differently to the same exercise programs. Many factors affect training response, including heredity, nutrition, fitness level, motivation, health habits (e.g., rest and sleep), maturity, hormone and enzyme levels, and environmental influences.

SETTING UP A PROGRAM

After you have given some thought to your goals, the needs of your sport, and evaluated your physical strength and weaknesses, you can refer to figure 3.1 and tables 3.1 and 3.2. They outline the methods and goals of various weight training programs.

Strength Training

The participants in this type of program are competitive weight lifters such as Olympic weight lifters, who perform the clean and jerk and snatch lifts, and power lifters, who specialize in three lifts: bench press, squat, and dead lift. This program is also used by power athletes such as football linemen, shot putters, and discus throwers.

These groups of athletes need a large amount of strength to be successful in competition. Their program is designed to increase strength. These athletes lift heavy weights for only a few repetitions, about two to six. When this type of training program is followed, the physiological changes that occur are an increase in the size of the individual muscle fiber and an increase in the ability of the nervous system to stimulate contraction of these fibers. These changes result in an increase in the force produced by the muscle.

Muscular Endurance Training

This program is used by endurance athletes to improve their stamina. The training program is designed to increase the size and number of blood vessels (vascularization) in the muscle and increase the efficiency of the heart and lungs. These changes are a function of increased muscular endurance and are achieved by doing many repetitions, about fifteen to twenty-five with light weights. This process pumps large amounts of

Figure 3.1 RELATIONSHIP BETWEEN THE NUMBER OF SETS AND INCREASES IN STRENGTH.

Reprinted from Getting Stronger *by Bill Pearl and Gary T. Moran. Copyright © 1986 Shelter Publications, Inc., Bolinas, CA. Reprinted by permission.*

Relative Strength Increase

Sets

Table 3.1

Sports Training Continuum		
Strength training	**All around sports training**	**Muscular endurance training**
Goal Strength & power	General conditioning (strength + endurance)	Muscular endurance (stamina)
Who trains this way Power lifters Olympic lifters Football linemen Shot putters Others	Most athletes General population	Swimmers Rowers Cyclists Distance runners Cross-country skiers Others
Physiological changes Increase in size of muscle fiber	Some increase in both size of muscle fiber and vascularization	Increase in vascularization, blood supply to muscle
Type of lifting Low reps (2–4–6) Heavy weights	Medium reps (8–10–12) Medium weights	High reps (15–25) Light weights

Source: Reprinted from *Getting Stronger* by Bill Pearl and Gary Moran © 1986 Shelter Publications, Inc., Bolinas, California. Reprinted by permission.

blood into the muscle in the short term, which increases muscle size. The process is known as pumping. Pumping produces significant increases in muscular endurance but only minimal increase in strength.

Bodybuilding

Many successful bodybuilders started out as power lifters or Olympic lifters, acquired significant muscle fiber size, and then switched their program to a bodybuilding regime involving pumping action to achieve their massive muscular definition and development. Many bodybuilders will use a strength (power lifting) program during portions of the year and then switch to the endurance program (bodybuilding) for the competitive portion of the year. This regimen allows them to increase both fiber size and vascularization.

Sport Training

Sport training is the type of weight training that is performed by most competitive athletes. This program is recommended for those individuals interested in maintaining fitness for everyday activities and informal sport and recreation. Table 3.2 summarizes

Table 3.2

A Summary of the Methods of Weight Training for Various Objectives (Using Free Weights)				
Variable	**Power**	**Strength**	**Local muscular endurance**	**Size**
Sets	4–6	4–6	Maximum	4–6
Repetitions**	3–8	3–8	25–40	Varies*
Method	Explosive, using compensatory acceleration	Moderate cadence	Slow, continuous cadence	Varies*
Rest intervals	Short pause with relaxation between reps, and 2–6 minutes between sets	Short pause with relaxation between reps, and 2–6 minutes between sets	Allow heart rate to return to manageable level between sets	Varies*

*In size training, variation is the key; for maximal size, use all of the methods listed, interspersing them through each set or between sets. For power lifters, size resulting from increased contracting elements of a muscle cell (strength system using about 8 reps per set) is most appropriate.

**In deference to the principle of overload, you should always attempt to use the appropriate amount of resistance. The last repetition in each set should be a near-maximal effort. For strength and power training the resistance should exceed 80 percent of your maximum capacity, for muscular endurance above 40 percent, and for size it should vary.

Source: Fredrick Hatfield, *Power Lifting, A Scientific Approach*. Contemporary Books, New York, 1985.

weight training methods with various objectives. (Refer to appendix A for more information on this topic.)

Most sports require a combination of strength, muscular endurance, and some measure of cardiorespiratory endurance. Most athletes benefit from a weight training program that yields gains in both strength and muscular endurance. This program is achieved by using a medium amount of resistance and performing a medium number of repetitions, about eight to twelve. The physiological changes that occur with this program are an increase in muscle fiber size and an increase in vascularization.

The sport training program is recommended as an initial or beginning program, even if one's goal is power lifting or body building. Also, if you have never lifted weights or are just returning to lifting, it is recommended that you follow a sport training program, as it will allow you to introduce your skeletal-muscular system and cardiorespiratory system to the rigors of resistance training without the levels of stress that the more specific programs (power lifting and endurance training) would place on you.

Power lifting places enormous stress upon tendons and ligaments as well as the muscle cells. These tissues need time to adjust to these high levels of stress, or injury can occur. Endurance training, because of its high repetitions, produces enormous quantities of biochemical fatigue products from cell metabolism. The buildup of these substances can cause significant muscle soreness, fatigue, and limited mobility. Because it takes time for vascularization to develop, you should work up to endurance training by first following a sport training program. Continue a sport training program for eight to ten weeks before shifting toward a strength or endurance program.

Before starting your exercise program you must be aware of three basic principles: intensity, duration, and frequency. Intensity refers to the degree of overload or stressfulness of the exercise, duration is the amount of time utilized for each exercise bout, and frequency is the number of exercises per week. Generally, the more intense, the longer, and more frequent the training program, the greater the benefits. Intensity and duration are interrelated, with the total amount of work accomplished being the important factor.

⟐ Critical Thinking 3-1

A student says he has been strength training for six weeks and has found that he is getting stronger but his muscles remain the same size.

How would you explain this phenomenon?

Selecting the Amount of Weight

Generally, to increase muscle strength, the intensity of effort should be near maximum with a low number of repetitions, and to gain muscle endurance, the intensity of effort should be lower with a high number of repetitions. The intensity level for strength gains is believed to be between one and six repetitions maximum. One repetition maximum (1 RM) is the maximum load that you can lift successfully one time through the full range of movement; two repetitions maximum (2 RM) is the amount you can lift successfully two times through the full range of movement, and so on.

Weight training research indicates that weight loads exceeding 75 percent of maximum are necessary for promoting strength gains, because the most important factor in strength development is intensity. Ten RM weight load usually corresponds to about 75 percent of that maximum.

An important factor in beginning your program is selection of the appropriate weight that should be lifted. The key is to select the amount of weight that allows you to perform the right number of repetitions for your program. For example, in the sport training program, we recommend that you perform three sets of the following repetitions (10-10-10).

See table 3.3 for standards, guidelines, and position statements regarding strength training.

Set 1—10 repetitions

Set 2—10 repetitions

Set 3—10 repetitions

Table 3.3

Standards, Guidelines, and Position Statements Regarding Strength Training

	Sets; RM	No. of exercises[a]	Frequency
Healthy sedentary adults			
1998 ACSM Position Stand (6)	1 set; 8–12 RM	8–10	2–3 d·wk^{-1}
1998 ACSM Guidelines (7)[b]	1 set; 8–12 RM	8–10	2 d·wk^{-1} minimum
1996 Surgeon General's Report (55)	1–2 sets; 8–12 RM	8–10	2 d·wk^{-1}
Elderly persons			
Pollock et al. (50)	1 set; 10–15 RM	8–10	2 d·wk^{-1} minimum
Cardiac patients			
1995 AHA Exercise Standards (27)	1 set; 10–15 RM	8–10	2–3 d·wk^{-1}
1995 AACVPR Guidelines (3)	1 set; 12–15 RM	8–10	2–3 d·wk^{-1}

Note: AHA, American Heart Association; AACVPR, American Association of Cardiovascular and Pulmonary Rehabilitation; RM, repetition maximum.
[a]Minimum one exercise per major muscle group, e.g., chest press, shoulder press, triceps extension, biceps curl, pull-down (upper back), lower back extension, abdominal crunch/curl-up, quadriceps extension, leg curls (hamstrings), calve raise.
[b]ACSM (7): guidelines developed for healthy, sedentary, and low-risk diseased populations.

References: 6. American College of Sports Medicine. The recommended quantity and quality of exercise for developing and maintaining cardiorespiratory and muscular fitness and flexibility in healthy adults. *Med. Sci. Sports Exerc.*, 30:975–991, 1998; 7. American College of Sports Medicine. *ACSM's Resource Manual for Guidelines for Exercise Testing and Prescription,* 3rd Ed. Baltimore: Williams and Wilkins, 1998, pp. 448–455; 55. U.S. Department of Health, and Human Services, *Physical Activity and Health. A Report of the Surgeon General.* Atlanta, GA: U.S. Department of Health and Human Services, Centers for Disease Control and Prevention, National Center for Chronic Disease Prevention and Health Promotion, 1996, pp. 22–29; 50. Pollock, M. L., J. E. Graves, D. L. Swart, and D. T. Lowentha I. Exercise training and prescription for the elderly. *South. Med. J.* 87:S88–S95, 1994; 27. Fletcher, G. F., G. Balady, V. F. Froelicher, L. H. Hartley, W. L. Haskell, and M. L. Pollock. Exercise standards: a statement for healthcare professionals from the American Heart Association. *Circulation* 91:580–615, 1995; 3. American Association of Cardiovascular and Pulmonary Rehabilitation. *Guidelines for Cardiac Rehabilitation Programs,* 2nd Ed. Champaign, IL: Human Kinetics Publishers, 1995, pp. 27–56.

You should choose a weight for set 1 that you can lift ten times (repetitions). You should work hard to perform the tenth repetition. If you could have done more repetitions, then the weight was too light. If you were able to do only six, eight, or nine repetitions, then the weight was too heavy.

The first few weight lifting sessions will be primarily testing sessions to determine the proper weight that you should lift. It is important that you keep accurate records (see record card, back cover of text) and have someone spot you during this period.

After your first set of ten repetitions, you should rest from one to two minutes before your second set. You may find that on your second set you are able to perform twelve repetitions of the same weight you used for the first set. If this occurs, then you will need to add weight (five to ten lbs.) for the second set to bring your repetitions down to ten. The same may occur with your third set. This increase in strength often occurs and is a result of the influx of blood and increased nerve stimulation to the muscle, making it better able to respond to the demands you make upon it.

To restate our example then, your program might look like this:

Set 1	10 repetitions	X amount of weight
Set 2	10 repetitions	X plus 5 pounds
Set 3	10 repetitions	X plus 10 pounds

Again, please note that the key to the program is the number of repetitions. If, after ten weeks, you want to shade your sport training program towards *strength development,* then you might do three sets of eight repetitions or a program as follows:

Set 1	10 repetitions	X amount of weight
Set 2	8 repetitions	X plus 10 pounds
Set 3	8 repetitions	X plus 15 pounds

If, after ten weeks of a sport conditioning program, you wanted to shade your program towards *endurance development,* you might choose the following type of program:

Set 1	10 repetitions	X amount of weight
Set 2	12 repetitions	X amount of weight
Set 3	12 repetitions	X plus 5 pounds

Strength-Testing Protocol for Repetition Maximum

A repetition maximum test should not be attempted unless an individual has developed the necessary skills in lifting and has had at least six weeks of strength conditioning.

1. A light warm-up of 5–10 repetitions at 40 to 60 percent of perceived maximum.
2. After a 1-minute rest with light stretching, 3 to 5 repetitions at 60 to 80 percent perceived maximum.
3. Step 2 will be close to the perceived 1 RM. A conservative increase in the weight is made and a 1-RM lift is attempted. If the lift is successful a rest period of three to five minutes is allowed. A rest period is most important before the maximal attempt. The 1 RM will usually be found within three to five maximal efforts.

After you have followed the sport training program for eight to ten weeks, then your skeletal-muscular and cardiorespiratory systems will be in better condition to shift toward a strength or endurance program if you so desire.

Remember! The number of repetitions and the appropriate amount of weight determine whether you are performing a strength, general, or endurance program, not how hard you work. How hard you work will determine your level of success and the amount of gain you achieve. We assume you are willing to work hard, or you would not be reading this book.

Remember the continuum:

Strength Development	2–4–6 repetitions
Sport Training	8–10–12 repetitions
Endurance Development	15–25 repetitions

How Often Should You Lift?

The general rule for weight lifting is to exercise the various muscle groups three times per week. Just as in a running or bicycling program, the best results are achieved when stress is applied in a hard day/easy day fashion. This approach allows for cellular changes to occur at an optimum rate and avoids overstressing or overtraining. In weight training we follow the hard/easy system by working hard one day and then following it with a day off. So a three-day-a-week program would follow a M–W–F or T–Th–Sat routine. The off-days allow the muscles time to recover from the stress that lifting imposes upon them.

Many experienced weight lifters lift more than three times per week (e.g., six days per week), but they will exercise a body part only three times per week. In this program the lifter would work his chest, back, and shoulders on M–W–F and his legs and arms on T–Th–Sat. This way each body part is exercised three times per week with a day off in between. This program is called a split-routine and is performed primarily by advanced lifters who perform multiple sets of multiple exercises for a specific body part. Examples of these exercises include regular bench press, inclined bench press, and declined bench press for chest development.

In summary, you should work each body part three times per week. You can do so in a routine in which you do all of your desired exercises three times per week, or a split-routine in which you perform a portion of your exercises three times per week and the remaining portion on the alternate days. For the beginning lifter, we recommend exercising three times per week, as it is mentally easier to gear yourself up to three workouts per week than six sessions per week.

How Many Sets?

The optimal number of sets to develop strength still remains controversial. The quality (intensity) and not the quantity (volume) may be the most important factor for developing muscular training programs. The use of a single set of an exercise is effective for individuals who are untrained or just starting resistance programs. One-set programs may also be used for maintenance programs. Strength changes have been found to be not different among one, two, or three sets of ten to twelve repetitions during the first several months of untrained individuals. In highly trained individuals, however, research indicates that single-set, low-volume programs do not achieve strength gains.

As seen in figure 3.1 you will experience gains with one set and even greater gains with two and three sets. After three sets there is a leveling off of the gains. Performing four or five sets of an exercise produces more gains than three sets, but the amount of this increase is less than occurs during the first three sets. In other words, you have to work harder for fewer results after three sets than you do for the first three sets. The law of diminishing returns prevails. Our recommendation is that you perform three sets of your major exercises. After you are conditioned to the exercises and want greater results, then you can go up to five sets. After five sets the curve flattens out, and little is gained for your efforts.

Overload

Muscle strength develops only when muscles are *overloaded*—forced to contract at maximum or near maximum tension. Muscle contractions at these tension levels produce physiological changes in the muscles, resulting in strength gains. If muscles are not overloaded to this degree, they do not increase in strength or in size (hypertrophy). Muscles adapt only to the load they are subjected to. A maximum overload results in maximum strength gains, whereas a minimum overload produces only minimum strength gains.

Progressive Resistance Exercise

Credit for the development of the first progressive resistance exercise program goes to Milo of Greece, 300 B.C. Milo picked up a calf each day as it grew into a full grown bull. Milo progressively lifted a heavier weight each day to overload the muscles and stimulate the muscles to build greater strength. The resistance progressively increased as the calf grew each day and stimulated strength increase. Likewise, the intensity of the load you lift must be progressively increased to insure future strength gains. If the intensity of the training load is not increased, only existing strength levels are maintained. With progressive overload the muscle responds with an increase in size (hypertrophy) and strength. The same overload response can be used to increase muscular endurance by progressively increasing the number of repetitions performed or the amount of resistance used. If training stops, the lack of stimulus will result in a loss of size (atrophy) and strength.

Specificity

The demands of the exercise must be sufficient to force muscles to adapt, and subsequent muscle adaptations are specific to the type of training performance. This concept is known as *specificity*. For example, aerobic activity develops aerobic capacity, and anaerobic activity develops anaerobic capacity.

Recent research indicates that muscle adaptations are specific to the type of training performed because exercise not only affects muscles but also nerve control of muscles. The nerve pathways appear to become more efficient with continued exercise. The efficiency, however, is specific only to the particular exercise.

During the first five weeks of resistance training, there is a marked improvement in the recruitment pattern by the central nervous system. As a result, strength increases will appear before increases in muscle size (hypertrophy).

Research also indicates that the joint angle of exercise, the type of exercise (i.e., isotonic, isometric, or isokinetic), and the speed and range of movement all produce a variety of specific muscle adaptations.

Muscles will adapt specifically to the type of stress that is imposed on them. For example, strength training such as Milo's improves strength, while performing many repetitions increases muscular endurance.

It is important that you assess your strengths and weaknesses and the requirements of your sport so that you can train as specifically as possible to maximize your performance increases. (See chapter 6 and appendix A.)

Application of Force

It is also important to maintain a consistent application of force by raising and lowering the weight in a controlled manner. This type of movement subjects the muscles to the same level of stress during both the lifting and lowering phases. Generally the lift phase should take about one to two seconds and the lowering phase approximately two to three seconds. Fast movements require more strength at the beginning of the lift and less force during the later portion of the movement. High speeds of lifting and lowering are less productive in strength development, with the added possibility of causing injury to muscle tissue.

Recommendations for the Aged

The American College of Sports Medicine has recommended that healthy persons of all ages and many patients with chronic disease can benefit from a single-set program of up to fifteen repetitions, performed a minimum of two days a week. Each session should consist of eight to ten different exercises that train the major muscle groups. The exercise should be preceded by at least a 15-minute warm-up. The large muscle groups should be exercised first, then the smaller groups. A 15-minute cooldown should follow the exercises. Each repetition should be performed slowly through the full range of motion, two to three seconds to lift and four to six seconds to lower the weight. There will be approximately a 10 to 15 percent increase in strength per week; therefore, it is necessary to increase the weight every two to three weeks as strength builds. Individuals with chronic disease, such as arthritis, may have to limit the range of motion of some exercises and use lighter weights with more repetitions.

Breathing

Inhale before a lift and exhale during the lift; then inhale as the weight is lowered. It is important to avoid holding your breath during force production (Valsalva maneuver). With proper breathing, cardiovascular stress from resistance exercise is minimal. Heart rate and blood pressure should rise only slightly if these procedures are followed.

Youth Guidelines

To guard against epiphyseal plate fractures, maximal or near maximal lifts should not be stressed for prepubescent programs. Proper form, especially in over-head lifts, should be emphasized. Three sets of ten to fifteen repetitions for most exercises is recommended.

ORDER OF EXERCISES AND RECOVERY

Progressive training becomes less effective when muscles become fatigued, since the training stimulus cannot be maintained at maximum level. Also, overloading a fatigued muscle may lead to soreness and injury. Therefore, follow three simple rules:

1. Exercise large muscle groups before smaller ones. Movements become fatiguing when the small muscles involved in the movement are fatigued. For example, when working the upper body, exercise the chest and back muscles before performing exercises that work primarily the arms or forearm. If not, the fatigued arm muscle may be the limiting factor rather than the chest or back muscles that you are trying to exercise.
2. Arrange your strength exercises so that successive exercises only minimally affect the muscle groups that were just trained previously.
3. Allow forty-eight hours between strength exercises for physiological recovery.

Combination of Exercises and Balance

To promote muscle balance, flexibility, and injury-free training, opposite muscle groups known as prime movers and antagonists should be exercised. For example, one should complement a quadriceps exercise (leg extension) with hamstring exercises (leg curl). There is a recommended procedure for combining exercises. You should exercise opposite muscle groups such as chest and back during the same workout. This approach ensures balance and harmony of muscle groups that work together in a movement.

A javelin thrower uses his or her chest and anterior (front) shoulder muscles to throw the javelin and also must use the upper back and posterior (back) shoulder muscles to slow the arm down after the javelin is released. If he or she develops the chest muscles alone, then he or she runs the risk of a strength imbalance and injury to back muscles.

Critical Thinking 3-2

An individual asks if it makes any difference what muscle groups you exercise initially when starting a strength-training program.

Explain to him the importance of muscle sequence.

The typical combinations of prime movers and antagonists are

Chest	–Back
Shoulder	–Lats
Biceps	–Triceps
Quadriceps	–Hamstring
Abdominals	–Lower back

Warm-Up and Cooldown

Before you start your strength-training program it is essential that you spend approximately fifteen minutes with a warm-up followed by a stretch regimen. You can warm up by marching in place, jogging, doing calisthenics, or swinging your arms back and forth and rolling your shoulders for a minute or two.

After the exercise make sure you cool down for ten minutes with a slow walk and more stretching.

Warm-ups are necessary to prepare the joint for the activity. Many lifters prepare for the joint movement by performing stretching exercises to move the joint through the range of motion. Often lifters perform a light first set to accomplish this. If you are cold and sore from previous workouts or have been inactive for a while, you should pay particular attention to your warm-up and include jogging and stretching.

Flexibility and Range of Motion

If you exercise through the full range of motion of the joint, you will maintain and likely increase your flexibility. Champion weight lifters and bodybuilders are among the most flexible athletes. The key is to lift through the entire range of motion of each joint. Flexibility exercises are included in chapter 10.

Breathing

It is very important that you breathe in a cyclic manner, both inhaling and exhaling with each repetition. Holding your breath throughout the lift can cause oxygen deprivation to the brain and can cause you to pass out. Obviously, this could be dangerous when lifting heavy weights over your head.

Holding your breath with a closed glottis during performance of resistance training is contraindicated (Valsalva maneuver). Blood pressure as high as 480/350 mmHg has been recorded during a double-leg press. Elevated blood pressure during lifting places an additional pressure on the heart and blood vessels. The simple principle is to exhale while lifting and inhale while lowering.

When performing a lift, inhale during the easiest part of the lift, *momentarily* hold your breath during the most difficult part, and then exhale when you can comfortably do so. When performing the bench press, for example, inhale as you lower the weight to your chest, momentarily hold your breath while you begin to press the weight upward, and then, during the effort phase of the pressing movement, exhale. As the weights you use become heavier, the momentary period of breath holding may become slightly longer. *You should never*, however, *hold your breath throughout the repetition cycle.* During heavy lifts you need that momentary pause in the breathing cycle (breath holding) to provide a stable support and anchor for the contracting muscles.

If while performing the bench press you exhaled during the beginning of the pressing movement (instead of holding your breath momentarily), the chest would compress during the exhalation at precisely the time you need a stable platform upon which the muscles can perform their contraction and movement.

Positioning

When performing lifts in a standing position (curls, overhead press, etc.), your feet should be a little wider than shoulder-width apart, and you should be balanced fore and aft. Many lifters find that wearing shoes or boots with a heel can help offset the shifting of their center of gravity when they lift heavy weights (see figure 10.8). Lifters sometimes use a board under their heels when performing squats to assist in balance. Hands should be placed approximately shoulder-width apart for most lifts, a little wider for the bench press. Thumbs should be wrapped around the bar to insure a stable grip.

Back

In most lifts, such as the dead lift and bent rowing, the back should be kept straight and the lift performed with the legs or arms. This method will help protect the back muscles from strain and injury.

Head

Keep the head and neck straight during almost all lifts. Twisting of the head, neck, and trunk causes injury, as the muscles are less efficient when the spine is twisted.

Safety

Safety should concern every athlete in the weight room. To be injured because you or someone else failed to exercise caution and lift safely is truly disheartening. Rules to follow include these:

1. Warm up properly
2. Do not try heavy resistance until you are familiar with the technique you are using.
3. Do not use heavy weights without a spotter (someone to help if you need help).
4. Collars should be used to insure that the weights do not slide off and unbalance the bar.
5. Do not jerk or twist when you lift as these movements significantly increase stress and risk of injury.

Table 3.4

General Principles

1. Warm up prior to lifting weights.
2. Include stretching exercises in your warm-up.
3. Stretching exercises should be done *slowly* through a *full* range of motion.
4. Do not try heavy resistances before you are familiar with the lifting technique you are using.
5. Include all the major muscle groups in your workout.
6. Insure that you involve opposing (prime mover/antagonist) muscle groups and aim for bilateral development.
7. For greater strength development, do fewer repetitions (eight or fewer); for a combined strength/muscular endurance response, work between eight and twelve reps.
8. Use a technique of lifting and a program workout that suits you personally—as long as it is wisely implemented. Vary the program in such a way so as to maintain interest in what you are doing.
9. Only by keeping accurate records (at least initially) can you effectively gauge your improvements and establish a routine.
10. Some caution might be taken while
    a. Performing back hyperextension exercises with weights.
    b. Doing *full* squats.
11. Don't forget that your weight training should be supplemented with an aerobic (cardiorespiratory endurance) activity, such as running, bicycling, or swimming.

6. Use care when performing the following exercises:

   a. Full squats—The structure of the knee is such that this exercise can cause ligament and tendon stress in some individuals. Half squats, to a ninety degree angle between thigh and leg, are recommended.

   b. Back hyperextensions—Back hyperextensions are a good exercise for strengthening the lower back; however, if too much weight is used too soon, the back muscles can tighten and spasm. Start with light weights and add resistance very gradually.

   c. Straight-leg sit-ups—Straight-leg sit-ups should be avoided as they place significant stress on the lower back. Sit-ups should be done with the knees bent to approximately ninety degrees or more.

   d. Dead lift—The dead lift is a good exercise for the thighs and buttocks, but you should keep the back straight and lift with the legs. You should keep your head up and eyes on the ceiling; squeeze your buttocks and tighten your abdominals when performing this lift.

7. Too much velocity generated while lifting may prove to be dangerous. Excessive speeds at the end of motion of a joint may result in loss of control and tissue damage.

EQUIPMENT

Many lifters use various accessories to aid their performance and safe lifting. These include

1. Weight lifting shoes or boots to aid stability.
2. Weight lifting belt to support the lower back.
3. Weight lifting gloves to insure a good grip and prevent blisters.
4. Weight lifting chalk used on hands to insure a good grip, especially when hands are wet.

Belts

Belts are effective in increasing intra-abdominal pressure, thus giving support to the spinal column while lifting. For resistance exercises not stressing the back, a belt is unnecessary. The belt should be worn for near maximal or maximal sets. During light sets it is not necessary to wear the belt. Beltless sets allow the abdominal muscles to receive a training stimulus, thus increasing their ability to protect the spinal cord. It is risky to suddenly perform lifting exercises without a belt if you are accustomed to wearing one while lifting.

Gloves

Weight training gloves are not required. However, they may be beneficial in preventing calluses and providing you with a firmer grip.

Shoes

An important factor in a weight training shoe is that it provides good lateral support. Running shoes with narrow heels and flexible shanks should not be used. Shoes that are designed for crosstraining or aerobic dance have a normal size heel and are more suitable for resistance training.

CHEATING

Cheating is the process of altering a lifting position to enable the lifter to lift more weight or to complete a repetition. An example is arching the back on the bench press. This arching changes the line of pull on the bone and transforms the flat bench press into a form of declined press. This procedure enables the lifter to handle more weight, as joint leverage is improved and the lower part of the pectoralis major is used more fully.

Another example is leaning back when doing the biceps curl to complete the exercise. Cheating is an advanced technique; novice lifters should use strict form on their lifts. Even advanced lifters should not cheat on all their sets but merely on the last few sets or last few repetitions of the last set.

Cheating is medically contraindicated. One should always proceed with caution because the increased joint motion can result in trauma to the tissue.

Advanced lifters use cheating to handle heavier weights than they can normally handle in the strict position. This step can result in their eventually being able to lift that weight with standard form. In short, there is a place for cheating, but it is for advanced lifters and should be used sparingly. Table 3.3 lists a summary of general strength training principles.

Glossary

Atrophy   Decrease in size and functional ability of muscle.
Cheating   The altering of the body's position to change leverage or use more muscle mass to complete a lift.
Duration   The amount of time utilized for each exercise bout.
Frequency   The number of exercises per week.
Hypertrophy   Increase in size and functional capacity of muscle.
Intensity   The degree of overload or stressfulness of the exercise.
Muscle Endurance   The ability of a muscle group to maintain a continuous contraction or repetition over a period of time.
Muscle Strength   The amount of force that can be exerted by a muscle group for one movement or repetition.
One Repetition Maximum   (1 RM) The maximum amount of weight you can successfully lift one time through the full range of motion.
Overload   Forcing a muscle to contract at maximum or near maximum tension.
Progressive Resistance   The progressive increase in load intensity (either weight or repetitions or both).
Specificity   The concept that exercises resemble the type of training performed.

Solutions to Critical Thinking

3-1. Early gains in muscle strength are the result of enhanced neuromuscular control. Increases in muscle size (hypertrophy) will appear a few weeks later.

3-2. Large muscle groups should be exercised before small muscle groups. If small muscle groups are initially exercised, they have a tendency to fatigue more easily, interfering with subsequent training of larger muscles. For example, upper chest and back muscles should be exercised before arms or forearms.

Review Questions

1. Why is it advisable to begin with a sport training program regardless of whether one's eventual goal requires power lifting or endurance training?
2. Discuss the criteria that make up strength and an endurance program.
3. What is meant by the overload principle?

References

Baechle, T. R. *Essentials of strength training and conditioning.* Human Kinetics, Champaign, IL, 1994.

Baechle, Thomas, ed. *Essentials of strength training and conditioning.* Human Kinetics, Champaign, IL, 1994.

Baechle, T. R., and B. R. Groves. *Weight training: Steps to success.* 2nd ed. Human Kinetics, Champaign, IL, 1998.

Bass, Charles. *Ripped—The sensible way to achieve ultimate muscularity.* Ripped Enterprises, Albuquerque, NM, 1980.

Darden, Ellington. *The nautilus book.* Contemporary Books, Chicago, 1982.

Darden, Ellington. *The nautilus woman.* Simon & Schuster, New York, 1983.

Field, R., and S. O. Roberts. *Weight training.* McGraw-Hill, Dubuque, IA, 1999.

Fleck, S. J., and W. J. Kraemer. *Designing resistance training programs.* 2nd ed. Human Kinetics, Champaign, IL, 1997.

Fleck, S. J., and W. J. Kraemer. 1988. Resistance training, basic principles. *Physician and Sports Medicine* 16 (3): 160–170.

Fox, E. L., and D. K. Mathews. *Interval training, conditioning for sport and general fitness.* Saunders, Philadelphia, 1974.

Gaines, Charles, and George Butler. *Pumping iron II: The unprecedented woman.* Simon & Schuster, New York, 1984.

Hatfield, Frederick C. *The complete guide to power training.* Fitness Systems, New Orleans, 1983. Lakewood, CA: Sports Conditioning Services, 5542 South Street, 90713.

Jarrell, Steve. *Working out with weights.* Anco, New York, 1982.

Kennedy, Robert. *Reps!—Building massive muscle!* Sterling Publishing Co., New York, 1985.

Kraemer, W. J., and S. J. Fleck. *Strength training for young athletes.* Human Kinetics, Champaign, IL, 1993.

Lombardi, V. P. *Beginning weight training: The safe and effective way.* Brown, Benchmark, Dubuque, IA, 1989.

McCartney, Neil. 1999. Acute response to resistance training and safety. *Medicine and Science In Sports and Exercise* 31–1: 32–37.

chapter 4

general programs

Objectives

After studying this chapter you should be able to

1. Describe a program to develop muscle endurance.

2. Describe a program to develop muscle strength.

3. Describe a program to develop aerobic capacity.

4. Describe a program for bodybuilding.

The following programs tables 4.1 through 4.4 have been selected for general conditioning for muscle strength, muscle endurance, and bodybuilding. You may make minor modifications to these programs depending upon how you respond to the exercise. Time is on your side, so don't overstress yourself for the first few weeks. Expect a little muscle stiffness and soreness the first few days. This is your body's way of telling you it has been a long time between workouts. This discomfort should go away in a short time. Tune into your body's signals while you exercise. You know more or less how you feel and how your body responds to exercise. You are the best judge as to what your body is capable of doing.

No single exercise can universally meet the needs of all individuals. However, no matter what exercise program you select, it should follow the sequence and fall within the time ranges shown in tables 4.1 through 4.4.

SPORT AND FITNESS CONDITIONING PROGRAMS

The goal of this program is to increase both strength and muscular endurance. This program is appropriate for most athletes and for those beginning a fitness program. The amount of resistance that is utilized will vary from individual to individual, but the principles remain the same. Perform this program three days per week.

You should consider supplementing your sport and fitness conditioning program with an aerobic conditioning program such as running, bicycling, or swimming. Perform the aerobic conditioning program three days per week, on days that alternate with those on which you do the sport and fitness conditioning program. (See chapter 12.)

Table 4.1

Sport and Fitness Conditioning Program			
Weight training program (M–W–F)			
Exercise	*Sets*	*Repetitions*	*Reference*
1. Bench press	3	10/10/10	fig. 10.8
2. Seated rowing	3	10/10/10	fig. 10.13
3. Bent-knee sit-ups	1	25–75	fig. 10.32
4. Half squats	3	10/10/10	fig. 10.46
5. Triceps pulldown	3	10/10/10	fig. 10.26
6. Seated dumbbell curl	3	10/10/10	fig. 10.23

After you have worked on the conditioning program for eight to ten weeks, you may choose to modify your program toward greater strength or muscular endurance development. The following two programs are designed towards those goals.

STRENGTH DEVELOPMENT PROGRAM

The goal of this program is maximum strength development. Perform it six days a week, following weight training program A three days a week, and weight training program B on three alternating days.

You should supplement your weight training program with a cardiorespiratory exercise program of three to five days per week in frequency. Your aerobic program should consist of ten to fifteen minutes of warm-up and flexibility exercises, twenty to forty minutes of aerobic exercise, and eight to ten minutes of cooldown. You might consider three days a week of cycling, swimming, or running as an adjunct to your weight training program. See chapter 12 for a circuit training aerobic program and appendix D for an aerobic running program.

> **Critical Thinking 4-1**
>
> An individual was told by a trainer that he had to start with three sets of exercise for each muscle group because one set would be a waste of time and effort.
>
> Explain to him the recent research in this area.

MUSCULAR ENDURANCE DEVELOPMENT PROGRAM

Maximum endurance development (three–six days per week). This program can be done either as a regular routine, three days per week, or as a split-routine, six days per week with upper body M–W–F and lower body T–Th–Sat. It is presented here as a split-routine.

This program utilizes supersets, a system whereby you alternate exercises, a and b, followed by a rest. You repeat that sequence until the appropriate number of sets are accomplished.

You should supplement your weight training program with a cardiorespiratory endurance program three to seven days per week. You might consider three days a week of cycling and/or three days a week of running as a warm-up to the weight training program.

BODYBUILDING

Bodybuilder programs are organized to increase muscle size, develop symmetry, and increase muscle definition. Bodybuilding programs contain more exercises than other resistance programs, as they focus on multiple exercises for various muscle groups. Bodybuilders generally progress from exercising large muscles to exercising small muscle groups. The loads utilized by advanced bodybuilders range from 1 to 40 RM. Beginning bodybuilders use a range of 7 to 20 RM. It is important to insure a large volume of exercise during training. High-intensity volume is important in producing hypertrophy. Exercises usually consist of three to six sets. However, sometimes as many as fifteen sets of different exercises can be performed for specific muscle groups. Rest periods between sets are no more than two minutes and sometimes less than one minute.

Advanced bodybuilders will focus on developing muscle mass through a strength training program (heavy weights, few repetitions) for part of the year or training cycle. This is followed by a medium weight, medium repetition program (8–12 rep) and finally a light weight, many repetition program (15–40 rep) for muscular hypertrophy and definition. This routine is the final stage before competition.

We caution the beginning bodybuilder against incorporating the very heavy weight and/or very high repetition portion of this advanced program, as it takes years of training to develop the strength of muscle tissue, tendons, and ligaments to withstand such

> **Critical Thinking 4-2**
>
> An athlete, in the process of rehabilitating a shoulder strain, wondered if there would be any problem if the weight lifted by the injured arm was lighter than the weight lifted by the healthy arm.
>
> What would you advise him?

Table 4.2

Strength Development Program

Weight training program A (M–W–F)

Exercise	Sets	Repetitions	Reference
1. Bench press	5	10/8/6/4/2	fig. 10.8
2. Seated rowing	5	10/8/6/4/2	fig. 10.13
3. Military press	3–5	10/8/6/(4/2)	fig. 10.15
4. Lateral pulldown	3–5	10/8/6/(4/2)	fig. 10.14
5. Crunch sit-ups	3	15–25	fig. 10.33
6. Triceps pullovers	3–5	10/8/6/(4/2)	fig. 10.24
7. Curls	3–5	10/8/6/(4/2)	fig. 10.22

Weight training program B (T–Th–Sat)

Exercise	Sets	Repetitions	Reference
1. Half squats	3–5	10/8/6/(4/2)	fig. 10.46
2. Sit-ups with weights	3	10–20	fig. 10.35
3. Leg extension	3	10/8/6	fig. 10.52
4. Leg flexion	3	10/8/6	fig. 10.53
5. Back hyperextension	3	10–20	fig. 10.38
6. Toe raises	3	10/8/6	fig. 10.54

Table 4.3

Muscular Endurance Development Program

Weight training program A (M–W–F)

Exercise	Sets	Repetitions	Reference
1. a. Bench press	3–5	(18/16)–14/12/10	fig. 10.8
b. Bent rowing	3–5	(18/16)–14/12/10	fig. 10.12
2. a. Upright rowing or inclined bench press	3	14/12/10	fig. 10.16
b. Lateral pulldown	3	14/12/10	fig. 10.14
3. Alternating elbow to knee sit-ups	1	50–100	fig. 10.34
4. a. Seated triceps Dumbbell curl	3	14/12/10	fig. 10.25
b. Standing biceps Dumbbell curl	3	14/12/10	fig. 10.22

Weight training program B (T–Th–Sat)

Exercise	Sets	Repetitions	Reference
1. a. Leg press	3	15/12/10	fig. 10.47
b. Back hyperextension	3	15/15/15	fig. 10.38
2. a. Hip flexion	3	12/12/10	fig. 10.48
b. Hip extension	3	15/12/10	fig. 10.49
3. a. Hip abduction	3	15/12/10	fig. 10.51
b. Hip adduction	3	15/12/10	fig. 10.50
4. Bent-knee sit-ups	1	50–100	fig. 10.32
5. a. Leg extension	3	15/12/10	fig. 10.52
b. Leg flexion	3	15/12/10	fig. 10.53

Table 4.4

Beginning body building program

Exercise	M/Th Sets	Upper body—chest and back Repetitions	Reference
1. Bench press	3–5	8–12	fig. 10.8
2. Inclined dumbbell flies	3	8–12	fig. 10.9
3. Declined bench press	3	8–12	fig. 10.10
4. Bent rowing	3–5	8–12	fig. 10.12
5. Seated pulley rows	3–5	8–12	fig. 10.13
6. Pec deck	3–5	8–12	fig. 10.11
7. Abdominal exercises	1–3	25	fig. 10.32
8. Crunches	1–3	25	fig. 10.33

Body building program

Exercise	Tue/Fri Sets	Lower body Repetitions	Reference
1. Half squat	3–5	8–12	fig. 10.46
2. Leg press	3–5	8–12	fig. 10.47
3. Leg extension	3	8–12	fig. 10.52
4. Leg flexion	3	8–12	fig. 10.53
5. Toe raise	3–5	8–12	fig. 10.54
6. Seated toe raises	3	15–25	fig. 10.55
7. Abdominal exercises	1–5	10–50	fig. 10.32
8. Crunches	1–3	25	fig. 10.33

Body building program

Exercise	Wed/Sat Sets	Upper body—shoulders and arms Repetitions	Reference
1. Standing press	3–5	8–12	fig. 10.15
2. Upright rowing	3	8–12	fig. 10.16
3. Lateral pulldown	6–8	8–12	fig. 10.14
4. Abdominal exercises	1–5	10–50	fig. 10.32
5. Crunches	1–3	25	fig. 10.33
6. Triceps pullover	3	8–12	fig. 10.24
7. Triceps pulldown	3	8–12	fig. 10.26
8. Seated triceps dumbbell curl	3	8–10	fig. 10.25
9. Standing barbell curl	3–5	8–12	fig. 10.22
10. Seated alternate dumbbell curls	3–5	8–12	fig. 10.23
11. Shoulder dips	3–5	8–15	fig. 10.17

high stress levels and volume. The beginning bodybuilder should stay in the 8–12 repetition range and cautiously work progressively toward the advanced program over time.

Remember, injuries slow or stop your progress; attempting to advance too rapidly ends up being counter-productive.

Solutions to Critical Thinking

4-1. The majority of evidence today indicates that for sedentary individuals and those beginning a resistance-training program, initially one set of exercises is as effective as three sets. However, for highly trained individuals one set is not sufficient to bring about increased gains in strength.

4-2. Initially he should use lighter weights for the injured arm until the muscle group has developed its pre-injury strength. He should go on exercising the healthy arm with the appropriate resistance level.

Review Questions

1. Are t

here any problems associated with combining an aerobic program with a strength-conditioning program?
2. If you are beginning a strength development program, what will be the initial number of sets for each body part?
3. What is the difference between muscle strength and muscle endurance?

References

Enoka, R. M. 1988. Muscle strength and its development. *Sports Medicine* 6:146–168.

Hickson, R. C. 1980. Interference of strength development by simultaneously training for strength and endurance. *European Journal of Applied Physiology* 45: 255–263.

Komi, P. V. *Strength and power in sport.* Human Kinetics, Champaign, IL, 1992.

Komi, P. V. 1986. Training of muscle strength and power: Interaction of neuromotoric, hypertrophic, and mechanical factors. *International Journal of sports medicine* 7:10–15.

Komi, P. V., ed. *Strength and power in sport.* Blackwell, 1993.

Pearl, Bill and Gary Moran. *Getting stronger.* Shelter, Bolinas, CA, 1986.

Perrin, David H. *Isokinetic exercise and assessment.* Human Kinetics, Champaign, IL, 1993.

Sobey, Edwin. *Strength training book.* Anderson World, Mountain View, CA, 1981.

Stone, M., and H. O'Bryant. *Weight training: A scientific approach.* Burgess, Minneapolis, MN,

Todd, Jan, and Terry Todd. *Lift your way to youthful fitness—The comprehensive guide to weight training.* Little, Brown, Boston, 1985.

Webster, David. *Body building—An illustrated history.* Arco Publishing, Inc., New York, 1979.

Westcott, Wayne. *Strength fitness physiological principles and training techniques.* Allyn & Bacon, Boston, 1983.

Westcott, W. L. *Building strength and stamina.* Human Kinetics, Champaign, IL, 1996.

Westcott, W. L., and T. R. Baechle. *Strength training past 50.* Human Kinetics, Champaign, IL, 1998.

chapter 5

motivation and mental conditioning

Objectives
After studying this chapter you should be able to

1. Describe the importance of motivation in achieving muscle strength and endurance.

2. Describe guidelines for staying committed.

3. Describe the process of mental preparation in strength training.

4. Define attention, focus, and concentration.

Motivation is the energy and driving force behind what we do in life. Its absence accounts for poor performance, underutilization of our abilities, and failure to achieve goals. Motivation lies at the heart of our decision to begin a task, to expend effort on the task, and to continue expending effort over a period of time. There is little use in maximized effort, however, unless we know where we are going. Motivation is, therefore, not only the energy that drives our behavior but plays a major role in establishing the goals toward which our energies are directed.

WHY WE DROP OUT

An important question that is often asked is "Why is it so difficult for many capable individuals to unlearn poor health habits and form new ones?" Is there some undiscovered personality trait that allows some individuals to be able to complete a weight loss program, give up cigarette smoking, and run three miles three times a week? Evidence indicates that two important questions have to be answered before embarking on a program. First, what is the perceived chance of achieving the outcome, and, secondly, what is the value that is placed on the outcome once it has been achieved? Am I capable of achieving increases in strength, and if I do, of what benefit will that increased strength be to me? Regarding the first question, evidence indicates that some individuals are more confident that they will be able to achieve their goals. If you believe you are capable of attaining a goal, you are more likely to achieve it. When faced with obstacles, people who entertain serious doubts about their ability to achieve a goal generally reduce their driving efforts toward their goal or give up altogether. Factors such as past success and encouragement play a vital part of your perception of success. The more you believe your effort will help you attain your goal, the greater your chance for success. An important point to remember is that the low fit or sedentary individual can look forward to substantial gains in muscular strength and endurance in only a few months of rigorous exercise.

A second consideration is what value we place on the outcomes of our effort. Social science research shows that humans act to maximize gains and minimize losses according to their perceptions of what constitutes a gain or a loss. We will act to ensure benefits to our well-being. We have basic needs that determine why we strive, work, and persevere. These needs must be fulfilled for us to lead a balanced life and to achieve challenging but obtainable goals. We all enjoy the satisfaction of achievement whether it comes from making something with our hands, earning a promotion at work, or lifting an extra ten pounds. A sense of mastery, a completion of a difficult task, leads to a feeling of self-confidence and well-being. In addition, the physical and psychological benefits outlined in chapter 1 should be important to you.

On the other hand, be cautious about exercise dependence. For example, some people spend most of their waking hours in the weight room. They clock in more time in their workout shorts than street clothes. They become obsessed and set higher and higher standards, which require more and more of their time, and they lose sight of the important reasons for exercising. Do not strive for unrealistic goals. Place exercise in proper perspective to your personal goals in life. The purpose for most individuals is to improve themselves and to achieve a realistic self-concept.

A FEW TIPS FOR STAYING COMMITTED

1. Make a list of the physiological and psychological benefits you expect to achieve from your program.
2. Think about past successes in your life, how you achieved them, why they were important to you, and their significance in the long and short term.
3. Evaluate your chances of success by evaluating your present status, your capabilities, and your limitations. Don't underestimate your potential. Remember! No one fails when he or she exercises.
4. Think how a training program will benefit you. Are you convinced that the physical and psychological changes that result from exercise will be beneficial?
5. Set both short- and long-term goals. Be honest with yourself about what you can accomplish. Set realistic and achievable goals.
6. Plan a strategy by making a list of what you need to do. This book will help you in this area.
7. Find a support group; you might find it beneficial to exercise with one or more friends. A group can provide feedback and personal support.
8. Vary your exercises to avoid boredom. Introduce variation, be creative, select exercises that bring out new skills, and extend and challenge old ones. Music also helps.
9. Stay within your limits and don't be obsessive about exercising. Don't worry about missing a few exercise periods. Don't be awed by others with more strength. Individualize your program. Don't compete with others.
10. Record your progress. *Keep records but don't keep score.*
11. Be patient. Nothing worthwhile happens overnight. There will be slumps and bad days and temporary loss in skill. Don't expect instant success. Change will occur.

CHANGING BEHAVIOR

It is difficult to change behavior without addressing the underlying causes; otherwise the same problems come back along with a new set of problems. Also, many of our behaviors tend to be adaptive and not maladaptations to everyday events. That is, we tend to make adaptations that enable us to get through each day with a minimum amount of stress. Another difficulty is that when we attempt to change our behavior in a positive way, we tend to find ways to undermine it. Certain changes make us feel less free, and feeling free is often more important than concerns about our health. However, if we are presented with informed choices for behavioral change, reinforced by results that we can experience and measure, we tend to stay committed.

Setting Goals

It is important to establish goals so that your progress toward a healthier life can be observed and measured. In order to do this, it is vital to develop a greater awareness of yourself and your environment. Focus on your lifestyle and convince yourself that you are capable of self-assessment and of taking action in the process of moving toward your goals.

Many individuals attribute their failure to achieve goals to lack of ability. They tend not to try again or persist; they stop trying. Research tells us that the reasons for failure can directly affect the ability to carry on. The most common reasons are lack of effort, ability, task difficulty, and luck. It is important to remember that motivation is changeable and under your control.

Critical Thinking 5-1

A student asks if it is necessary to set goals before embarking on a resistance-training program.

What could you tell this student about the importance of short- and long-term goal setting?

Some important aspects of goal setting include the following:

1. Select a goal you can definitely attain if you exert sufficient effort.
2. Remember your level of success in achieving your goal is directly linked to the amount of effort you exert. Your willingness to undergo some discomfort is vital to achieving your goals.
3. If successful or unsuccessful in realizing your goals, determine why.
4. When you have reached your goals, establish new ones.

Foremost in this procedure is the establishment of measurable short- and long-term goals. For example, short-term goals could be determining your target heart rate, degree of flexibility, range of motion, or the amount of resistance to use for weight training. Examples of long-term goals could be jogging a mile in ten minutes, reaching the recommended muscle strength for your age and sex, or reducing your body fat by 5 percent. It is also important to set new goals as the previous ones are reached.

Some Important Aspects of Goal Setting

1. Establish your own realistic goals.
2. Put them in writing.
3. Your goal must be attainable.
4. Your goal must be measurable.
5. Your goal should have target dates.
6. Your goal should allow for change.
7. Your goal should state the amount of effort as well as outcome.

WHY DO PEOPLE LIFT?

The reasons that people lift weights are as varied and numerous as the people who lift. The weight room may be the most democratic of settings in all of sports and society. People of both sexes and all ethnic, socioeconomic, and age groups lift weights. They may lift to improve sport performance, improve physical appearance, improve fitness level, enjoy a physical activity, or a combination of some or all of the above.

Regardless of the reason or reasons, almost everyone who lifts weights experiences an improved self-image. Strength truly builds confidence. An increase in self-confidence can go a long way in improving one's sport performance, physical appearance, and outlook on life.

MENTAL PREPARATION

Today's athlete can find no more fertile area in which to improve his or her performance than that of psychological preparation. The importance of this avenue for improving both training and contest performance has been known for years. In the United States many professional and university teams use sport psychologists to help improve individual and team performance. In addition, many individual athletes not associated with teams are using sport psychology techniques and exercises to improve their training and performance.

We will concentrate primarily on the psychological techniques that are most pertinent to improve weight training performance, but we urge you to look further into additional techniques and exercises that may be pertinent to your particular sport or activity. A recommended reading list is given at the end of this chapter.

In weight training the majority of our efforts go towards training. Thus, if we can use some psychological techniques successfully, we can improve our training efforts, and gains will be greater.

ATTENTION, FOCUS, AND CONCENTRATION

The terms attention, focus, or concentration refer to the ability to direct our thoughts and efforts to a specific task and ignore extraneous stimuli. In weight training, you must be able to focus your attention on the lift in order to achieve maximum performance. This process is enhanced by limiting external stimuli that divert your attention and by narrowing your attention to the lift.

VISUALIZATION AND IMAGERY

One technique that can be useful in focusing your attention is visualization. It is commonly used by many athletes today. The process involves rehearsing the lift in your mind and seeing (visualizing) yourself performing the lift. You imagine through mental rehearsal the process of lowering the weight, the feeling of its weight, the power with which you stop the weight and change its direction upward, and the force of exertion as you press it upward. In your mind's eye you watch yourself doing this as you feel the sensation of doing so. You are rehearsing a successful lift. This is a particularly good technique to use when you are trying for a maximum lift.

Table 5.1

Changing Negative Thoughts to Positive Ones	
Negative thoughts	**Change to positive thoughts**
I can't . . .	I can do it. I have done it many times before.
I won't be at my best because . . .	I have done everything I can do to prepare.
The heat is so bad I cannot do anything . . .	The heat creates a greater challenge.
I am really nervous and anxious . . .	The last time I felt this way, I performed my best.
I am afraid that I will make a fool of myself . . .	Unless I face the challenge and take the risk, I'll never know what I can accomplish.
I don't want to fail . . .	What is absolutely the worst thing that could happen to me? I could lose. If so, I will work harder to try to prevent that.
What is the worst thing that could happen?	I will be disappointed if things do not turn out as I want them to; however, I'll work harder to ensure success.
You stupid jerk . . .	Why don't you try to do _____ next time? It might be a better approach than the one you are using now.
I don't think I am prepared . . .	I have practiced and trained hard for this performance so I am prepared to do well.
I am tired, I can't go on . . .	It is almost over, I know I can finish. The difficult part has passed.
I am getting worse instead of better . . .	I need to set daily goals and evaluate my progress on a regular basis.
I have failed to get beyond this point every time I have faced it . . .	I can learn from my mistakes. This time I will do what I need to do to be successful.
I don't care whether I win or lose . . .	I have put too much time and effort into preparing for this event not to put forth everything I can to be successful.
I lost again. I'll never be a winner . . .	I can learn from losing. I need to talk with a coach to get some help regarding those things I need to improve.
I will never be as good as . . .	With more work, I can improve my skills and my performance.
It is not fair. I work just as _____ but I don't do as well . . .	I may have to work harder than some to accomplish the same level. I am willing to work as hard as I have to because I want to succeed.
I never seem to be able to do this . . .	This time I am going to think through and mentally prepare so that I can do it . . .

Adapted from *The Athletes Guide to Sports Psychology,* by Harris and Harris.

POSITIVE SELF-THOUGHTS

One of the obstacles to better performance for almost every athlete is the recurrent appearance of negative thoughts. Negative thoughts occur because of the influence of past experiences, listening to the negative thoughts of others, or listening to our own self-doubts. The results of these inputs are that we often focus on a negative outcome rather than a positive outcome.

We often fail to lift a certain weight because we have convinced ourselves that we cannot do so. The way to deal with negative thoughts or self-doubts is to immediately change those thoughts to positive ones so that you are rehearsing success rather than failure.

GUIDELINES

The following is a list of guidelines that you should follow during your exercise program.

Begin Gradually and Progress Slowly. Results will show up in about two or three months; don't be in a rush.

Always Check your Heart Rate During and Immediately After Exercise. Your heart rate response will tell you if you are doing too much, too soon, or too little.

Apply the Progressive Overload Principle. Gradually overloading a body system will lead to an increase in its capacity.

Exercise a Minimum of Three to Four Times Weekly for Thirty Minutes or More. Exercise duration below this will not substantially increase your capacity.

Alternate Light and Heavy Training. This will allow adequate recovery between workouts and reduce the risk of injury.

Warm Up Before Each Exercise Session. Warm-up will increase the work capacity of your muscles and heart and reduce the risk of injury.

Cool Down After Each Exercise Session. This will allow you to maintain the blood flow from the exercised muscles to the heart and decrease recovery time.

Use the Appropriate Training Program Outlined in Each Chapter. The start of your exercise program should be based on the outcome of your fitness evaluation found in chapter 3.

Glossary

Attention/Focus/Concentration The ability to direct our thoughts and effort to a specific task and ignore extraneous stimuli.
Imagery The mental picture we focus upon during visualization, such as the successful completion of a lift. These images help us in the process of performing our intended tasks.
Motivation The basic reason why we strive, work, and persevere toward our goals.
Visualization The process of forming a mental picture of an act that we will perform. Visualization can also be described as the act of rehearsing the successful completion of an act that we wish to perform.

Solutions to Critical Thinking

5-1. The old saying "You can't get lost if you don't know where you are going" applies here. It is essential to set short- and long-term goals and maintain progress records in order to properly evaluate you body's response to a resistance-training program. A short-term goal may be to exercise three times a week for eight weeks. A long-term goal may be to bench press your body weight.

Review Questions

1. What are some of the reasons for the high percentage of dropouts from exercise programs?
2. What advice would you give an individual beginning a strength-training program in order for him or her to stay committed?
3. Why is it important to set goals when embarking on a resistance-training program?

References

Coakley, J. S*port in society: Issues and controversies*. 6th ed. McGraw-Hill, Dubuque, IA, 1998.

Cox, R. H. *Sport psychology*. 4th ed. McGraw-Hill, Dubuque, IA, 1998.

Garfield, Charles A., and Hal Z. Bennett. *Peak performance—Mental training techniques of the world's greatest athletes*. J. P. Tharcher, Los Angeles, CA, 1984.

Garfield and Bennett. *Peak performance, mental training techniques of the world's greatest athletes*. J. P. Tharcher, Los Angeles, 1984.

Harris and Harris. *The athletes guide to sports psychology: Mental skills for physical people*. Leisure Press, New York, 1984.

Jerome, John. *Staying with it*. The Viking Press, New York, 1984.

McGlynn, George H. *Dynamics of fitness, a practical approach*. McGraw-Hill, Dubuque, IA, St. Louis, 1999.

Suinn, R. M. *Psychology in sports: Methods and applications*. Burgess, Minneapolis, MN, 1980.

Williams, Jean M. *Applied sports psychology*. Mayfield Press, Palo Alto, CA, 1986.

chapter 6

evaluation and self-assessment

Objectives

After studying this chapter you should be able to

1. Describe the importance of fitness evaluation.
2. Define muscle strength and endurance.
3. Define cardiovascular endurance.
4. Define body density.
5. Define flexibility.
6. Explain tests for muscle strength and endurance.
7. Explain tests for cardiovascular endurance.
8. Explain tests for body density.
9. Explain tests for flexibility.

It is essential that you make an objective evaluation of your present muscle strength and endurance in order to determine the focus of your training program. Muscle endurance is to some degree dependent upon muscle strength. However, it is possible to have a high level of muscle strength and a low level of muscle endurance. Also, this evaluation will enable you to set reasonable strength training goals and prevent unnecessary stress on your body's systems.

Also included in a complete physical fitness evaluation are tests of cardiorespiratory endurance, body composition, and flexibility. Because of the many variables necessarily found in fitness tests, such as sex, age, height, flexibility, and motivation, these tests are not precise measures and are subject to error. They should be used only as general guidelines for outlining your fitness program and as general indicators of how you compare with others of your age and sex.

MUSCLE STRENGTH TEST

Muscle strength can be easily assessed by the one-repetition maximum test (1 RM), the maximum amount of weight you can successfully lift once. Four tests are utilized: bench press (figure 6.1a and b), leg press (figure 6.2a and b), biceps curl (figure 6.3a and b), and shoulder press (figure 6.4a and b). For each, determine the greatest weight that you can lift just once for that particular lift. Begin with a weight that you can lift comfortably. Then keep adding weight until you can lift the weight correctly just one time. If you can lift the weight more than once, more pounds should be added until the true 1 RM is reached.

For each muscle group, divide the total amount of weight lifted by your present body weight in pounds to determine the percentage of weight lifted. Now find your percentages in table 6.1. This table is based upon the percentage of your body weight you can lift for each of the exercises.

(A more comprehensive muscle strength list may be found in appendix B.)

MUSCULAR ENDURANCE

Table 6.2 can be used to assess your muscular endurance.

The norms are based on a college-age population. (See chapter 10 for proper exercise positions.)

a.
b.

Figure 6.1 (*a*) BENCH PRESS (universal description).

From a supine position on the bench, grasp the bar with an overhand grip with the hands approximately shoulder-width apart. (*b*) Extend the elbows fully, but do not lock them. Progressively increase the weight until you can no longer make the lift.

a.
b.

Figure 6.2 (*a*) LEG PRESS.

Place your feet on the pedals and grasp the handles on the seat. (*b*) Press your feet forward to elevate the weight and return. Inhale while lowering the weight and exhale while lifting it. Progressively increase the weight until you can no longer make the lift. Avoid hyperextending or locking knees.

PRECAUTION REGARDING THE ONE RM MAXIMUM STRENGTH TEST

Older individuals, those who have been sedentary for some time, and those with a low level of strength should not attempt the 1 RM test for maximum strength until approximately week eight of their training program. After eight weeks they will have developed sufficient skill, flexibility, and familiarization with lifting so that there is little chance of possible injury with the 1 RM test. The 10 RM level (see chapter 3) should be used in training up until the eighth week. Your 10 RM at a particular weight is equal to approximately 75 percent of your 1 RM. This can be used to estimate an individual's 1 RM in situations when a 1 RM attempt is inappropriate. Physically active college

Critical Thinking 6-1

An individual beginning a weight-resistance program has been told by a friend that he should take a 1 RM test before starting his program.

What would you caution him about?

Table 6.1

Muscle Strength Tests

Male	Percentage of weight lifted	Very poor	Poor	Average	Good	Very good	Excellent	Superior
Fitness level								
Bench press	_____	50	75	100	110	120	140	150
Leg press	_____	160	180	200	210	220	230	240
Biceps curl	_____	30	40	50	55	60	70	80
Shoulder press	_____	40	50	67	70	80	110	120

Female	Percentage of weight lifted	Very poor	Poor	Average	Good	Very good	Excellent	Superior
Fitness level								
Bench press	_____	40	60	70	75	80	90	100
Leg press	_____	100	120	140	145	150	175	190
Biceps curl	_____	15	20	35	40	45	55	60
Shoulder press	_____	20	30	47	55	60	60	80

Source: From *Health and Fitness through Physical Activity* by M. L. Pollock, J. H. Wilmore, and S. M. Fox. Copyright © 1978 by John Wiley and Sons. Reprinted with permission of the publisher.

Table 6.2

Dynamic Muscular Endurance Test Battery

Percent of body weight lifted

Exercise	Men	Women	Repetitions (max = 15)
Arm curl	0.33	0.25	_____
Bench press	0.66	0.50	_____
Lateral pulldown	0.66	0.50	_____
Triceps extension	0.33	0.33	_____
Leg extension	0.50	0.50	_____
Leg curl	0.33	0.33	_____
Bent-knee sit-up			_____
		Total repetitions (max = 105) =	_____

Total repetitions	Fitness category*
91–105	Excellent
77–90	Very good
63–76	Good
49–62	Fair
35–48	Poor
<35	Very poor

*Based on data for 250 college-age men and women.

Source: Heyward, V. *Design for Fitness*. Minneapolis: Burgess, 1984, p. 47. Used by permission.

a.   b.

Figure 6.3   (*a*) BICEPS CURL.

Grasp the bar with your hands shoulder-width apart, using an underhand grip. Bring the bar to a position of rest against your thigh, with your elbows fully extended and your feet spread shoulder-width apart. (*b*) Using only your arms, raise the bar to your chest and then return to the starting position. Keep your back straight and always return to a position where your elbows are fully extended. Progressively increase the weight until you can no longer make the lift.

a.   b.

Figure 6.4   (*a*) SHOULDER PRESS (universal description).

Sit with your feet on the floor. Bend your knees and grasp the bar with an overhand grip, hands spread approximately shoulder-width apart. (*b*) With your elbows under the bar, assume a flat back, press the bar over your head as you exhale (do not forcefully lock elbows), and return to your starting position. Progressively increase the weight until you can no longer make the lift.

students may be given the 1 RM test during the second or third week. However, the test for muscular endurance can be safely administered during the first weeks of the training program.

STRENGTH EVALUATION

The reason for monitoring strength is to help in the evaluation and progression of resistance-training programs. Programs as well as goals can be quite diverse. The amount of strength development is dependent upon the exercise prescription, time available, and objectives of the program. Regular assessment of strength capabilities allows the exercise prescription to be properly evaluated and changes to be made when appropriate.

Decisions have to be made to insure a proper cost-benefit ratio. Strength development does not continue at a constant rate of increase or magnitude of change over a long-term training program. In some situations, for example, small changes in strength require large amounts of training when a person is close to his or her theoretical limit.

It is important to get a baseline reading for muscular strength before the start of your strength-training program, in addition to proper instruction in lifting methods.

PUSH-UPS

Start in a standard "up" position for a full push-up, with your weight on your toes and hands. (If you have limited upper body strength, you can perform this test with your knees bent and your weight on your knees and hands.) Figure 6.5a and b illustrates both positions. Your partner should place his or her fist on the floor beneath your chest. Lower yourself until your chest touches your partner's fist. Keep your back straight while rising to an "up" position. Count the number of consecutively performed push-ups and then refer to table 6.3 to determine your fitness level.

a.

b.

Figure 6.5 (*a*) and (*b*) PUSH-UPS.

Table 6.3

Push-Up Test

Standard push-up (weight on toes)

	Fitness level						
Age (years)	Superior	Excellent	Very good	Good	Average	Poor	Very poor
15–29	Above 51	51–54	45–50	35–44	25–34	20–25	15–19
30–39	Above 41	41–44	35–40	25–34	20–24	15–20	8–14
40–49	Above 36	35–39	30–35	20–29	14–19	12–14	5–11
50–59	Above 31	31–34	25–30	15–24	12–14	8–12	3–7
60–69	Above 26	26–29	20–25	10–19	8–9	5–7	0–4

Modified push-up (weight on hands and knees)

	Fitness level						
Age (years)	Superior	Excellent	Very good	Good	Average	Poor	Very poor
15–29	Above 48	46–48	34–45	17–33	10–16	6–9	0–5
30–39	Above 38	33–37	25–33	12–24	8–11	4–7	0–3
40–49	Above 33	29–32	20–28	8–19	6–7	3–5	0–2
50–59	Above 26	21–25	15–21	6–14	4–5	2–3	0–1
60–69	Above 20	15–19	5–15	3–4	2–3	1–2	0–

Source: From *Health and Fitness through Physical Activity* by M. L. Pollock, J. H. Wilmore, and S. M. Fox. Copyright © 1978 by John Wiley and Sons. Reprinted with permission of the publisher.

Figure 6.6 HEAD AND SHOULDER RAISE.

HEAD-AND-SHOULDER RAISE

Lie on your back with arms across your chest. Your knees should be bent at about ninety degrees with both feet flat and no more than eighteen inches in front of the buttocks (see figure 6.6). Don't forget to breathe, to assist in muscular contraction. Complete as many raises as possible in one minute. Warm up with a few raises before the test. Curl your neck and upper back until your trunk reaches a thirty to forty degree angle with the exercise surface, then return to the starting position.

Refer to table 6.4 to determine your fitness level.

Table 6.4

Head-and-Shoulder Raise Score

Age (years)	Very poor	Poor	Average	Good	Very good	Excellent	Superior
Males							
17–29	0–17	17–35	36–41	42–47	48–50	51–55	55+
30–39*	0–13	13–26	27–32	33–38	39–43	44–48	48+
40–49	0–11	11–22	23–27	28–33	34–38	39–43	43+
50–59	0–8	8–16	17–21	22–28	29–33	34–38	38+
60–69	0–6	6–12	13–17	18–24	25–30	31–35	35+
Females							
17–29	0–14	14–28	29–32	33–35	36–42	43–47	47+
30–39*	0–11	11–22	23–28	29–34	35–40	41–45	45+
40–49	0–9	9–18	19–23	24–30	31–34	35–40	40+
50–59	0–6	6–12	13–17	18–24	25–30	31–35	35+
60–69	0–5	5–10	11–14	15–20	21–25	26–30	30+

*The value of ages over thirty is estimated.

Source: Reprinted by permission of the Cooper Institute for Aerobic Research, Dallas, Texas, 75265.

Table 6.5

Modified Sit-and-Reach

	Score at age				
	20–29	30–39	40–49	50–59	60+
Men					
High	≥19	≥18	≥17	≥16	≥15
Average	13–18	12–17	11–16	10–15	9–14
Below average	10–12	9–11	8–10	7–9	6–8
Low	<9	<8	<7	<6	<5
Women					
High	≥22	≥21	≥20	≥19	≥18
Average	16–21	15–20	14–19	13–18	12–17
Below average	13–15	12–14	11–13	10–12	9–11
Low	<12	<11	<10	<9	<8

Source: Reprinted by permission from *ACSM Resource Manual for Guidelines for Exercise Testing and Prescription* (p. 165) by S. Blair, P. Painter, R. R. Pate, L. K. Smith, and C. B. Taylor, 1988, Philadelphia: Lea and Febiger, which was adapted from *The Y's Way to Physical Fitness* (pp. 106–111) by L. A. Golding, C. R. Myers, and W. E. Sinning (Eds.), 1982, Rosemont, IL: YMCA of the USA.

MODIFIED SIT-AND-REACH TEST

The modified sit-and-reach test is an excellent measure of trunk **flexibility** (the extent and range of motion around the joint). (See figure 6.7.) Before attempting the test, warm up by jogging briefly.

Method

1. Place a yardstick on the floor with the zero mark closest to you. Tape the yardstick in place at the fifteen inch mark. See figure 6.7.
2. Warm up properly. See chapter 13.
3. Ask a partner to help you keep your legs straight during the sit-and-reach test. However, it is important that the partner not interfere with your movement.
4. Sit on the floor with the yardstick between your legs, your feet ten to twelve inches apart, and your heels even with the tape at the fifteen-inch mark.
5. With the index fingers of both your hands together, reach forward as far as possible, keeping your knees in contact with the floor.
6. Note the distance you are able to reach. Find your score in table 6.5.

Figure 6.7 MODIFIED SIT-AND-REACH.

DETERMINE YOUR CARDIORESPIRATORY ENDURANCE LEVEL

The chief means of evaluating cardiorespiratory efficiency is to determine the body's capacity to consume oxygen at a maximum rate. The assessment of oxygen uptake through laboratory testing is the most accurate method but requires a good deal of time and sophisticated equipment and is impractical for self-testing. The one and a half mile run test can be used to measure the amount of maximum oxygen uptake by determining the heart rate response to the exercise.

1.5 MILE RUN

The 1.5 mile test can be run on an oval track or on a straightaway. You should perform this test only if you have been training to run this distance and are in good physical condition. If you become overtired while running, slow down to a jog or walk. Do not unduly overstress yourself. Keep track of the amount of time it takes you to run 1.5 miles, and then find your estimated maximum oxygen uptake in table 6.6a and your fitness level in table 6.6b.

WALKING TEST

The walking test can be performed by low-fit individuals who cannot attempt the 1.5 mile test. To perform the test find a measured track or a flat course where you can measure a mile. Take time to warm up for several minutes, first by stretching thoroughly or walking. Your walking shoes should have a roomy toe box, flexible soles with good traction, and a stiff heel cup for stability. Running shoes have too much padding, which make your feet wobble.

Time yourself as you walk the mile as fast as you can without experiencing signs of exhaustion such as nausea or shortness of breath. When you finish, record your heart rate. (Take your pulse for fifteen seconds and multiply by four.) Cool down by walking slowly for a few minutes.

Table 6.6a

1.5 Mile Run Test	
Time in minutes and seconds	**Estimated max VO$_2$ in ml/kg/min**
7:30 or less	75
7:31–8:00	72
8:01–8:30	67
8:31–9:00	62
9:01–9:30	58
9:31–10:00	55
10:01–10:30	52
10:31–11:00	49
11:01–11:30	46
11:31–12:00	44
12:01–12:30	41
12:31–13:00	39
13:01–13:30	37
13:31–14:00	36
14:01–14:30	34
14:31–15:00	33
15:01–15:30	31
15:31–16:00	30
16:01–16:30	28
16:31–17:00	27
17:01–17:30	26
17:31–18:00	25

Adapted from K. H. Cooper, "A Means of Assessing Maximal Oxygen Intake," *Journal of the American Medical Association* 203 (1968):201.

Table 6.6b

1.5 Mile Run Test[1]					
Age group (yrs)	**High**	**Good**	**Average**	**Fair**	**Poor**
10–19	Above 66	57–66	47–56	38–46	Below 38
20–29	" 62	53–62	43–52	33–42	" 33
30–39	" 58	49–58	39–48	30–38	" 30
40–49	" 54	45–54	36–44	26–35	" 26
50–59	" 50	42–50	34–41	24–33	" 24
60–69	" 46	39–46	31–38	22–30	" 22
70–79	" 42	36–42	28–35	20–27	" 20

[1]The average maximal O$_2$ uptake of females is 15 to 20 percent lower than that of males. To find the appropriate category for females, locate the score in the above table and shift one category to the left; e.g., the "Average" category for males is the "Good" category for females.

Table 6.7 will compare your current fitness level to "moderate" fitness. If you walk the mile in less time than the range shown for that heart rate, your fitness level is high. If it took you longer than that range, your fitness level is low. An older person needs a lower heart rate than a younger person in order to score as equally fit. This is because

Table 6.7

One-Mile Walking Test			
Age	**Heart rate**	**Time showing moderate fitness[1]**	
		Men (175 lbs.)	*Women (125 lbs.)*
20–29	110	17:06–19:36	19:08–20:57
	120	16:36–19:10	18:38–20:27
	130	16:06–18:35	18:12–20:00
	140	15:36–18:06	17:42–19:30
	150	15:10–17:36	17:12–19:00
	160	14:42–17:09	16:42–18:30
	170	14:12–16:39	16:12–18:00
30–39	110	15:54–18:21	17:52–19:46
	120	15:24–17:52	17:24–19:18
	130	14:54–17:22	16:54–18:48
	140	14:30–16:54	16:24–18:18
	150	14:00–16:26	15:54–17:48
	160	13:30–15:58	15:24–17:18
	170	13:01–15:28	14:55–16:54
40–49	110	15:38–18:05	17:20–19:15
	120	15:09–17:36	16:50–18:45
	130	14:41–17:07	16:24–18:18
	140	14:12–16:38	15:54–17:48
	150	13:42–16:09	15:24–17:18
	160	13:15–15:42	14:54–16:48
	170	12:45–15:12	14:25–16:18
50–59	110	15:22–17:49	17:04–18:40
	120	14:53–17:20	16:36–18:12
	130	14:24–16:51	16:06–17:42
	140	13:51–16:22	15:36–17:18
	150	13:26–15:53	15:06–16:48
	160	12:59–15:26	14:36–16:18
	170	12:30–14:56	14:06–15:48
60+	110	15:33–17:55	16:36–18:00
	120	15:04–17:24	16:06–17:30
	130	14:36–16:57	15:37–17:01
	140	14:07–16:28	15:09–16:31
	150	13:39–15:59	14:39–16:02
	160	13:10–15:30	14:12–15:32

[1]For every ten pounds over 175 pounds for men or over 125 pounds for women, time must be fifteen seconds faster. For every ten pounds under those weights, time can be fifteen seconds slower.

Source: Reprinted by permission of the Cooper Institute for Aerobic Research, Dallas, Texas, 75265.

younger people have a higher maximum heart rate. They can end the test with a faster pulse rate and still have as much cardiac capacity and reserve as an older person who tests at a slower pulse.

If you fall within the moderate fitness range in table 6.7, then you can begin your walking-jogging program (appendix D) at starting level two to three (average). If your score is two or more minutes over the moderate fitness range for your age, your starting level should be one to two (poor-very poor). If you are two minutes under the moderate fitness range, your starting level is four to five (good-very good). If you are four minutes or more under, your starting level can be five to seven (excellent-superior).

TEST FOR BODY COMPOSITION

Body composition refers to the proportion of lean body tissue to total body weight. The recommended percentage of body fat for adult males is 12 to 17 percent, for adult females 19 to 24 percent.

The skinfold test for determination of body fat is based on the relationship of subcutaneous fat (fat just below the skin) to total lean body tissue. The method is subject to errors of as much as 3 to 15 percent, plus or minus the actual body fat percentage.

To perform the test you need a pair of skinfold calipers. Hold the skinfold between the thumb and index finger. Release the tension on the calipers slowly so that they pinch the skinfold as close as possible to your fingers. Three measures are required for both male and female: the chest, thigh, and abdomen for the male, and the triceps, thigh, and iliac crest for the female. See figures 6.8 through 6.12.

Figure 6.8 CHEST SKINFOLD MEASUREMENT.

Locate a point over the outside edge of the pectoralis major mucsle just adjacent and medial to the armpit. The skinfold should run diagonally betwen the shoulder and the opposite hip.

Figure 6.9 THIGH SKINFOLD MEASUREMENT.

Locate a vertical skinfold in the anterior midline of the thigh, halfway between the hip and the knee joint. Place your body weight on the opposite leg while taking the measurement.

Figure 6.10 ABDOMEN SKINFOLD MEASUREMENT.

Locate a vertical skinfold adjacent to the umbilicus.

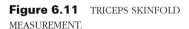

Figure 6.11 TRICEPS SKINFOLD MEASUREMENT.

Locate a vertical skinfold on the back of the arm halfway between the tip of the acromion process (bony projection on the tip of the shoulder) and the olecranon process (rear point of the elbow), with the arm hanging in a relaxed position.

Figure 6.12 ILIAC CREST SKINFOLD MEASUREMENT.

Locate a vertical skinfold over the iliac crest (point of the hip) in the midaxillary line (middle of the armpit).

After taking the three skinfold measurements appropriate to your sex, total the measurements on the nomogram in figure 6.13. Use the straight edge to connect the point on the left that corresponds to your age with the point on the far right that corresponds to the sum of your three skinfold measurements. Then read the percentage of body fat from the center male or female scale.

Figure 6.13

Nomogram for the determination of percentage of body fat for the sum of the chest, abdomen, and thigh skinfolds of males fifteen years of age and above, and for the sum of the triceps, thigh, and iliac crest skinfolds of females fifteen years of age and above. (See next page.)

Adapted from W.B . Baun, M. R. Baun, and P. B. Raven. "A Nomogram for the Estimate of Percent Body Fat from Generalized Equations," Research Quarterly for Exercise and Sport 52(1981):380–84. *Reprinted by permission of the American Alliance for Health, Physical Education, Recreation and Dance, 1900 Association Drive, Reston, Virginia 22091.*

🌀 **Critical Thinking 6-2**

A female swimmer said that her most recent skinfold test had shown a 2 percent increase in body fat from her previous test six months prior. She mentioned that she has reduced her caloric intake and has engaged in a rigorous aerobic exercise program four times a week for six weeks since her first test.

What would cause the increase in body fat?

Unfortunately the skinfold test is subject to error. In some cases a 3 percent error can result when different people evaluate the same person using skinfold calipers. In addition, dehydration can affect the skinfold test by as much as 10 to 15 percent.

Table 6.8

Body Fat Score			
Male percentage of body fat	**Fitness level**	**Female percentage of body fat**	**Fitness level**
10	Very lean	13	Very lean
11–12		13–15	
12–14	Lean	17–18	Lean
14–15		18–22	
15–17	Acceptable	22–28	Acceptable
17–18	Fat	28–30	Fat
20+	Obese	30+	Obese

Reprinted from *Getting Stronger* by Bill Pearl and Gary T. Moran. Copyright © 1986 Shelter Publications, Inc., Bolinas, CA. Reprinted by permission.

Figure 6.14 NOMOGRAM FOR DETERMINING BMI.

B. T. Burton and W. R. Forster, Health Implications of Obesity. An NIH Consensus Development Conference, *Journal of the Dietetic Association,* 85 (1985): pages 1117–21.

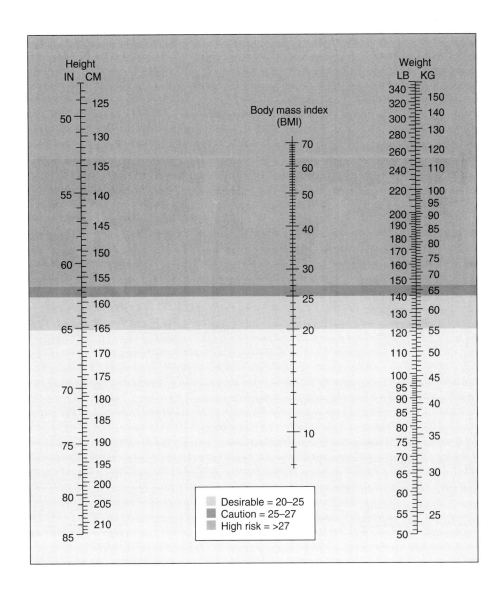

BODY MASS INDEX

If you don't have a skin caliper, **body mass index** offers an alternative way to define obesity. To calculate body mass index, divide your weight in kilograms by height in meters squared. The nomogram in figure 6.14 does this calculation for you. When the body mass index exceeds twenty-five, obesity-related health risks begin for men and women.

Mark your height and your weight on the corresponding scales, using a ruler or straight edge. Draw a line connecting those two points, then read your BMI from the middle scale.

Glossary

Body Composition   The proportion of body fat to lean body tissue.
Cardiorespiratory Efficiency   The ability of the heart to deliver oxygen to all of the organs of the body.
Flexibility   The extent and range of motion about a joint.
Muscle Endurance   The ability of a muscle to produce force continually over a period of time.
Skinfold Test   The method of estimating body fat by measuring subcutaneous fat with skinfold calipers.

Solutions to Critical Thinking

6-1. Attempting a 1 RM test at the beginning of a resistance program without proper strength and skill can result in serious injury. It is recommended that the individual should wait at least six to ten weeks before attempting a carefully prescribed 1 RM test.

6-2. Skinfold tests may have an error factor of 3 percent, especially if another individual takes the reading. In addition, if the test was taken when she was dehydrated this may also cause a recording error from 10 to 15 percent.

Review Questions

1. What are some of the precautions you would take to reduce the chance of errors utilizing the skinfold test?
2. What are the basic components of physical fitness?
3. What are some of the problems associated with administering a 1 RM test?

References

American College of Sports Medicine: *ACSM's guidelines for exercise testing and prescription*. 5th ed. Williams & Wilkins, Baltimore, 1995.

DeVries, H., and T. Houch. *Physiology of exercise*. Brown & Benchmark, Dubuque, IA, 1994.

Fox, E. 1973. A simple technique for predicting maximal aerobic power. *Journal of Applied Physiology* 35:914–916.

Howley, E., and B. D. Franks. *Health fitness: Instructors handbook*. Human Kinetics, Champaign, IL, 1992.

Jackson A., and M. Pollock. 1985 Practical assessment of body composition. *Physician and Sports Medicine* 13:76–90.

Lohman, T. 1987. The use of skinfold to estimate body fatness in children and youth. *Journal of Alliance for Health, Physical Education, Recreation, and Dance* 58:98–102.

McGlynn, G. *Dynamics of fitness: A practical approach* McGraw-Hill, Dubuque, IA, 1999.

Williams, M. *Lifetime fitness and wellness*. Wm. C. Brown, Dubuque, IA, 1996.

chapter 7

m u s c l e s

Objectives

After studying this chapter you should be able to

1. Describe the structure of a skeletal muscle.
2. Describe the physiology of a muscle contraction.
3. Define hypertrophy and atrophy.
4. Describe muscle soreness.

The basic function of skeletal muscles is to contract. This contraction enables human movement to occur. Over 600 skeletal muscles provide us with the capability to perform all manner of voluntary movement. Each voluntary muscle is a separate structure in its own right, containing connective tissue, nerves, and blood vessels. The muscles make up approximately 42 percent of the body weight in men and 36 percent in women.

STRUCTURE OF SKELETAL MUSCLE

If you were to closely examine a skeletal muscle, you would find that each muscle has its own outer covering of connective tissue called epimysium. As seen in figure 7.1, the extension of the outer connective tissue at the end of the muscle forms the tendon, which connects and anchors the muscle to the bone. If the epimysium is peeled away from the body of the muscle, a number of bundles called fasciculi are revealed. Each bundle is surrounded by its own connective tissue structure called perimysium. Contained within this muscle bundle are the individual muscle fibers. Each fiber (some the size of a human hair) is surrounded by a covering of connective tissue called endomysium.

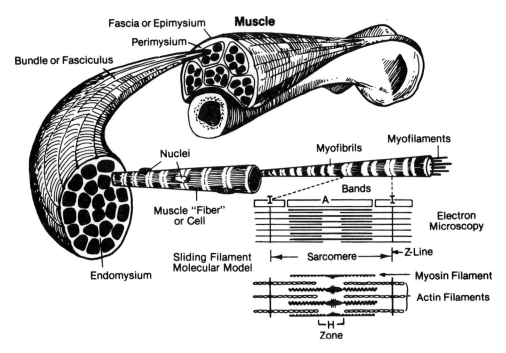

Figure 7.1 STRUCTURAL DESIGN OF HUMAN SKELETAL MUSCLE.

From Jack H. Wilmore and David L. Costill, Training for Sport and Activity, *3rd ed. Copyright © 1988 Wm. C. Brown Publishers, Dubuque, Iowa. All Rights Reserved. Reprinted by permission.*

Each muscle fiber is composed of hundreds of cylindrical-shaped structures called myofibrils. A sheath or membrane covers each fiber, separating it from the surrounding fluid. The myofibrils contain the tiny protein filaments whose actions are responsible for the contraction of the myofibrils and, in turn, the muscle. The myofibrils are immersed in the fluid portion of the fiber called sarcoplasm. The sarcoplasm contains enzymes to power the mitochondria, which are the power packs of the cell. Myofibrils contain two kinds of protein filaments, thick ones composed of the protein myosin and thin ones composed of the protein actin. These proteins are geometrically aligned throughout the muscle.

As seen in figure 7.2, the smallest unit of the myofibril is the sarcomere, which is the distance between two Z-lines. When the muscle is stimulated by the nervous system, this small unit will contract. The A-band, the dark portion of the sarcomere, consists of both actin and myosin filaments with the actin filaments attached to the Z-lines. The tiny projections extending from the myosin filaments or the actin filaments are called the myosin cross bridges (fig. 7.3). These tiny cross-bridges are instrumental in the shortening of the muscle. When the muscle contracts, the actin filament slides over the myosin filament toward the center of the sarcomere in a coupling process where the myosin cross-bridges form a temporary bond with the actin filaments. This coupling process is dependent on the release of calcium ions stored in a membranous structure called the sarcoplasmic reticulum. Active sites on the actin filaments are covered by troponen and tropomyosin proteins. When the calcium ions are released, they bind with troponen and cause a change in tropomyosin so that it exposes active sites on the actin filament. When coupling takes place, the cross-bridges swivel in a manner that causes the actin filaments to slide over the myosin filaments. This process activates the enzyme ATPase (adenosine triphosphatase) that breaks down ATP (adenosine triphosphate) stored on the cross-bridges. ATP provides energy for the

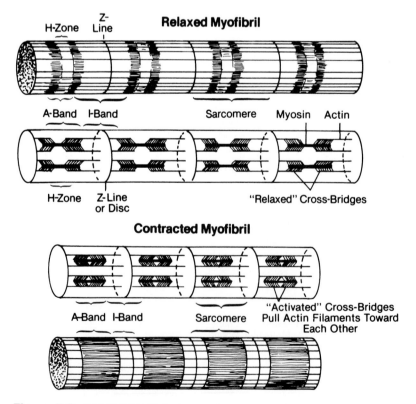

Figure 7.2 THE SEQUENCE OF EVENTS THAT TAKES PLACE WITHIN A MYOFIBRIL DURING CONTRACTION.

Figure 7.3 MYOSIN MOLECULES HAVE PROJECTIONS THAT EXTEND TOWARD NEARBY ACTIN FILAMENTS.

From Jack H. Wilmore and David L. Costill, Training for Sport and Activity, *3d ed. Copyright © 1988 Wm. C. Brown Publishers, Dubuque, Iowa. All Rights Reserved. Reprinted by permission.*

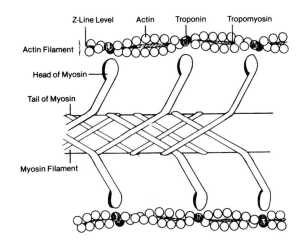

ANTERIOR VIEW OF SUPERFICIAL SKELETAL MUSCLES.

POSTERIOR VIEW OF SUPERFICIAL SKELETAL MUSCLES.

Brachialis

Temporalis

Occipitalis

Sternocleidomastoid

Trapezius

Deltoid

Teres minor

Teres major

Triceps brachii

Brachio-radialis

Infraspinatus

Rhomboideus

Latissimus dorsi

External oblique

Gluteus medius

Gluteus maximus

Adductor magnus

Gracilis

Vastus lateralis

Biceps femoris

Semitendinosus

Semimembranosus

Sartorius

Gastrocnemius

Calcaneal tendon

Soleus

Peroneus longus

action between actin and myosin. For more shortening to occur, the cross-bridges must break bonds already formed and bind to other active sites reloaded with ATP on the actin filament. This process is called recharging. When neural stimulation stops, calcium ions are pumped back into the sarcoplasmic reticulum, the cross-bridges uncouple, and the muscle relaxes.

AGONIST AND ANTAGONIST

Muscles and muscle groups work in harmony to produce a movement. When the leg is extended, the muscle responsible for that movement is called the agonist or prime mover. Another muscle, the antagonist, has to relax to allow for smooth movement. In leg extension movements, the quadriceps are the agonists, and the hamstrings are the antagonists. The antagonists are also capable of resisting agonist action and are responsible for movement in the opposite direction. The antagonists of the prime mover that extends the leg are responsible for flexing it. If both agonists and antagonists contract at the same time, the part they act upon will remain stationary. Smooth coordinated movements depend upon the prime mover and antagonist working in harmony. It is therefore important to strengthen both groups of muscles and not one at the expense of the other.

TENDONS

Tendons are the extension of the outer cover of the muscle and anchor the muscle to the bone. They have the appearance of white glistening cords or bands.

LIGAMENTS

Ligaments are strong flexible bands or capsules of fibrous tissue that help hold the bones together at the joints. They play a significant role in determining the range of motion of the joint.

ATROPHY

Critical Thinking 7-1

A student was not sure at what level he should resume his training after a lay-off of three weeks. He had been training for six weeks prior to this break.

What is your advice?

With a lack of neural stimulation and exercise, a wasting process may take place in which the muscle becomes smaller and weaker. This process, called atrophy, is often apparent when a limb has been in a cast or immobilized for an extended period of time.

SLOW- AND FAST-TWITCH MUSCLE FIBERS

Human muscles contain three types of muscle fibers: a slow-twitch Type I *red fiber* and two types of fast-twitch Type II *white fibers*. Each fiber type is structurally and chemically equipped to perform work for long or short periods of time. For example, fast-twitch fibers are preferentially used for short-term, high-intensity exercises such as sprinting, while slow-twitch fibers are used during longer, less intensive exercise such as long-distance running.

Exercise cannot change the types or numbers of fibers in your muscles, as these characteristics (or traits) are inherited. However, the efficiency of both red and white muscle fibers can be increased through proper training methods. A specific type of exercise must be used to improve the efficiency of a given fiber type. For example, to increase the metabolic potential of fast-twitch fibers, high intensity exercise of few repetitions must be used. Conversely, exercises of longer duration with lower intensities increase the metabolic potential of slow-twitch fibers.

Fast-twitch fibers produce greater force than slow-twitch fibers. As a result, individuals with a greater cross sectional area of fast-twitch fibers are capable of generating greater strength. Fast-twitch units, however, are quick to fatigue from very intense contractions, which demand high rates of force development.

HYPERTROPHY

Hypertrophy is an increase in the size and functional capacity of a muscle. There are two types of hypertrophy, transient and chronic. Transient hypertrophy is caused by the pumping action of the muscle and results in fluid accumulation in the muscle. This temporary enlargement disappears shortly after termination of exercise. In chronic (or true) hypertrophy the muscle growth results from enlargement of the muscle fiber. This growth is directly related to the increased synthesis of protein that increases the thickness of the myofibrils. Tension overload may also stimulate proliferation of connective tissue, capillarization, and satellite cells that surround the muscle fibers and improve the *structural integrity of ligaments and tendons.* The greatest hypertrophy is seen in those muscles that in everyday activity do the least work in relation to their genetic potential. The tension a muscle develops during exercise is a stimulus for increased uptake of amino acids and enhanced synthesis of protein. In addition, it is thought that a breakdown and buildup process takes place. This theory holds that intensive training breaks down muscle protein that then rebuilds between training sessions and leads to a super compensation and an increase in muscle size. However, the exact cellular mechanism by which resistance training results in increased muscle size is still unknown.

THE FAR SIDE By GARY LARSON

"I don't know what to tell you, Mr. Miller, but something has definitely gone awry with your workout program."

The degree of hypertrophy will depend not only on the severity of the overload but the total duration of the overload. However, one must be cautioned about individual exceptions to this principle. For instance, individuals with a large number of fibers may have an advantage in terms of their capacity for training over those with fewer fibers, particularly in bodybuilding. Also, evidence indicates that bodybuilders who engage in high-volume, low-intensity training gain increased size of slow-twitch fibers and increased capillarization. Power lifters who engage in low-volume, high-intensity training gain increased size of fast-twitch fibers with decreased capillarization.

HYPERPLASIA

Hyperplasia is an increase in the number of muscle fibers. Considerable controversy still exists regarding whether or not heavy resistance training results in an increase in muscle fibers (hyperplasia). Recent research has criticized the methodology used in former studies that found some evidence of fiber splitting. The differences in research results may be due to differences in the mode of training as well as methodology. The consensus is that weight training or other exercises do not result in an increase in the number of muscle fibers; rather they increase the size and functional capacity of existing fibers.

MUSCLE SORENESS

Many individuals engaged in rigorous exercise encounter muscle soreness. Two different patterns of soreness are apparent. The first type is soreness that occurs during the latter stages of, or immediately after, exercise. This type of soreness is thought to result from high hydrostatic pressure caused by fluid from the blood entering the muscle tissue. The second type of soreness generally appears twelve to forty-eight hours after a strenuous exercise. We have all had the unpleasant experience of waking up the next morning barely able to move after a previous day's exercise.

Muscle soreness that occurs approximately twelve to twenty-four hours after exercise may be caused by an influx of calcium ions into the mitochondria. Leukocyte

Critical Thinking 7-2

An individual has complained that one day after beginning his strength-training program he suffered severe muscle soreness.

Explain to him the physiological basis for muscle soreness.

Table 7.1

Weight Exercises and Major Muscles Involved

Biceps—Barbell curls, dumbbell curls, pull-ups, reverse curls.

Triceps—French curls, tricep extensor (standing or lat machine). Bar-dips, military press, bench press, pullovers (bent arm).

Brachialis—Reverse curls, upright rowing.

Deltoids—Military press, behind the neck press, dumbbell press, upright rowing, pullovers (bent arm), lateral raise (standing), bent rowing.

Flexor carpi—Wrist curls, curls, grip machine.

Pectoralis—Bench press, lateral raise (incline or supine), pullovers and press, lat pull (machine).

Trapezius—Shoulder shrugs, behind the neck press.

Rhomboids—Bent rowing, shoulder shrugs, lat pull (machine).

Latissimus dorsi—Lat pull (machine), bent rowing, dumbbell rowing, pullovers (bent arm).

Serratus—Pullovers (bent or straight arm).

Abdominals—Sit-ups (all varieties), scissor kick (incline), leg lifts (hanging), leg pullovers (incline).

External obliques—Side bending (dumbbell or barbell), stiff-legged side lift.

Erector Spinae—Stiff-legged dead lift, dead lift, back hyperextensions.

Gluteus Maximus—Squats, leg press (machine).

Quadriceps—Squats, leg press (machine), knee extension (machine).

Hamstrings—Knee flexions (machine), squats.

Gastrocnemius and soleus—Toe raises (leg press machine or standing).

infiltration may also result in an inflammatory response. Soreness is more prevalent in eccentric contractions because fewer muscle fibers are activated than in concentric contractions. This may cause edema, swelling, and inflammation.

Generally muscle soreness after exercise can be limited if there is a good pre- and post-warm-up and stretching. Stretching can also bring some relief from existing pain in the muscle. Easy swimming or cycling can help reduce soreness.

Glossary

Actin   Thin contractile protein in muscle fibers.
Agonist   Muscle responsible for movement.
Antagonist   Muscle that relaxes to allow agonist to contract.
Atrophy   Decrease in the size of muscle tissue.
Epimysium   Fibrous connective tissue surrounding skeletal muscle.
Fasciculus   Bundles of muscle fibers enclosed by connective tissue, which make up a skeletal muscle.
Fast Twitch   Fast-twitch Type II muscle fibers physiologically adapted for short-term, high-intensity exercise.
Hyperplasia   An increase in the number of muscle cells.
Hypertrophy   Enlargement in muscle size.
Ligament   Connective tissue that attaches bone to bone.
Muscle Soreness   Muscle pain resulting from chemical or physical changes in the muscle tissue.
Myosin   Thick contractile filaments that make up the muscle fibers.
Slow Twitch   Slow-twitch Type I muscle fibers physiologically adapted for endurance activity with a high capacity to use oxygen.
Tendon   A cord of connective tissue that attaches muscle to bone.

Solutions to Critical Thinking

7-1.   A period of three weeks, in this case without training, is not sufficient to result in losses of muscle strength and endurance. However, he should start with a slightly lighter resistance the first few sessions and then resume his normal training load without fear of injury.

7-2. Delayed muscle soreness twenty-four to forty-eight hours after beginning an exercise program is a common phenomenon. It is generally brought about by calcium into the cells and in some cases microscopic tears in the muscle fibers. Stretching before and after the exercise can substantially reduce some of the soreness in addition to ice application. Eccentric contractions (negative work) usually cause greater soreness than concentric contractions. If the soreness lasts longer than a few days, he should seek medical advice.

Review Questions

1. What are some of the differences between a slow-twitch and fast-twitch muscle fiber?
2. What is the physiological basis for delayed muscle soreness?
3. What causes skeletal muscle to increase in size (hypertrophy) as a result of strength training?

References

Booth, F. W., and D. B. Thomason. 1991. Molecular and cellular adaptation of muscle in response to exercise: Perspectives of various models. *Physiological Review* 71:541–585.

Castro, M. J., D. J. McCann, J. D. Shaffrath, and W. C. Adams. 1995. Peak torque per unit cross-sectional area differs between strength-trained and untrained young adults. *Medicine and Science in Sports and Exercise* 27:397–403.

Komi, P. V. 1984. Physiological and biomechanical correlates of muscle function: Effects of muscle structure and stretch-shortening cycle on force and speed. *Exercise Science Sports Review* 12:81–121.

McCarthy, J. P., J. E. Agre, B. K. Graf, M. A. Pozniak, and A. C. Vailas. 1995. Compatibility of adaptive responses with combining strength and endurance training. *Medicine and Science in Sports and Exercise* 27:429–436.

Nardone, A., C. Romano, and M. Schieppatgi. 1989. Selective recruitment of high-threshold human motor units during voluntary isotonic lengthening of active muscles. *Journal of Physiology* 409:451–471.

Rooney, K. J., R. D. Herbert, and R. J. Balnave. 1994. Fatigue contributes to the strength training stimulus. *Medicine and Science in Sports and Exercise* 26:1160–1164.

Sale, D. G. 1988. Neural adaptation to resistance training. *Medicine and Science in Sports and Exercise* 20 (Suppl.):135–145.

Shephard, R. J., E. Bouhlel, H. Vandewalle, and H. Monod. 1988. Muscle mass as a factor limiting physical work. *Journal of Applied Physiology* 64:1472–1479.

Soest, A. J. van, and M. F. Boibbert. 1993. The role of muscle properties in control of explosive movements. *Biol. Cybern* 69:195–204.

Treuth, M. S., G. R. Hunter, T. Kekes-Szabo, R. L. Weinsier, M. I. Goran, and L. Berland. 1995. Reduction in intra-abdominal adipose tissue after strength training in older women. *Journal of Applied Physiology* 78:1425–1431.

Welle, S., C. Thornton, and M. Statt. 1995. Myofibrillar protein synthesis in young and old human subjects after three months of resistance training. *American Journal of Physiology* 268:E422–427.

training concepts

Objectives

After studying this chapter you should be able to

1. Define strength, power, and speed.
2. Describe force potential.
3. Describe nerve control of skeletal muscles.
4. Define isotonic, isometric, eccentric, concentric, and isokinetic contraction.

Strength training has finally emerged from the dark ages of ignorance and uncertainty. In recent years a great deal of excellent research has occurred in the areas of muscle cell physiology and muscle training techniques. As a result, a substantial body of knowledge has been established that supports a number of basic muscle training concepts.

STRENGTH, POWER, AND SPEED

There has always been a great deal of interest in the amount of maximal force or strength potential of muscles. *Muscle strength* (the amount of force that can be exerted by a muscle group for one movement or repetition) has always been considered to be an essential basis of athletic skill. Strength training by its nature emphasizes the force component of a movement but not the acceleration component essential in power. Recently, however, new interest has arisen in the maximal rate that a muscle can generate and transfer mechanical energy, which is expressed as power. Power is basically the product of strength and speed (power = force × distance/time). It is obvious from this formula that muscle power is dependent on the interaction of strength and speed. An increase in either force or speed will result in increased power. However, strength will play only a minor role unless the athlete can apply it explosively over a short period of time. The great majority of sports require power and, though strength is an essential ingredient of power, speed must receive special consideration. For example, the strongest football lineman may not necessarily be the best if he doesn't have the speed that allows him to outmaneuver and outleverage his opponent. The quickness of the first step in basketball, changing direction in football, and the explosiveness out of the starting blocks in sprinting also point out the critical interaction between muscle force and speed.

The effects of strength training on muscle speed are not well understood. However, speed training is different from strength training. Strength training requires a high level of resistance that prohibits fast movement. Speed, on the other hand, can best be enhanced by repeatedly practicing the specific movements required in the particular sport skill. Because speed depends upon activating the appropriate neuromuscular pattern involved in a particular skill, it is important to train at velocities of movement similar to or faster than those of the specific sport movement. Speed is defined as strength guided by skill. To increase speed, one needs to increase strength and to maintain or increase skill.

Another consideration sometimes overlooked when the emphasis is on strength is that high power efforts typically involve high movement velocities that are coupled with brief contraction time. In rapid movement there is little kinesthetic feedback to the individual regarding the amount of force generated. It is possible that many athletes who train with weights become conditioned to make their best efforts when they can sense the force they are developing. It is tempting to speculate that successful athletes may be those who have learned to use upper motor centers for performing maximum power contractions without relying on kinesthetic feedback or relying on a critical feedback period of short duration.

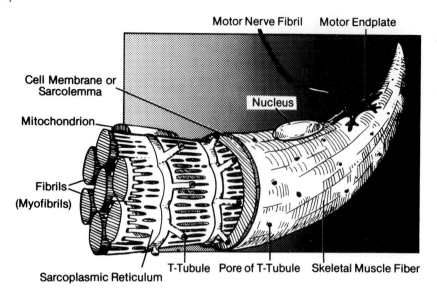

Cell Membrane or Sarcolemma

Mitochondrion

Motor Nerve Fibril   Motor Endplate

Nucleus

Fibrils (Myofibrils)

Sarcoplasmic Reticulum   T-Tubule   Pore of T-Tubule   Skeletal Muscle Fiber

Nerve impulse transmission. From Jack H. Wilmore and David L. Costill, *Training for Sport and Activity.* 3d ed.

Copyright © 1988 Wm. C. Brown Publishers. Dubuque, Iowa. All Rights Reserved. Reprinted by permission.

Strength

An enhanced arousal level and accompanying nerve disinhibition and/or possible neural facilitation are the probable explanations for the unexplained feats of strength performed in emergency situations. In such situations an individual is capable of achieving his or her individual maximum level of strength. Significant changes in neural facilitation also occur in the early stages of strength training programs, which partly account for rapid increases in strength in these stages.

Neuromuscular Facilitation

A *motor unit* consists of a motor nerve cell (neuron) that originates in the spinal cord and all the muscle fibers supplied by that neuron. The number of muscle fibers innervated by a single motor nerve varies from a few in some eye muscles to as many as a thousand in the large thigh muscle. All of the muscle fibers within a given unit are of the same fiber type. The muscle fibers are located throughout the muscle and all contract simultaneously when stimulated by the nervous system. Even though patterns of motor unit activity are still not well understood, it is apparent that different patterns are optimal for different activities.

Force Potential

There are basically three ways in which training overload can enhance the maximal strength of muscles. These are the number of motor units called into action, the frequency of the nerve impulses, and the coordination of nerve impulses. Increased frequency of nerve impulses results in increased force and decreased frequency in decreased force. The degree of muscle tension is dependent upon the number and frequency of motor units activated by the central nervous system. The more units recruited, the stronger the maximal contraction. Finally, nerve impulses have to be properly synchronized to allow for unified contraction, which is essential for maximum force.

Nerve Impulses and Strength

Both excitatory and inhibitory stimuli descend from the brain to the motor nerves. One explanation for increases in strength is that through training one can learn to decrease the inhibitory impulses from the brain to the muscles, thus allowing for a greater recruitment of force. In other words, physical training may be responsible for various adaptations of the brain and spinal cord. Another factor to consider is that certain muscle groups can be maximally activated through voluntary muscle

Critical Thinking 8-1

A parent is concerned about the safety and benefit of a strength-training program for her eleven-year-old son.

What could you tell her to satisfy her concerns?

contraction while others cannot. It may be that those muscles that can be more voluntarily activated receive greater stimulation from the brain. Unfortunately, evidence in this area is somewhat incomplete.

Muscle Cross Section

One of the best indicators of the maximum strength capability of a muscle is its cross sectional area. The larger the cross section, the greater the potential strength of the muscle and vice versa. This fact is particularly true in isolated muscles where there is an extremely high correlation between cross sectional area and maximal force. However, the relationship is much less in the whole organism than in the isolated muscle. Also, it has been found that increases in strength as a result of training may sometimes be disproportionate to muscle size and due possibly to improved neural facilitation. This observation may explain why women are able to make significant increases in strength with small changes in cross sectional muscle size.

Muscle Length

There is an optimum length of a muscle at which it can generate its greatest force. Muscles are generally their strongest at a length slightly longer than their normal resting length in their fully extended position. Muscles are weaker at shorter and longer lengths than the optimum.

Weight-Resistance Methods

As a general rule, a muscle worked close to its maximum capacity will increase in strength. The overload can be applied by a wide variety of weight lifting equipment, free weights, ropes, isokinetic devices, pulleys, and so on. Strength improvement is governed primarily by the intensity of the overload and not the method, though certain methods may be more appropriate in some circumstances than others. Isotonics, isometrics, eccentric, and isokinetic contractions are the most widely used techniques for increasing strength and endurance in muscles.

MUSCLE CONTRACTION

Isotonic Exercise

Isotonic exercise is exercise that is performed against resistance while the load remains constant. The resistance varies with the angle of the joint, for example, lifting free weights (barbells) or weight stacks, such as those used in the universal gym. Free weights are most popular among today's athletes as they feel that the motions are most similar to sport skill movements.

Eccentric Loading

Eccentric loading is sometimes referred to as a negative contraction because the muscle lengthens as it develops tension. An example would be letting yourself down slowly from a chin-up. This type of exercise tends to produce more muscle soreness, possibly due to micro tears in the muscle fibers and tendons, than other techniques. It is not superior to other isotonic methods but is used mainly as a supplement to other training techniques.

Isometric Exercise

An isometric exercise is a contraction performed against a fixed or immovable resistance, where tension is developed in the muscle, but there is no change in the length of the muscle or the angle of the joint. Isometric exercise is also called static contraction. An example would be holding a heavy weight in one position for a fixed amount of time or pushing against a wall.

It appears that with isometric exercise strength development is specific only to the joint angle stimulated during training. As a result, isometric exercise does not increase strength throughout the range of movement. Isometric exercise also may inhibit the ability of the muscle to exert force rapidly, such as is necessary in the shot put and discus events. In addition, isometric exercise increases pressure in the chest cavity, which results in reduced blood flow to the heart, lungs, and brain, along with increased blood pressure. Consequently, isometric exercises are not recommended for individuals with cardiovascular problems. There also may be some decrease in muscular endurance as isometric restricts peripheral blood flow during the static contraction.

Isokinetic Exercise

An isokinetic exercise is a contraction in which the muscle contracts maximally at a constant speed over a full range of the joint movement against a variable resistance. Isokinetic means equal motion, which is interpreted to mean equal rate of motion or equal speed. An isokinetic contraction can be accomplished only with the use of special equipment, such as a minigym that utilizes "accommodating resistance." In other words, the harder you pull, the harder the gym resists you—the resistance is always related to the applied force.

Unlike with other types of resistance training in isokinetic exercise, there is no set resistance to meet. Rather the velocity of movement is controlled. The resistance offered by the machine cannot be accelerated and any force applied against the equipment results in equal reaction of force. This makes it possible for a person to exert maximum effort throughout the full range of movement. Another advantage is that isokinetic equipment allows one to approximate the same force and same velocity as that encountered in athletic competition. Isokinetic resistance also provides a safer alternative to other exercise programs, especially during the process of muscle rehabilitation. Isokinetic exercise may also be used to quantify a muscle group's ability to generate torque or force, and is also useful as an exercise modality in the restoration of a muscle group's pre-injury level of strength.

When training isokinetically, it is necessary to exert as much force against the resistance as possible for maximal strength gains to occur. It is easy to "cheat" and not go through the workout at high intensity. Cheating may be hindered if there is a partner around to supply motivation.

High-velocity training is not as specific as slow exercise training in bringing about strength gains. Training at fast velocities tends to increase strength at and below the exercise velocity. Exercise at slow velocities tends to produce strength increases specific to training velocities.

It is apparent that many combinations of sets and repetitions of isokinetic training will result in increases in strength. Examples of isokinetic equipment are the Cybex, Lido, Mirac, Biodex, Kincom, and Orthotron.

Isokinetic exercise has become popular because it provides a speed-specific indication of the absolute strength of the muscle group being trained, thus enabling one to more closely replicate some specific athletic skills. The most effective strength gains have come from speeds of approximately sixty degrees (measure of distance) per one second or less. Recent research, however, has indicated that training at fast speeds of movement generally increases strength at all speeds of movement.

> **Critical Thinking 8-2**
>
> A young woman who is five feet 10 inches and weighs one hundred sixty pounds said that on a height-weight chart she was considered to be overweight. She has been weight training for over a year and feels that her weight is appropriate for her size.
>
> Explain the problems associated with determining proper body weight from height-weight charts.

ADVANTAGES AND DISADVANTAGES OF WEIGHT-RESISTANCE PROGRAMS

Isotonic, isometric, eccentric, and isokinetic exercise all have their advantages and disadvantages. As long as the muscle is overloaded, however, it will gain in strength.

Isotonic Exercise

Advantages

1. It generally produces strength gains throughout the full range of movement.
2. Progress in strength gains is easy to evaluate because of numbered free weights and universal stacks.
3. Strength exercises can be developed to duplicate a variety of sports skills.
4. If free weights are used, balance and symmetry are enhanced.

Disadvantages

1. The equipment is cumbersome.
2. There is a greater potential for accidents.
3. Most strength gains occur at the weakest point of the movement and are not uniform throughout.

Eccentric Exercise

Advantages

1. It is as effective in strength gains as isotonic and isometric exercise.
2. It increases motivation of some individuals who enjoy lifting heavier resistance.
3. It may increase one's skill by lowering resistance slowly.
4. It can duplicate a variety of movements.

Disadvantages

1. It can cause greater post-exercise soreness than other methods.
2. A partner as spotter is needed to lift heavier resistance.

Isometric Exercise

Advantages

1. Little time is required for training.
2. Expensive and cumbersome equipment is not needed.
3. Exercise can be performed anywhere—in home, office, or on vacation.

Disadvantages

1. Strength gains are not produced throughout the full range of movement.
2. Strength gains are difficult to evaluate; that is, no numbered weights or gauges are customarily used.
3. It increases the pressure in the chest cavity, causing reduced blood flow to the heart, lungs, and brain.
4. It is not as efficient in producing strength gains as isotonic and isokinetic methods.
5. It is not effective in producing increases in skilled movements.
6. Motivation is difficult to maintain.
7. Muscular endurance may decrease.

Isokinetic Exercise

Advantages

1. It produces maximum resistance through the full range of movement.
2. It increases strength throughout the full range of movement.
3. It may result in less injury and soreness than isometric and isotonic exercise.
4. The uniqueness of the equipment may increase motivation.

5. Strength gains are easy to determine.
6. It is adaptable to specific movement patterns.
7. It permits skill improvement.

Disadvantages

1. The equipment is very expensive, with limited availability.
2. Research is still incomplete with regard to motor patterns and force-velocity relationships.
3. Applicability to sport-specific ballistic skills may be limited and may be best for tension skills (e.g., swimming and running).
4. A high level of motivation is required to give full effort to each exercise.

Glossary

Eccentric   Exercise in which the muscle lengthens as it develops tension.
Isokinetic   A contraction in which the muscle contracts maximally at a constant speed over a full range of joint movement against a variable resistance.
Isometric   A contraction performed against a fixed or immovable resistance where tension is developed in the muscle, but there is no change in the length of the muscle or angle of the joint.
Isotonic   Exercise against resistance while the load remains constant, with the resistance varying with the angle of the joint.
Muscle Strength   The amount of force that can be exerted by a muscle group for one movement or repetition.
Power   The product of strength and speed.
Speed   Strength guided by skill.

Solutions to Critical Thinking

8-1. The American Academy of Pediatrics has stated that a properly supervised and prescribed strength program can increase strength and endurance, decrease the chance of injuries, and increase the child's sports performance. It is important that the program be adjusted to the physiological age of the child because of the wide variety of growth patterns in pre-pubescent children. To avoid the possibility of epiphyseal plate (growth plate) fractures, near maximum lifts should not be attempted; proper form should be learned and ten to fifteen repetitions should be utilized. A high number of repetitions can also cause injury to the growth plate, ligaments, and tendons.

8-2. Height-weight charts are notoriously erroneous, especially if a person has a great deal of lean muscle and large diameter bones for his or her height. To put this young woman's mind at rest, you should recommend a more valid test such as underwater weighing or a skinfold test. Also remind her that a person may be found to be overweight, according to some measures, but not over-fat.

Review Questions

1. Discuss the components of muscle power.
2. What is the difference between a concentric and eccentric muscle contraction?
3. What are the advantages of utilizing isokinetic exercises?

References

Castro, M. J., D. J. McCann, J. D. Shaffrath, and W. C. Adams. 1995. Peak torque per unit cross-sectional area differs between strength-trained and untrained young adults. *Medicine and Science in Sports and Exercise* 27:397–403.

Chu, D. *Jumping into polymetrics.* Leisure Press, Champaign, IL, 1994.

deVries, H. A., and T. J. Housh. *Physiology of exercise for physical education, athletics and exercise science.* 5th ed. McGraw-Hill, Dubuque, IA, 1993.

Hall, S. J. *Basic biomechanics.* 3rd ed. McGraw-Hill, Dubuque, IA, 1999.

Komi, P. V. 1984. Physiological and biomechanical correlates of muscle function: Effects of muscle structure and stretch-shortening cycle on force and speed. *Exercise Science Sports Review* 12:81–121.

McCarthy, J. P., J. E. Agre, B. K. Graf, M. A. Pozniak, and A. C. Vailas. 1995. Compatibility of adaptive responses with combining strength and endurance training. *Medicine and Science in Sports and Exercise* 27:429–436.

Nardone, A., C. Romano, and M. Schieppatgi. 1989. Selective recruitment of high-threshold human motor units during voluntary isotonic lengthening of active muscles. *Journal of Physiology* 409:451–471.

Osternig, L. R., R. H. Robertson, R. K. Troxel, and P. Hansen. 1990. Differential responses to proprioceptive neuromuscular facilitation (PNF) stretch techniques. *Medicine and Science in Sports and Exercise* 22:106–111.

Powers, S. K., and E. T. Howley. *Exercise physiology.* 3rd ed. McGraw-Hill, Dubuque, IA, 1997.

Robergs, R. A., and S. O. Roberts. *Exercise physiology: Exercise, performance, and clinical applications.* Mosby-Year Book, St. Louis, 1997.

Robergs, R. A., and S. O. Roberts. *Fundamental principles of exercise physiology: For fitness, performance, and health.* McGraw-Hill, Dubuque, IA, 2000.

Rooney, K. J., R. D. Herbert, and R. J. Balnave. 1994. Fatigue contributes to the strength training stimulus. *Medicine and Science in Sports and Exercise* 26:1160–1164.

Sale, D. G. 1988. Neural adaptation to resistance training. *Medicine and Science in Sports and Exercise.* 20 (Suppl.):135–145.

Shephard, R. J., E. Bouhlel, H. Vandewalle, and H. Monod. 1988. Muscle mass as a factor limiting physical work. *Journal of Applied Physiology* 64:1472–1479.

Soest, A. J., van, and M. F. Boibbert. 1993. The role of muscle properties in control of explosive movements. *Biological Cybernetics* 69:195–204.

Wade, M. G., and J. A. W. Baker. *Introduction to kinesiology: The science and practice of physical activity.* McGraw-Hill, Dubuque, IA, 1994.

Welle, S., C. Thornton, and M. Statt. 1995. Myofibrillar protein synthesis in young and old human subjects after three months of resistance training. *American Journal of Physiology* 268:E422–427.

chapter 9

advanced training

Objectives

After studying this chapter you should be able to

1. Describe the pyramid system.
2. Describe single sets.
3. Describe the multi-poundage system.
4. Describe the super pump system.
5. Describe super sets.
6. Describe burnouts.
7. Describe partial repetition.
8. Describe circuit training.
9. Describe periodization.
10. Describe forced repetition.
11. Describe negative work.
12. Describe split-routine.
13. Describe plyometrics.

Once you have mastered the basic techniques of strength training and have developed a high level of strength and endurance, you may be tempted to enter into advanced training.

No unanimity of opinion exists on the best training system, but generally success in weight training will depend on your progression and quality of work.

The following systems and techniques are commonly used today by advanced weight lifters. Optimal gains, strength, and hypertrophy can be achieved by mixing various training programs and manipulating the training variables.

PYRAMID SYSTEM

The pyramid system is the most popular system for strength and power development. Progression from a low weight to a higher weight with a decreasing number of repetitions is the hallmark of this system. Following in table 9.1 is an example of a pyramid system.

The athlete may then work his or her way back down to lower weights and higher repetitions.

Table 9.1

Pyramid System		
Set Number	Number of Repetitions	Weight (in lbs)
1	10	155
2	8	185
3	6	205
4	4	225
5	2	245
6	1	255

SINGLE SET SYSTEMS

Single set systems consist of the performance of one set of each exercise, eight to twelve repetitions. These are not as efficient in producing strength and endurance gains as multiple sets for highly trained individuals. However, single sets should be utilized by beginners and sedentary persons.

MULTI-POUNDAGE SYSTEM

The multi-poundage system requires the assistance of one or two spotters. The individual performs 4 to 5 RMs. Then the spotter removes twenty to forty pounds from the bar. The individual then performs four to five more repetitions, and continues this procedure for several sets. The number of sets depends upon the original resistance used. This program is used primarily to increase muscular endurance.

SUPER PUMP SYSTEM

The super pump system is primarily for bodybuilders. The individual starts off with fifteen to eighteen sets for each body part and one to three exercises for each muscle group per training session. There is a fifteen-second rest period between sets of five to six repetitions. These exercises are useful primarily for the large muscles in the arms, chest, and shoulders.

SUPER SETS

In the super set system the lifter performs one exercise and quickly follows it with another exercise, then rests. The individual works on the two exercises alternately until a desired number of sets has been completed. Adding a third exercise to this routine is called trisets.

BURNOUTS

In the burnout system, after you complete what is normally your last set, you take some weight off the bar and immediately do an additional set. You continue doing sets with less weight each time and without rest for up to five or six sets or until exhaustion.

PARTIAL REPETITIONS

At the end of the last repetition, usually of the last set of an exercise, when the lifter is unable to perform another full repetition, he or she performs one-half, one-third, or one-fourth of a repetition until these cannot be continued.

FORCED REPETITION

After the last full repetition of the last set, the spotter helps the lifter perform another one to three repetitions by assisting the lifter as needed to complete the repetitions.

NEGATIVE WORK

After the last set has been completed, additional weight is added to the bar and the lifter with the aid of spotters slowly lowers the weight. The spotters then raise the weight and the lifter lowers it again. This process may be repeated for three to five repetitions and several sets.

SPLIT-ROUTINE

Rather than performing the entire workout program in one day, many lifters break up their programs into alternate day routines. A lifter may work the upper body on Monday, Wednesday, and Friday, and the lower body on Tuesday, Thursday, and Saturday. This routine results in more workouts per week but each workout is shorter. Many athletes find that they can perform higher intensity workouts with this method.

POWER AND SPEED EXERCISES

Power is the ability of muscles to produce high levels of force in a short time (explosive strength). For example, two individuals can lift 200 pounds a distance of four feet, but one can lift it faster than the other; in this case we say the one who lifts it faster has more power. Power is basically the product of strength and speed. By increasing either one, you can increase power. For example, a discus thrower's power can be increased by improving arm, shoulder girdle, and back strength, all muscles involved in the sport, or by improving the speed with which the movement is accomplished.

In many sports, power is more important than strength. The ability to put the shot, high jump, and long jump all require power.

Speed is the ability to perform a particular movement very rapidly. It is a function of distance and time. The fastest way to improve speed is not only to increase strength but also to improve skill. There comes a time, however, after the skill is well learned that simply practicing and refining the skill no longer yield increases in speed. At this point increased strength of the muscles primary to the sport movement, coupled with continued practice of the skill, can result in increased speed.

PLYOMETRICS

Plyometrics are exercises in which the muscle is loaded suddenly and forced to stretch before the contraction of movement occurs. The greater the stretch put on the muscle from its resting length immediately before the concentric contraction, the greater the resistance the muscle can overcome. Plyometrics emphasize the speed of the eccentric phase. The rate of stretch is more critical than the magnitude of stretch. These exercises were developed to enable the muscle to reach maximum strength in as short a time as possible. Examples include jumping off a box onto the ground and rebounding as quickly as possible. The deceleration and acceleration of body weight provides the overload. Upper body plyometrics include medicine ball throws, catches, and several types of push-ups.

The term stretch-shortening cycle is beginning to replace the term plyometrics. Stretch-shortening cycle occurs when the sequence of muscle activity goes quickly from eccentric to concentric contraction, and the muscle is stretched just prior to the concentric contraction. In other words, the muscle is stretched slightly and then shortened. The slight stretching that occurs will store elastic energy, causing a more forceful concentric contraction. Also more muscle fibers may be recruited. Virtually all

Table 9.2

	Low intensity	Medium intensity	High intensity	Shock
In-place Jumps	• Squat jump • Split squat jump • Cycled split squat jump (Also: ankle bounce, ice skater, lateral cone jump)	• Pike jump • Double-leg tuck jump (Also: jump-up, lateral hop)	• Double-leg vertical power jump • Single-leg vertical power jump • Single-leg tuck jump	
Standing jumps		• Standing triple jump (Also: standing long jump)		
Short-response hops		• Double- and single-leg zigzag hop and double-leg hop	• Single-leg hop and double- and single-leg speed hop	
Long-response hops		• Double-leg hop	• Single-leg hop and double and single-leg speed hop	
Short-response bounds		• Alternate leg bound • Combination bound		
Long-response bounds		• Alternate leg bound • Combination bound		
Shocks				• In-depth jump • Box jump
Upper body plyometrics	• Medicine ball sit-up • Plyometric sit-up (Also: two-hand overhead forward throw, clap push-ups)	• Medicine ball push-up (Also: overhead backward throw, underhand forward throw, Russian twist)		• Drop-and-catch push-up

Plyometric Drills, Classified by Intensity Level

jumping exercises involve a stretch-shortening cycle. Plyometrics have been shown to increase vertical jumping ability. The number of exercises and height are still in doubt. Plyometrics have little effect on hypertrophy and body composition.

Individuals should be introduced slowly in training programs and should keep the volume of training low. Heavy individuals may need to use a smaller training volume, that is, number of jumps, than the training volume of light individuals because of greater resistance in body weight and smaller relative lean muscle mass.

Weight training and, most importantly, plyometrics are best for developing power and speed. Plyometrics place more emphasis on the neuromuscular system. To increase power you must train the larger and faster motor units that are related to the activity. To do this you must overload the muscles at high speeds.

Plyometric exercises are beneficial in sports that require the application of maximal force during high speed movements, sometimes referred to as speed-strength. The individual should be well into a strength-training program before attempting plyometrics. Refer to table 9.2 for plyometric intensity levels and to figure 17.1 for plyometric exercise machine.

Definitions of Plyometric Exercises

Jump—A movement that concludes with a two-foot landing.
Jump in place—Vertical jump performed in place (tuck, pike, split squat, squat, power jumps).

Critical Thinking 9-1

A volleyball player was hesitant about utilizing plyometrics for fear that the exercise would build unnecessary bulk and negatively affect her jumping ability.

Explain to her the benefits of plyometric exercise.

Standing jump—A maximal jump that may be linear, vertical, or lateral.

Hop—A move that starts and concludes with a one-foot or two-foot landing of the same foot or feet (short hop, ten repetitions; long hop, thirty repetitions or more).

Bound—Series of movements in which one lands successfully on alternate feet (short-response bound, twenty-five–thirty meters; long-response bound, sixty meters or more).

Shock—In-depth jump and box jumps (few use this method).

Caution—This combination of high force and speed produces very significant loads on the muscles, tendons, and ligaments. These structures need to be well conditioned to both force and speed before plyometric exercises are attempted. Proper technique and form are very important in performing these exercises in order to reduce the impact shock and to protect the joints and joint structure.

PERIODIZATION

The underlying principle of periodization is related to Hans Selye's general adaptation syndrome. Selye's theory states that there are three phases of the body's adaptation when it is confronted with a stress stimulus, in this case, resistance training. The first phase is termed the shock or alarm phase, which lasts one to two weeks. Soreness and stiffness may develop, with a slight decrease in performance. In the second phase, adaptation to the training and performance demands increases. This phase is sometimes called super-compensation. The third phase is staleness, for the body no longer adapts to the new stimulus, which results in overwork, staleness, and exhaustion.

The key to periodization is to reduce the risk of overtraining and subsequent staleness and keep the exercise stimulus effective in order to maintain a high level of performance.

Periodization consists of four phases in each training cycle, not including active rest. The overall training period is referred to as a macrocycle, which may range from three months to four or five years. Within the macrocycle are two or more mesocycles consisting of a few weeks to a few months. Each mesocycle is broken down to a number of microcycles of about a week in length. A mesocycle is made up of three periods: preparatory, competition, and transitional.

Following a season of competition is a period of transition, which includes active rest for a period of one to four weeks. During this time the individual may participate in a variety of leisure sports activities. Only low-volume and light resistance training should be engaged in during this time of recovery from the stress of competition.

The preparatory phase that follows the transition phase includes a hypertrophy phase, strength phase, power phase, and peaking phase. The hypertrophy phase consists of high-volume, low-intensity exercise, three to five sets of eight to twelve repetitions, fifty to seventy-five percent, 1 RM. The strength phase consists of moderate volume and increased intensity, three to five sets of five to six repetitions, 80 to 88 percent, 1 RM. The power phase consists of low-volume, high-intensity exercise, the major goal being to bring about increases in maximum strength, three to five sets, two to four repetitions, 90 to 95 percent (high intensity), 1 RM. The peaking phase consists of very low volume and high intensity, where the goal is to peak strength for a particular competition, one to three sets, one to three repetitions, 100 percent, 1 RM.

Periodization can be used also for cardiorespiratory training. It consists of gradually reducing volume while increasing intensity to accomplish specific sports requirements. The concept of periodization with its four phases makes it possible to develop a resistance training program for any sport.

STRENGTH AND POWER

Hypertrophy	3–5 sets	8–20 RM
Strength	3–5 sets	2–6 RM
Power	3–5 sets	2–3 RM
Peaking	1–3 sets	1–3 RM

It is vital to understand how to manipulate intensity and volume for specific sports. Variation in training is essential to maintain motivation and reduce monotony and boredom.

Most sports have a schedule that includes an off-season, preseason and an in-season period.

Table 9.3

Typical Training Mesocycle for a Sprinter		
Season designation	**Period/phase designation**	**Training schedule**
Off-season	**Preparatory period**	
	• Hypertrophy/endurance phase	*Flexibility training:* ballistic, static, or proprioceptive neuromuscular facilitation (PNF) stretching
		Resistance training: specific or nonspecific exercises of high volume and low intensity
		Metabolic training: aerobic activities
		Speed training: high-volume, low-intensity technique training
	Transition (optional)	All training of low volume and low intensity
	• Strength phase	*Flexibility training:* ballistic, static, or PNF
		Resistance training: specific exercises of moderate volume and intensity
		Metabolic training: interval work
		Speed training: moderate-volume and moderate-intensity technique training, including towing and downhill activities
Preseason	**• Power phase**	*Flexibility training:* ballistic, static, or PNF stretching
		Resistance training: specific exercises of low volume and high intensity
		Metabolic training: short work intervals of maximal and near-maximal intensity with full recovery intervals
		Speed training: high-intensity, low-volume activities
	Transition period (optional)	All training of low volume and low intensity
In-season	**Competition period**	*Flexibility training:* ballistic, static, or PNF stretching
		All training of low volume and high intensity
		Resistance training: low-volume, high-intensity, sport-specific exercises
		Metabolic training: race-specific intervals with full or near-full recovery between intervals
Off-season	**Transition period**	*Optional:* recreational games; light, unsupervised training

From Dan Wathan, Periodization, concepts and applications, in *Essentials of Strength Training and Conditioning,* ed. Thomas Baechle. Champaign, IL: Human Kinetics, 1994.

Off-season—Period between last contest and six to eighteen weeks prior to first contest.
Preseason—Six to eight weeks prior to first contest.
Competitive period—All contests scheduled for that season.

The majority of athletes today use some kind of cycling in their training. By manipulating the load and frequency of exercise, the volume of exercise can be controlled. Training cycles may progress from high volume/low intensity to low volume/high intensity. This gives the body time to recover and adjust to training demands while still allowing for a maximal exercise stimulus; the body is able to meet the high demands encountered during competition. (See appendix G for examples of training cycles.)

Examples of Cycles

4 weeks	10 RM	3–4 days a week
4 weeks	8 RM	4 days a week
4 weeks	4 RM	5 days a week
4 weeks	1–3 RM	6 days a week

Another option is to vary the number of weeks for each different training load.

3 weeks	10–12 RM
7 weeks	8 RM
4 weeks	3 RM
2 weeks	1–3 RM

It is extremely difficult to maintain a peak level of fitness for more than a few weeks during the in-season. It is important to develop a training cycle that peaks the individual for the most important contest. Low volume and greater intensity are essential for the most critical events.

Glossary

Burnout   Continued sets with reduction in resistance until exhaustion.
Circuit Training   A combination of strength and/or endurance exercises performed in sequence at various stations.
Forced Repetitions   Performing additional repetitions with assistance when muscle can no longer complete movement.
Multi-Poundage System   Progressive reduction in training load.
Negative Work   Exercise in which spotters raise the weight, lifter slowly lowers the weight.
Partial Repetition   Performing an exercise without moving the weight through the complete range of motion at either the beginning of a repetition or at the end of a repetition.
Periodization   Calendar year broken down into various training cycles.
Plyometrics   Exercise in which the muscle is loaded suddenly and forced to stretch before the contraction for movement occurs.
Pyramid System   Progression from low weight to higher weight with decreasing number of repetitions.
Single Set   The performance of one set for each exercise.
Split-Routine   A routine in which certain parts of body are worked on one day and other parts on alternate days.
Super Pump System   Fifteen to eighteen sets for each body part. And one to three exercises for each muscle group.
Super Sets   Alternating back and forth between two exercises until the prescribed number of sets are completed.

Solutions to Critical Thinking

9-1. Plyometric exercise will increase the specific speed of contraction and will enhance her vertical jumping, but will not result in hypertrophy and changes in body composition.

9-2. If an individual only exercises the prime mover (i.e., biceps curl) this muscle will become stronger while the antagonist is placed under increased stress as a joint stabilizer. The antagonist should also be trained to aid in performances, enhancement, and injury prevention. In this circumstance, in addition to the biceps curl the triceps pulldown should also be utilized.

Review Questions

1. Why have plyometric exercises gained in popularity among athletes?
2. Why is it important to include periodization in your resistance program?
3. Give an example of the pyramid system to develop strength and power.

References

Bobbert, M. F. 1990. Drop jumping as a training method for jumping ability. *Sports Medicine* 9:7–22.

Chu, D. *Jumping into plyometrics.* Leisure Press, Champaign, IL, 1994.

Fowler, N. E., Z. Trzaskoma, A. Wit, L. Iskra, and A. Lees. 1995. The effectiveness of a pendulum swing for the development of leg strength and counter-movement jump performance. *Journal Sports Science* 13:101–108.

Garhammer, J. 1991. A comparison of maximal power outputs between elite male and female weightlifters in competition. *International Journal Sport Biomechanics* 7:3–11.

Garhammer, J. 1980. Power production by Olympic weightlifters. *Medicine and Science in Sports Exercise* 12:54–60.

Komi, P. V., ed. *Strength and power in sport.* Blackwell Scientific Publications, London, 1992.

Mastropaolo, J. A. 1992. A test of the maximum-power theory for strength. *European Journal of Applied Physiology* 65:415–420.

Maugham, R. J., J. S. Watson, and J. Weir. 1983. Relationship between muscle strength and muscle cross-sectional area in male sprinters and endurance runners. *European Journal of Applied Physiology* 50: 309–318.

McGlynn, George H., and Gary T. Moran. *Cross-Training for sports.* Human Kinetics, Champaign, IL, 1997.

Silvester, L. J., C. Stiggins, C. McGown, and G. R. Bryce. 1982. The effects of variable resistance and free-weight training on strength and vertical jump. *National Strength Conditioning Association Journal* 3:30–33.

Starson, R. S., F. C. Hagerman, and R. S. Hikida. 1981. The effects of detraining on an elite power lifter. *Journal of Neurological Sciences* 51:247–257.

Tesch, P. A., and L. Larsson. 1982. Muscle hypertrophy in bodybuilders. *European Journal of Applied Physiology* 49:301–306.

United States Olympic Committee. *USOC drug education handbook.* United States Olympic Committee, Colorado Springs, 1989.

Welbergen, E., H. C. G. Kemper, J. J. Knibbe, H. M. Toussaint, and L. Clijsen. 1991. Efficiency and effectiveness of stoop and squat lifting at different frequencies. *Ergonomics* 34:613–624.

chapter 10

exercises

Objectives

After studying this chapter you should be able to

1. Describe a strength exercise for the chest.
2. Describe a strength exercise for the back.
3. Describe a strength exercise for the shoulder.
4. Describe a strength exercise for the trunk.
5. Describe a strength exercise for the hips.
6. Describe a strength exercise for the thighs.
7. Describe a strength exercise for the calf muscles.

This chapter provides a selection of the most effective and popular exercises for various body parts. (See figures 10.1 through 10.55.) These include exercises with free weights and machines. The section includes weight training exercises for chest, back, shoulder, arms (biceps, triceps, and forearms), trunk (abdominals and lower back), hips, and thigh and calf.

CHEST, UPPER BACK, AND SHOULDER EXERCISES

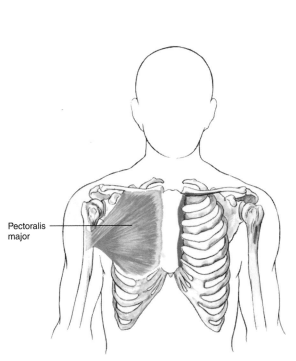

Figure 10.1 PECTORALIS MAJOR MUSCLE.

Figure 10.2 RHOMBOID MUSCLES.

Figure 10.3 TERES MINOR MUSCLE.

Teres minor

Teres major

Anterior view with teres major insertion

Figure 10.4 TERES MAJOR MUSCLE.

Latissimus
dorsi

Figure 10.5 LATISSIMUS DORSI MUSCLE.

Figure 10.6 TRAPEZIUS MUSCLE.

Figure 10.7 DELTOID MUSCLE.

Figure 10.8 BENCH PRESS.

Muscles Used:

Primary: *Pectoralis Major.* (See fig. 10.1.)
Additional: *Anterior Deltoid, Biceps Brachii, Triceps Brachii.*

The weight is lowered to the chest and returned to the starting position. Hands are slightly wider than shoulder width; thumbs should be wrapped around the bar, with feet flat on floor.

Figure 10.9 INCLINED DUMBBELL FLY.

Muscles Used:

Same as in bench press, with more emphasis on the upper Pectoralis Major fibers. (See fig. 10.1.) Lower the dumbbells to the side with a wide elbow position, then return to starting position.

Figure 10.10 DECLINED BENCH PRESS.

Muscles Used:

Primary: *Same as in bench press but with more emphasis on lower portion of Pectoralis Major.*
(See fig. 10.1.)

The weight is lowered to the chest and returned to the starting position. Hands are slightly wider than shoulder width; thumbs should be wrapped around the bar, with feet flat on floor.

 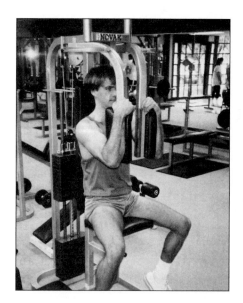

Figure 10.11 PEC DECK MACHINE.

Muscles Used:

Pectoralis Major with emphasis on the inner/medial fibers. (See fig. 10.1.)

From the starting position bring your arms together until the machine arms nearly touch, then return to starting position.

Figure 10.12 BENT ROWING.

Muscles Used:

Primary: *Upper back musculature, Rhomboid Major and Minor, Teres Major and Minor.* (See figs. 10.2, 10.3, 10.4.)

Additional: *Posterior Deltoid Latissimus Dorsi.*

Place feet shoulder-width apart. Hands should be about shoulder-width apart with knees slightly bent. The bar is lifted to the chest and then lowered. Be careful not to twist or jerk the lower back. The exercise can be done with the head resting on a bench or table to help support the lower back.

Figure 10.13 SEATED PULLEY ROWS.

Muscles Used:

Same muscles as in bent rowing. (See figs. 10.2, 10.3, 10.4.)

Knees are bent and the back is held straight. The hand grip is brought to the chest and then returned to the starting position.

Figure 10.14 LATERAL PULLDOWN.

Muscles Used:

Latissimus Dorsi. (See fig. 10.5.)

A wide grip is taken on the bar and then the bar is pulled to shoulder level. For heavy resistance, a seated position can be used to enable a restraining bar to be placed above the knees in order to keep the body down.

Figure 10.15 PRESS (MILITARY PRESS).

Muscles Used:

Primary: *Trapezius, Deltoid.* (See figs. 10.6, 10.7.)
Additional: *Supraspinatus, Levator Scapulae.*

Feet are placed flat on the floor approximately shoulder-width apart. The hand grip is slightly wider than shoulder-width. The bar is pressed overhead and then returned to the starting position.

In figure 10.15 a weight rack is used that provides a safety measure for heavy weights. When lifting high resistances in this lift, a weight belt may be used to support the lower back.

If a weight rack is not used, the weight is brought from a floor resting position up to the on-shoulder position in what is called a clean movement.

Figure 10.16   UPRIGHT ROWING.

Muscles Used:

Primary: *Trapezius, Deltoid.* (See figs. 10.6, 10.7.)
Additional: *Supraspinatus, Levator Scapulae.*

A close, narrow grip is used. The bar is brought up to just below chin level and returned to the starting position.

Figure 10.17   SHOULDER DIPS.

Muscles Used:

Primary: *Anterior Deltoid Pectoralis Major.* (See figs. 10.1, 10.7.)
Additional: *Triceps Brachii, Biceps Brachii.*

This exercise is performed on parallel bars. From the upright position, lower yourself to as low a position as possible, then push up to the upright position. The exercise may be performed with weights held by the feet and legs (see fig. 10.17).

ARM EXERCISES

Figure 10.18 BICEPS BRACHII MUSCLE.

Long head
Short head } Biceps brachii

Figure 10.19 BRACHIALIS MUSCLE.

Brachialis muscle

Triceps

O, Medial head

Flexor carpi
ulnaris

Figure 10.20 TRICEPS BRACHII MUSCLE.

Figure 10.21 FLEXOR CARPI ULNARIS MUSCLE.

Figure 10.22 CURL.

Muscles Used:

Primary: *Biceps Brachii, Brachialis.* (See figs. 10.18, 10.19.)
Additional: *Coracobrachialis, Brachioradialis, Anterior Deltoid.*

Feet and hands shoulder-width apart. The bar is brought up to the shoulders and returned to the starting position. Keep your back straight and knees slightly bent to discourage cheating.

Figure 10.23 SEATED ALTERNATE DUMBBELL CURLS.

Muscles Used:

Same as in curl. (See figs. 10.18, 10.19.)

Seated position with feet and knees wide apart. The elbow of the lifting arm is in tight to the thigh. The opposite hand rests on the opposite thigh. After the target number of repetitions is achieved, the weight is switched to the other hand.

Figure 10.24   TRICEP PULLOVERS.

Muscles Used:

Primary: *Triceps Brachii.* (See fig. 10.20.)
Additional: *Pectoralis Major, Latissimus Dorsi.*

This exercise is especially effective for working the long head of the Triceps.

Lie on a bench with the feet on the bench or flat on the floor. Hold the dumbbell with both hands and bring it up from the floor to a position directly above the head. Return it to near the floor.

Figure 10.25   SEATED TRICEPS DUMBBELL CURLS.

Muscles Used:

Primary: *Triceps Brachii.* (See fig. 10.20.)
Additional: *Deltoid.*

From a seated position, using one arm at a time, bring the dumbbell down to a position between the shoulder blades (scapulae) and return to the starting position.

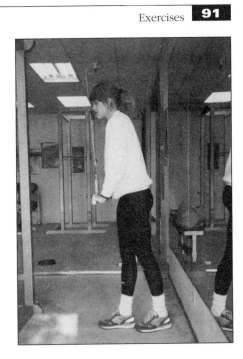

Figure 10.26   TRICEP PULLDOWNS.

Muscles Used:

Primary: *Triceps Brachii.* (See fig. 10.20.)
Additional: *Posterior Deltoid, Latissimus Dorsi.*

Use a narrow grip. Bring the bar down close to the body to a position in front of the hips with the arms fully extended. Be careful of using the trunk in an effort to handle more weight.

Figure 10.27   FOREARM CURLS.

Muscles Used:

Primary: *Forearm Flexors, Flexor Carpi Radialis, Flexor Carpi Ulnaris.* (See fig. 10.21.)
Additional: *Flexor Digitorum Profundus, Flexor Digitorum Superficialis.*

Rest the forearms on the thighs for support. Hold the bar with a palm-up grip, and flex the hands and wrist upwards. A reverse, palm-down grip can be used to perform a reversed forearm curl for development of the posterior forearm muscles.

LOWER BACK AND ABDOMINAL EXERCISES

Figure 10.28   RECTUS ABDOMINUS MUSCLE.

Pectoralis major

Latissimus dorsi

Rectus abdominis
(covered by sheath)

Rectus abdominis
(sheath removed)

External oblique
abdominal

Internal oblique
abdominal

Transverse
abdominis

Serratus
anterior

Linea alba

Umbilicus

Iliac crest

Inguinal canal
and ligament

Figure 10.29   ABDOMINAL MUSCLES.

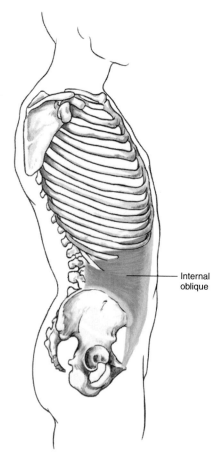

Internal
oblique

Figure 10.30   TRANSVERSUS
ABDOMINIS MUSCLE.

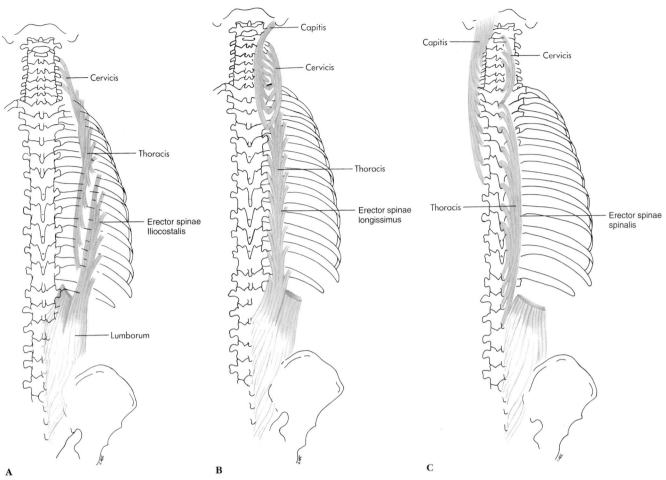

A   **B**   **C**

Figure 10.31   ERECTOR SPINAE (SACROSPINALIS) MUSCLE. **A,** Iliocostalis; **B,** longissimus; **C,** spinalis.

Figure 10.32   LIE WITH ARMS ACROSS CHEST.

Muscles Used:

Primary: *Rectus Abdominis.* (See fig. 10.28.)
Additional: *Internal Obliques, External Obliques, Transverse Abdominis.*

Start flat on the floor with feet secured under a dresser, pads, or sit-up board. A spotter also can hold your feet. Bend knees to at least a ninety-degree angle to place less stress on the lower back. Lie with arms across chest. Straight-up sit-ups work primarily the rectus abdominis while twisting sit-ups add work for the oblique muscles.

Figure 10.33 CRUNCHES.

Muscles Used:

Same as in head-and-shoulder raise. (See fig. 10.28.)

Place legs on a bench. Start this sit-up flat on the floor and bring torso up until elbows touch the knees.

Figure 10.34 ALTERNATE KNEE TOUCHING SIT-UPS.

Muscles Used:

Abdominal Group. (See fig. 10.29.)

Starting flat on the floor, raise upward and touch your elbow to your opposite knee. Repeat for the opposite elbow and knee. This exercise is excellent for oblique development.

Figure 10.35 SIT-UPS WITH WEIGHTS.

Muscles Used:

Abdominal Group. (See fig. 10.29.)

Start flat on the floor and move to a fully trunk upright position. The use of weights adds resistance for greater strength development.

Figure 10.36 SIDE BEND WITH DUMBBELL.

Muscles Used:

Primary: *Transverse Abdominis.* (See fig. 10.30.)
Additional: *Internal Obliques, External Obliques.*

From an upright standing position, bend to the side, stretching the opposite side. Try to concentrate on isolating the musculature to slowly return to the upright position.
Be careful not to use too heavy a weight as this area will increase in size.

Figure 10.37 SEATED BAR TWISTS.

Muscles Used:

Primary: *Transverse Abdominis.* (See fig. 10.30.)
Additional: *Internal Oblique, External Obliques.*

From a seated or standing position with a bar or broomstick on your shoulders and your hands spread wide and grasping the bar, twist to one side and reverse twist to the other.
Try to isolate the abdominal muscles while performing this exercise.

a.

b.

c.

Figure 10.38 (*a* & *b*) BACK HYPEREXTENSION (*c*) WITH WEIGHTS.

Muscles Used:

Primary: *Erector Spinal Group.* (See fig. 10.31.)

Using a back hyperextension machine, start from the down (flexed) position and move upward into a hyperextended position. This exercise can be performed with light weights to build greater strength. Take care, however, as the lower back muscles are subject to spasms. Use only light weights.

LOWER BODY EXERCISES

Figure 10.39 HIP MUSCLES.

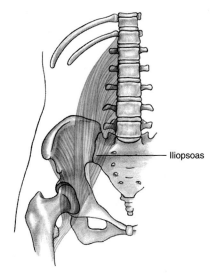

Figure 10.41 ILIOPSOAS MUSCLE.

- Iliopsoas

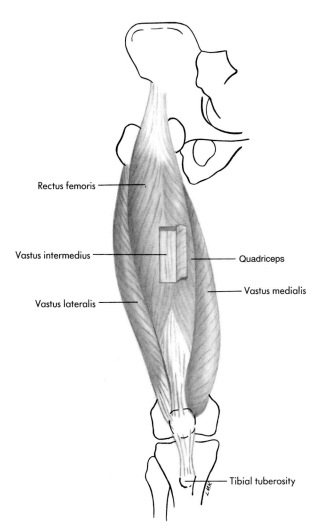

Rectus femoris

Vastus intermedius

Quadriceps

Vastus medialis

Vastus lateralis

Tibial tuberosity

Figure 10.40 QUADRICEPS MUSCLES.

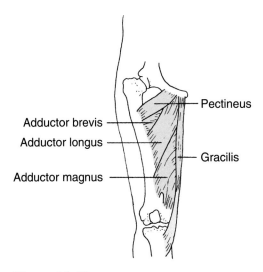

Pectineus

Adductor brevis

Adductor longus

Gracilis

Adductor magnus

Figure 10.42 ADDUCTOR MUSCLES.

Figure 10.43 HAMSTRING MUSCLES.

Semitendinosis

(long head)
Biceps femoris
(short head)

Semimembranosus

Hamstring

Medial head

Lateral head

O, Posterior surfaces
of two condyles of
femur

Gastrocnemius

I, Posterior surface
of calcaneus

Figure 10.44 GASTROCNEMIUS MUSCLE.

Figure 10.45 SOLEUS MUSCLE.

Soleus

Figure 10.46 (*a & b*) HALF SQUAT.

Muscles Used:

Primary: *Gluteals, Quadriceps, Hamstrings.* (See figs. 10.39, 10.40, 10.43.)

The safest way to perform squats is to use a squat rack, as shown in figure 10.46. Starting from an upright position with the bar on your shoulders, bend at the knees and slightly lower yourself to a position of a ninety degree angle between your thigh and leg. This is a half squat. Full squats put great stress on the knees and can produce injuries in susceptible individuals. We recommend half squats.

Figure 10.47 LEG PRESS.

Muscles Used:

Primary: *Quadriceps*. (See fig. 10.40.)
Additional: *Hamstrings, Gluteals*.

Adjust the seat so that there is a ninety degree angle or less at the knees. From this position press until legs are extended.

Figure 10.48 HIP FLEXION.

Muscles Used:

Primary: *Iliopsoas*. (See fig. 10.41.)
Additional: *Rectus Femoris, Quadriceps Group*.

Face away from the weight pulley. Extend your leg behind you, then bring the leg forward.

Figure 10.49 FOUR-WAY HIP EXTENSION.

Muscles Used:

Primary: *Gluteals*. (See fig. 10.39.)
Additional: *Hamstrings*.

Place your leg in front of you, then bring your leg backwards into a hyperextended position behind you.

Figure 10.50 HIP ADDUCTION.

Muscles Used:

Primary: *Adductor Group*. (See fig. 10.42.)
(Groin Muscles)

Stand with legs wide apart, then bring one leg inward and across in front of the support leg.

Figure 10.51 HIP ABDUCTION.

Muscles Used:

Primary: *Gluteus Medius and Minimus.* (See fig. 10.39.)
Additional: *Tensor Fascia Latae.*

From a position slightly in front of the support leg, move the leg outward to the side.

Figure 10.52 LEG EXTENSION.

Muscles Used:

Quadriceps. (See fig. 10.40.)

Move the legs from a flex position to an extended position, pause momentarily, and return. Start with your legs at a right angle and pause with your legs straight.

Figure 10.53 LEG FLEXION.

Muscles Used:

Primary: *Hamstrings (Semitendinosus, Semimembrinosus, Biceps Femoris).* (See fig. 10.43.)

Lying prone on the bench with your heels behind the pads, flex the legs and bring your heels toward your buttocks.

Figure 10.54 TOE RAISE.

Muscles Used:

Primary: *Posterior Calf groups, Gastrocnemius, Soleus.* (See figs. 10.44, 10.45.)
Additional: *Tibialis Posterior.*

Starting from a position in which your heels are lower than your forefeet, press upwards using the calf muscles until you are standing on your toes.

Figure 10.55 SEATED TOE RAISES.

Muscles Used:

Same as in toe raise. (See figs. 10.44, 10.45.)

Slide your feet halfway down the foot platform so that the balls of your feet are on the platform but your heels are off. Press forward and back from a toes-back to a toes-forward position.

Review Questions

1. Discuss the most efficient exercises to develop abdominal muscle strength. What muscles are involved?

2. What are the precautions that one must take to insure safety in completing an over-head lift?

3. Discuss two exercises useful in developing arm strength.

References

Arnheim, D. D., and W. E. Prentice. *Principles of athletic training*. 10th ed. McGraw-Hill, Dubuque, IA, 2000.

Atha, J. 1981. Strengthening muscle. *Exercise Sport Science Review* 9:1–73.

Baechle, T. R. *Essentials of strength training and conditioning*. Human Kinetics, Champaign, IL, 1994.

Baechle, T. R., and B. R. Groves. *Weight training: Steps to success*. 2nd ed. Human Kinetics, Champaign, IL, 1998.

Bobbert, M. F., P. A. Huijing, and G. J. van Ingen Schenau. 1987. Drop jumping. I. The influence of jumping technique on the biomechanics of jumping. *Medicine and Science in Sports Exercise* 19:332–338.

Darden, E. *The Nautilus advanced bodybuilding book*. Simon & Schuster, New York, 1984.

DeLorme, R., and F. Stransky. *Fitness and fallacies*. Kendall/Hunt, Dubuque, IA, 1990.

Enoka, R. M. 1988. Muscle strength and its development. *Sports Medicine* 6:146–168.

Field, R., and S. O. Roberts. *Weight training*. McGraw-Hill, Dubuque, IA, 1999.

Fleck, S. J., and W. J. Kraemer. *Designing resistance training programs*. 2nd ed. Human Kinetics, Champaign, IL, 1997.

Gonyea, W. J., and D. Sale. 1982. Physiology of weight lifting. *Archives of Physical Medicine and Rehabilitation* 63:235–237.

Komi, P. V. *Strength and power in sport*. Human Kinetics, Champaign, IL, 1992.

Komi, P. V. 1986. Training of muscle strength and power: Interaction of neuromotoric, hypertrophic, and mechanical factors. *International Journal of Sports Medicine* 7:10–15.

Kraemer, W. J., J. F. Patton, S. E. Gordon, E. A. Harman, M. R. Deschenes, K. Reynolds, R. U. Newton, N. T. Triplett, and J. E. Dziados. 1995. Compatibility of high-intensity strength and endurance training on hormonal and skeletal muscle adaptations. *Journal of Applied Physiology* 78:976–989.

Lesmes, G. R., D. Costill, E. F. Coyle, and W. J. Fink. 1978. Muscle strength and power changes during maximal isokinetic training. *Medicine Science Sports* 10:266–269.

Linderman, J., T. D. Fahey, L. Kirk, J. Musselman, and B. Dolinar. 1992. The effects of sodium bicarbonate and pyridxine-alpha-ketoglutarate on short-term maximal exercise capacity. *Journal of Sports Science.* 10:243–253.

Lombardi, V. P. Beginning weight training: The safe and effective way. Brown, Dubuque, IA, 1989.

McDonagh, M. J. N., and C. T. Davis. 1984. Adaptive response of mammalian skeletal muscle to exercise with high loads. *European Journal of Applied Physiology.* 52:139–155.

MacDougall, J. D., G. R. Ward, D. G. Sale, and J. R. Sutton. 1977. Biochemical adaptation of human skeletal muscle to heavy resistance training and immobilization. *Journal of Applied Physiology.* 43:700–703.

Mastropaolo, J. A. 1992. A test of the maximum-power theory for strength. *European Journal of Applied Physiology* 65:415–420.

Moritani, T., and H. A. deVries, 1979. Neural factors versus hypertrophy in the time course of muscle strength gain. *American Journal of Physical Medicine,* 58:115–130.

Nardone, A., C. Romano, and M. Schieppatgi. 1989. Selective recruitment of high-threshold human motor units during voluntary isotonic lengthening of active muscles. *Journal of Physiology* 409:451–471.

National Strength and Conditioning Association. 1989. Strength training for female athletes: A position paper: Part I. *National Strength Conditioning Association Journal* 11:43–56.

O'Shea, P. 1964. Effects of selected weight training programs on the development of strength and muscle hypertrophy. *Research Quarterly.* 37:95–102.

Welbergen E. H., C. G. Kemper, J. J. Knibbe, H. M. Toussaint, and L. Clijsen. 1991. Efficiency and effectiveness of stoop and squat lifting at different frequencies. *Ergonomics* 34:613–624.

Westcott, W. L. *Building strength and stamina.* Human Kinetics, Champaign, IL, 1996.

chapter 11

women and weight training

Objectives

After studying this chapter you should be able to

1. Describe the effect of strength training on women.

2. Describe the physical differences between men and women that are significant in strength training.

3. Define amenorrhea.

4. Describe exercise guidelines for pregnancy.

5. Describe the female athlete triad.

6. Describe eating disorders.

Female participation in physical activities has increased markedly over the past few years as outdated social mores regarding women's involvement in exercise and sport have changed.

Increasingly, more and more women are lifting weights. To those of us who have enjoyed the benefits of weight training, the increase in women's weight training is not at all surprising. Having known the benefits for years, we realized that as women began to lift they too would enjoy and desire the benefits of weight training.

One reason why the increase has been so dramatic is that women have found that through weight training they have become stronger. Being stronger improves your confidence, your self-image, and your concept of what goals can be achieved. In few, if any, athletic endeavors are these experiences so quickly enjoyed, dramatic in effect, and repeatedly reinforced.

Let's look at some special training considerations for women and their impact on weight training.

PHYSIOLOGY

Men's and women's response to cardiorespiratory training is nearly identical. When it comes to skeletal-muscular training, however, some differences in response to training do occur. These differences are not a function of muscle physiology but rather hormonal influences.

Women have a smaller amount of muscle mass and greater amount of subcutaneous fat stores that tend to lessen muscle definition. Women on average have about three-quarters the amount of absolute strength of males; however, their percentage of strength increases as a result of training is approximately the same. Also, female bodybuilders have dramatically high lean to fat ratios in comparison with other female athletes. Women are smaller than men, have less muscle mass, and have approximately two-thirds overall of absolute strength of men. The strength is related to anatomical differences between average men and women. Body height, weight, muscle fiber size, the proportion of hip width and the proportion of body fat to body weight all determine levels of strength. Women's upper body strength is less than that of men both absolutely (45 percent) and relative to total body weight or lean body mass (55 percent). However, leg strength when expressed relative to body weight or lean body mass is nearly equal in men and women. Women have the same number of type I and type II fibers as men. However, they have more fat between the muscle bundles (fascicles) than men do. A body composed of more muscle and less fat has the potential to exert more power. In men, for instance, broader shoulders support more muscle tissue and increased leverage, which is an advantage over narrow shoulders of women. However, women have the same potential for developing force per unit of muscle tissue. Men at rest have approximately ten times more testosterone than women, which accounts for the increase in hypertrophy in men completing resistance programs.

This male sex hormone is also present in women but in significantly less amounts. The influence of testosterone on skeletal muscles is, with the aid of training, to increase muscle mass. Because women have lower levels of testosterone, the increase in muscle mass (hypertrophy) that they experience with weight training is significantly less. Very few women increase dramatically in muscle mass as a result of weight training. Those that do may have an unusually high level of testosterone in their systems or may be using anabolic steroids (see chapter 16). A major misconception is that women need different strength resistance programs than those of men. Women's adaptations to resistance programs are the same as those of men for most variables. Therefore, women's programs should be the same as those for men, except the total amount of absolute resistance will be less.

Muscle building increases women's strength and improves overall balance, thus reducing the risks of falls. Increased strength also leads to increased physical activity, which keeps bones stronger. The greater bone density aids in reducing the chances of fractures and reduces risk of osteoporosis. Women typically lose about one-fourth of their bone mass by age 70, putting them at risk for fractures. In addition, women's resistance programs can decrease normal pre-menstrual symptoms such as breast enlargement, appetite craving, bloating, and mood changes. Menstrual irregularities may be more prevalent in women performing strenuous resistance activity. They will cease once strenuous resistance training is stopped.

Most women respond to weight training by increasing their strength, endurance, and muscle tone, but they do so without the significant increases in muscle mass that men experience. Very few women need to worry about becoming "too big" or "masculinized" as a result of weight training. However, with exceptional overload and volume they may increase muscle mass.

If a woman chooses to use anabolic steroids to raise her testosterone level, she will respond to training in the same manner as a man and will produce muscle mass increases in a similar fashion. There are, however, side effects to using anabolic steroids that may be unacceptable to her, such as deepening voice, increase in body hair, acne, high blood pressure, and other problems (see chapter 16).

Men, on the other hand, exceed women in maximum oxygen consumption during exercise. This is believed to be due to greater cardiac output, blood volume, and oxygen-carrying capacity of the blood. Also, because men have more lean muscle in relation to total body weight than women, they have about thirty to forty percent greater absolute strength. Their overall stores of energy-rich compounds, such as ATP, PC, and glycogen, also are greater.

Women's response to physical training in terms of cardiorespiratory endurance, muscle metabolism, and strength however, is similar to that of men.

> **Critical Thinking 11-1**
>
> A competitive woman swimmer was concerned that increasing her strength-training program would result in larger muscles, which she has seen in men who engage in strength training.
>
> Explain to her the physiological differences between men and women resulting from resistance training.

PHYSICAL DIFFERENCES

The bone structure of the female pelvic girdle is wider than a male's to facilitate the birthing process. Women's knees, however, are approximately the same distance apart as a man's. This combination results in a greater convergence angle and stress, and, thus, a greater likelihood that women will experience knee problems when performing squats, particularly deep or full squats. Women should gradually increase the resistance they use in these lifts to prevent this problem.

Percentage of Body Fat

Women have a higher percentage of body fat than men. This is true in the general population (men, 12 to 17 percent; women, 19 to 24 percent) as well as in comparing male and female athletes (men, 4 to 10 percent; women, 10 to 14 percent). Exercise can reduce body fat, and this reduction occurs without sex discrimination. Women often, however, start with a higher percentage and retain a higher percentage even when highly trained (as compared to a highly trained male).

Menstruation

The cause of exercise amenorrhea (cessation of menstruation) is still unknown. However, a number of theories exist, including increased testosterone and decreased ovarian function, loss of body fat, and active pituitary functioning. Presently, there is a strong indication that a change in hypothalamic functioning may be responsible. Sufficient calcium replacement is essential for individuals encountering amenorrhea.

Most women who cease menstruation appear to suffer no physiological problems, but the long-term effects are unknown. If amenorrhea does occur, cutting back on training, eliminating stress, and raising the percentage of body fat above 10 percent are recommended.

EXERCISE GUIDELINES FOR PREGNANCY

1. Exercise intensity should not go beyond the 70 percent threshold level. The American College of Obstetricians and Gynecologists cautions against heart rates exceeding 140 beats per minute.
2. Exercise should be stopped if there is any pain or bleeding.
3. Adequate intakes of iron, calcium, and vitamins should be insured before and during pregnancy.
4. Avoid bouncing, jarring, and twisting activities that put your abdomen in jeopardy.
5. If you feel tired or experience discomfort, stop and rest.
6. You should not exercise so intensely that you are unable to talk.
7. Don't exercise while lying on your back after the fourth month. This can block the blood supply to the uterus and depress fetal heart rate. If you need to rest, lie on your side.
8. Don't exercise vigorously in hot weather (core body temperature should not go above 101 degrees Fahrenheit).
9. Drink plenty of water before, during, and after exercise.
10. Your exercise program should be started well in advance of your pregnancy.
11. Research is not confirmed regarding the detrimental effects of a pregnant mother being involved in such activities as gymnastics and yoga.

If a pregnant woman has medical problems, disease, or other complications, she should seek advice from an obstetrician before undertaking a rigorous physical exercise program. Rhythmic, moderate activity is well advised and safe for both mother and fetus.

EXERCISE AFTER CHILDBIRTH

Women who have just given birth should start exercising as soon as possible if there were no complications and if they have received medical clearance from their physician. They should start slowly because their red blood cell count may be a little low, resulting in feelings of fatigue and shortness of breath. Gradually, over four to six weeks, they should be able to work up to the exercise routine they maintained before they became pregnant. If, during exercise, they feel themselves getting overly tired, they shouldn't force themselves to complete the exercise. Moderation is the key until their bodies start responding and they feel as though they can exercise without undue stress.

OSTEOPOROSIS

Osteoporosis is a disease in which bone tissue degenerates. It ranks closely behind arthritis as a major chronic disease of older people, especially women. Susceptibility to the disease appears to increase with menopause. It may be that the estrogen decreases that accompany menopause hasten the destruction of bone tissue and also decrease the body's absorption rate of calcium, which is vital for the integrity of the bones.

There is a wide variation in bone density among women. Physical activity, calcium intake throughout life, ability to adapt to low-calcium diets, and fluoride intake are all associated with higher bone density. On the other hand, a lack of regular menstruation, premature menopause, use of some medications, and prolonged bed rest are associated with low bone density. It is important, therefore, not to focus attention on calcium alone when a number of factors play a significant part in this disease. Evidence from the National Institute of Health indicates that taking calcium supplements after menopause has only a marginal effect on bone loss. The NIH recommends that all adults consume 1,000 milligrams of calcium daily, and post-menopausal women who are considered to be at high risk for the development of osteoporosis should consume an additional 500 milligrams.

Some success has resulted from a combination of increased calcium intake with an aerobic exercise program. Weight training with light weights supplemented with the proper diet may prove to be an answer, as training has been shown to increase bone density in all age groups regardless of gender.

FEMALE ATHLETE TRIAD

Some women and girls are at risk for a newly defined syndrome known as the female athlete triad. A combination of factors, together or alone, comprise the triad: amenorrhea, osteoporosis and disordered eating. Recent evidence indicates that from 15 to 62 percent of female athletes suffer from eating disorders. The American College of Sports Medicine also has recognized that male athletes in weight regulated and endurance sports may be at risk for disordered eating and osteoporosis. Extensive exercise and anorexia nervosa in men have been associated with low male hormone levels and osteoporosis.

Long-term consequences of the triad are not yet fully understood. However, women build 60 to 70 percent of their calcium supply in their bones between the ages of eleven and eighteen. Young women who do not allow normal amounts of calcium to be deposited in their bones may suffer irreversible bone loss. Also, the athletes with amenorrhea have reduced levels of estrogen, which results in the loss of bone mass. This loss can occur in the early twenties and is generally irreversible, leading to osteoporosis.

The American College of Sports Medicine warns that the delayed onset of menstruation or the absence of three or more consecutive cycles after the onset is neither a desirable nor abnormal result of exercise. It may be a symptom of an underlying medical problem.

> **Critical Thinking 11-2**
>
> A female athlete has been diagnosed as having a serious eating disorder and amenorrhea.
>
> What health problems could that lead to?

EATING DISORDERS' WARNING SIGNS

1. Preoccupation with food, calories and weight
2. Wearing baggy clothes or layered clothing
3. Relentless excessive exercise

4. Avoiding food-related social activities
5. Noticeable weight loss or gain
6. Excessive concern about weight
7. Bathroom visits after meals
8. Increasing criticism of one's body

Medical Center Orthopedics, 12 May 1999, Louisville, Kentucky

Glossary

Amenorrhea   Abnormal cessation of menstruation.
Anabolic Steroids   Synthetic hormones that are similar to the male hormone testosterone.
Female Athlete Triad Syndrome   A potentially serious problem involving a combination of eating disorders, amenorrhea, and osteoporosis.
Hypothalamus   Portion of brain controlling hormonal functioning among many other responsibilities.
Menopause   The natural cessation of menstruation occurring near age fifty.
Osteoporosis   A loss in bone materials and density, producing brittleness and softness of the bone.

Solutions to Critical Thinking

11-1. The reason that men will evidence increased muscle size (hypertrophy) from strength training is that they have larger amounts of testosterone circulating in their bodies. Women have very small amounts of testosterone and experience much less muscle growth.

11-2. This athlete has symptoms of the female athlete triad. She is at risk for calcium loss in the bones and subsequently osteoporosis.

Review Questions

1. What symptoms are associated with the female athlete triad syndrome?
2. What are some different physiological adaptations between men and women resulting from resistance training?
3. What are some of the important exercise guidelines during pregnancy?

References

Bell, R., and M. O' Neill. 1994. Exercise and pregnancy: A review. *Birth* 21(2):85–95.

Clapp, J. F., and S. Dickstein. 1984. Endurance exercise and pregnancy outcome. *Medicine and Science in Sports and Exercise* 16:556–562.

Fahey, T. D., and G. Hutchinson. *Weight training for women.* Mayfield, Mountain View, CA, 1992.

Hakkinen, K., A. Pakarinen, and M. Kallinen. 1992. Neuromuscular adaptations and serum hormones in women during short-term intensive strength training. *European Journal of Applied Physiology* 64:106–111.

Kirkley, George W. *Weight lifting and weight training.* Anco, New York, 1982.

Kulpa, P. J., B. M. White, and R. Visscher. 1987. Aerobic exercise in pregnancy. *American Journal of Obstetrics and Gynecology* 156:1395–1403.

Kuramoto, A. K., and V. G. Payne. 1995. Predicting muscular strength in women: A preliminary study. *Research Quarterly for Exercise and Sport* 66:168–172.

Lance, Kathryn. *Getting strong—A woman's guide to realizing her physical potential.* The Bobbs-Merrill Co., New York, 1978.

Layne, Jennifer E., and Miriam E. Nelson. 1999. The effects of progressive resistance training on bone density. *Medicine and Science in Sport and Exercise* 31-1:25–30.

Leon, Edie. *Complete woman weight training guide.* Anderson World, Mountain View, CA, 1976.

Lyon, Lisa, and Douglas Kent Hall. *Lisa Lyon's body magic.* Bantam Books, New York, 1981.

Miller, A. E. J., J. D. McDougall, M. A. Tarnoplosky, and D. G. Sale. 1992. Gender differences in muscle fiber characteristics. *European Journal of Applied Physiology* 66:254–262.

Morton, M. J., M. S. Paul, and J. Metcalfe. 1985. Exercise during pregnancy. *Medical Clinics of North America* 69:97–107.

National Strength and Conditioning Association. 1989. Strength training for female athletes: A position paper: Part I. *National Strength Conditioning Association Journal* 11:43–56.

Nyburg, K. H., L. K. Backrach, B. Lewis, K. Kent, and R. Marcus. 1993. Low bone mineral density at axial and appendicular sites in amenorrheic athletes. *Medicine and Science in Sports and Exercise* 25:1197–1202.

O'Shea, J. P. *Scientific principles and methods of strength fitness.* Addison-Wesley, Reading, MA, 1979.

Pirie, Lynne, and Bill Reynolds. *Getting built—A woman's body building program for strength, beauty and fitness.* Warner Books, New York, 1984.

Shangold, M., and G. Merkin, eds. *Women and exercise: Physiology and sports medicine.* 2d ed. F. A. Davis, Philadelphia, 1994.

Taaffe, D. R., L. Pruitt, J. Reim, G. Butterfield, and R. Marcus. 1995. Effect of sustained resistance training on basal metabolic rate in older women. *Journal of American Geriatric Society* 43:465–471.

Wells, C. L. *Women Sport and performance.* Human Kinetics, Champaign, IL, 1985.

chapter 12

cardiorespiratory fitness

Objectives

After studying this chapter you should be able to

1. Describe cardiorespiratory fitness.
2. Describe the target heart rate method.
3. Define aerobic and anaerobic exercise.
4. Describe intensity, duration, and frequency of cardiorespiratory training.
5. Define cooling down.
6. Describe the American College of Sports Medicine Recommendations about Exercise.
7. Describe pre-exercise screening.

The body's ability to deliver oxygen and nutrients rapidly and efficiently to all vital organs such as the heart, nervous system, and working muscles is the basis of cardiorespiratory endurance. A well-conditioned heart and efficient respiratory system are essential to a high level of physical fitness. Table 12.1 lists the benefits of cardiorespiratory training on the body.

MAXIMUM OXYGEN UPTAKE

The main function of the heart and circulatory system is to provide blood, which is necessary to maintain the proper functioning of all body cells. In terms of exercise, the heart's main concern is its ability to deliver oxygen to the working cells of the body and to rid the cells of waste products. The greatest amount of oxygen used by the cells during maximum exercise per unit of time is referred to as **maximum oxygen uptake.** Maximum oxygen uptake is one of the best indexes of cardiorespiratory fitness. Training may be a twenty percent contributing factor in determining maximum oxygen uptake, whereas the remaining 80 percent is thought to be genetically determined.

The amount of blood pumped out per beat **(stroke volume)** at rest for the average individual is approximately 70 to 90 milliliters. During rigorous activity, the average heart may pump 100 to 120 milliliters per beat. The trained individual, however, may have a stroke volume at rest of 100 to 120 milliliters and a maximum

Table 12.1

Benefits of Cardiorespiratory Training		
Cardiorespiratory Training Increases	**Cardiorespiratory Training Produces**	**Cardiorespiratory Training Decreases**
Tolerance to stress	Lower resting heart rate	Obesity-adiposity
Arterial oxygen content	Physical conditioning of muscles	Arterial blood pressure
Electron transport activity	Greater oxygen utilization	Heart rate
Efficiency of the heart	Greater stroke volume	Vulnerability to dysrhythmias
Blood vessel size		Stress response
Efficiency of blood circulation	Lower heart rate for submaximal work	Need of heart muscle for oxygen

capability during exercise of 150 to 170 milliliters. This gives the trained individual a decided advantage, since the more efficient your heart, the greater its ability to maintain exercise levels for long periods of time with less stress. The hearts of some trained individuals may be capable of pumping out as much as 30 to 35 *liters* a minute. This amount is six times the total volume of the blood in the body, which indicates the truly exceptional efficiency of the heart.

CARDIORESPIRATORY ENDURANCE

Cardiorespiratory endurance is the body's ability to sustain prolonged vigorous exercise. Muscular endurance, though partly dependent on the cardiorespiratory system, refers to the ability of a muscle or muscle group to sustain prolonged movement. Muscular endurance is related to muscular strength and is specific to the muscles that are being exercised.

AEROBIC-ANAEROBIC

All-out exercises lasting two minutes or less without stopping are referred to as anaerobic exercises (without oxygen). Such exercises as sprinting, tennis, handball, and weight lifting are examples of anaerobic exercises. For all-around physical fitness anaerobic exercise should be accompanied by continuous vigorous exercise lasting beyond two minutes, such as jogging, cycling, and swimming, which train the aerobic system (with oxygen). It is important to do aerobic training before participating in anaerobic activities such as strength training.

Figure 12.1 shows the relative amounts of aerobic versus anaerobic fitness required in different sport activities.

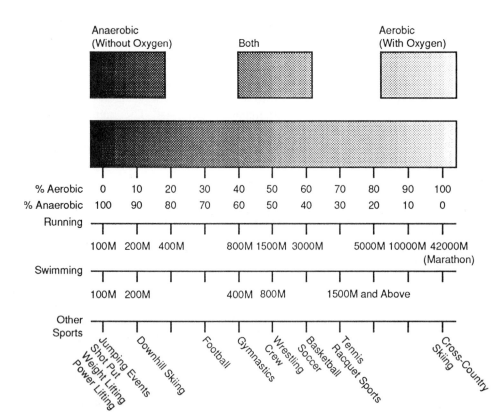

Figure 12.1 RELATIVE AMOUNTS OF ANAEROBIC VERSUS AEROBIC FITNESS REQUIRED IN DIFFERENT SPORT ACTIVITIES.

In the running and swimming events, researchers generally agree that at around three minutes (until about seven or eight minutes) there are relatively equal requirements in both the aerobic and anaerobic pathways for muscle energetics.

From Aerobic Weight Training *by Frederick C. Hatfield. Ph.D. Copyright © 1985 Contemporary Books, Inc. Reprinted by permission of Contemporary Books, Inc.*

ENERGY SYSTEMS

The first energy source involves two energy-rich compounds—**ATP (adenosine triphosphate)** and **PC (phosphocreatine)**—that are stored directly in the muscle tissue. When the muscle is stimulated through exercise, ATP and PC break down and release immediate energy for muscle contraction. Energy from ATP and PC, however, is available only for a brief period because only very small amounts of these compounds are stored in the muscle. This concept is known as **anaerobic** (without oxygen).

A second energy source during exercise is supported by sugar, which is stored in the muscles in the form of glycogen. When glycogen is broken down, the released energy produces more ATP. However, when glycogen is burned in the absence of oxygen, it gives off an end product called lactic acid, which results in muscle fatigue. For this reason, this energy source is limited to activities that last approximately one to two minutes. If exercise continues beyond this time, the body is required to draw upon oxygen, the third energy source available during exercise.

The oxygen system can use both glycogen and fats as fuel for the production of ATP. Lactic acid, along with the accumulation of calcium 2+ (ions) and heat, are major factors in muscle fatigue. However, when oxygen is used through a complex process that occurs in the muscle cells, the oxygen prevents the buildup of lactic acid and promotes the resynthesis of ATP for energy. This system is referred to as **aerobic** (with oxygen) and is used primarily in endurance activities, such as long-distance running, skiing, and swimming.

INTENSITY

For a training effect to occur in the cardiovascular and muscular system, the exercise program must consist of activities that produce an overload on these systems. For cardiovascular training the threshold level is 70 percent of your maximum heart rate, as previously outlined. A threshold level of 60 percent is used for post-heart-attack victims, obese persons, or persons with a history of sedentary living.

TRAINING EFFECT

Monitoring your heart rate is a very effective way of determining exercise intensity. This approach is referred to as the threshold effect or training heart rate effect. Research by Karvonen found that a training level of 70 percent of your maximum heart rate, approximately 60 percent of your maximum oxygen uptake level, is considered to be a minimal level of intensity necessary to increase cardiovascular endurance.

Determining your target heart rate is relatively simple. First you determine your maximum heart rate by subtracting your age from 220. This method is not an exact measure because the formula predicts rather than assesses. As a result, there is a possibility of a ten beat per minute error. Next, subtract your resting pulse rate from your predicted maximum heart rate, then multiply the difference by 70 percent. Add this product to your resting heart rate; the result will give you your target heart rate level. The resting heart rate is determined by taking your pulse in the morning before you get out of bed. Because of daily fluctuations you should average this figure for three to five days.

The following is an example of determining the target heart rate level for a twenty-year-old individual with a resting heart rate of seventy beats per minute:

220 − 20 = 200 beats per minute (maximum heart rate) where 20 is the individual's age.
200 − 70 = 130 (70 is the resting heart rate in this example)
130 × .70 = 91 (.70 is the desired intensity)
91 + 70 = 161 beats per minute where 70 is the resting heart rate

The target heart rate level in this example is 161 beats per minute.

Three basic principles are important to insure proper cardiovascular training effects: intensity, duration, and frequency.

Also refer to tables 12.2 and 12.3 which relate energy to type and intensity of exercise.

Table 12.2

Approximate Energy Cost (in Kilocalories) of Various Physical Activities

Sport or Activity	Kilocalories Expended per Minute (kcal/min) of Activity
Climbing	10.7–13.2
Cycling 5.5 MPH	4.5
9.4 MPH	7.0
13.1 MPH	11.1
Dancing	3.3–7.7
Football	8.9
Golf	5.0
Gymnastics	
Balancing	2.5
Abdominal exercises	3.0
Trunk bending	3.5
Arm swinging, hopping	6.5
Rowing 51 str/min	4.1
87 str/min	7.0
97 str/min	11.2
Running	
Short distance	13.3–16.6
Cross-country	10.6
Tennis	7.1
Skating (fast)	11.5
Skiing, moderate speed	10.8–15.9
Uphill, maximum speed	18.6
Squash	10.2
Swimming	
Backstroke	11.0
Breaststroke	11.5
Crawl (55 yd/min)	14.0
Wrestling	14.2

Source: Reprinted by permission of the American Alliance for Health, Physical Education, Recreation and Dance, 1900 Association Drive, Reston, Virginia 22091.

Table 12.3

Typical Criteria for the Classification of Exercise Intensity

Exercise Intensity Classification	Criteria Heart Rate	Energy Expenditure (kcal/hr)	Perceived Exertion
Very light	<110	<110	Very, very easy
Light	110–120	111–270	Easy, no pain or discomfort
Moderate	121–150	270–400	Somewhat difficult and slight discomfort
Heavy	151–160	401–550	Difficult, uncomfortable, and some pain
Very heavy	161–180	550–669	Very difficult and painful
Exhaustive	>180	>700	Extremely difficult and painful

Source: From Hage, Phillip, "Perceived Exertion: One Measure of Exercise Intensity," in *The Physician and Sports Medicine,* September 1981, pp. 136–46. © 1981 McGraw-Hill Healthcare Group. Reprinted by permission.

DURATION

How long you exercise depends primarily on the intensity of the exercise and your long-range goals. Beginners should exercise for a minimum of fifteen to twenty minutes. As fitness level improves, the exercise session can be increased from thirty to sixty minutes. Maintaining your target training effect level during the thirty to sixty minutes of exercise will improve your cardiorespiratory endurance. Longer work periods are necessary only for those interested in competing in such activities as long-distance running or swimming. Strength training should be approximately fifteen minutes in duration. Generally, longer exercise sessions over thirty-five minutes produce greater fitness benefits. However, low-fit individuals should start out with five- to ten-minute sessions equivalent to approximately 100 kilocalories per session and work up to expenditures of 200 to 300 kilocalories per workout. (A kilocalorie is the amount of heat necessary to raise one kilogram of water one degree Celsius.) Longer duration exercises tend to improve the muscle's ability to use fat. Presently there is no evidence to indicate that additional health benefits are derived from workouts that exceed 60 minutes (600 kilocalories). Therefore it is recommended that low-fit individuals' exercise should last long enough to burn 100 to 200 kilocalories; medium-fit, 200 to 400; and high-fit individuals, 400 or more kilocalories. There is considerable evidence now to indicate that exercise needs to exceed 7.5 kilocalories a minute to reduce the risk of heart disease.

Do not attempt to increase your weekly training intensity or volume more than 10 percent weekly. In addition, do not attempt new times or distances until you can do two-thirds of the new time and distance comfortably.

FREQUENCY

You don't have to knock yourself out seven days a week to achieve cardiorespiratory endurance. Workouts three to five days a week are sufficient. It is important to allow yourself twenty-four to forty-eight hours for rest and recovery between exercise bouts.

Overstressing the body is one of the worst things you can do, and one way to do that is by strenuously exercising only once a week. This kind of regimen is worse than no exercise at all. Strenuous exercising once a week can greatly stress your cardiorespiratory system without producing any benefits. If you cannot exercise at least three times a week, then your once- or twice-a-week exercise should be moderate, with the main objectives of relaxation and burning up a few extra calories. In addition it may lower the risk of coronary heart disease.

Another thing to keep in mind is that if you miss a day or two in your exercise routine, you should never try to make it up. This is a dangerous practice, especially for middle-aged people. The important consideration here is not to become obsessive about exercising. Some people, whose main goal in exercising is to avoid having a heart attack, become so rigidly goal-directed that any interference in their exercise schedule results in anxiety. This is not the object of exercise. Your exercise program should be enjoyable and relaxing. Avoid rigidly structured schedules that lead to anxiety and tension. And remember, don't "pile it on" if you miss a day.

These three workouts should be spaced evenly through the week to avoid long periods of nonactivity. A typical schedule is as follows:

3-day schedule
RUN M–W–F

5-day schedule
RUN M–W–F   or   RUN T–Th–Sat
BIKE T–Th   BIKE Sun–F

7-day schedule
RUN M–W–F
BIKE T–Th–Sat
SWIM Sun

COOLING DOWN

You should continue to exercise at a low intensity (stretching and walking eight to ten minutes) following a rigorous workout. (See table 12.4.) This step will allow your body to adjust to a resting state. Cooling down prevents the blood from pooling in the lower extremities, which could reduce the amount of blood returning to the heart and disrupt the cardiac cycle. Cooling down also helps reduce muscle soreness, dizziness, and the amount of biochemical fatigue products in the blood.

Critical Thinking 12-1

A middle-aged person has time only to jog once a week to develop fitness.

Explain the problem associated with once a week jogging.

Critical Thinking 12-2

A college wrestler has a habit of taking a cold shower immediately after practice.

What is the danger in this procedure?

Table 12.4

Sequence and Time Ranges for Basic Fitness Program		
Stage	**Duration**	**Activity**
Warm-up, flexibility	10–15 minutes	Walking, slow jogging
Aerobic exercise	20–40 minutes	Bicycling,
		Walking,
		Jogging,
		Swimming
Cooldown	8–10 minutes	Walking, stretching

Table 12.5

Muscle Strength and Cardiovascular Circuit-Training Program	
Duration	Ten weeks
Frequency	Three days per week
Circuits/session	Circuit A: 3; Circuit B: 2
Time/circuit	Circuit A: 7 1/2 min; Circuit B: 15 min
Total time/session	Circuit A: 22 1/2 min; Circuit B: 30 min
Load	40 to 55 percent of 1 RM
Repetitions	As many as possible in thirty seconds
Rest	Fifteen seconds between stations

Muscle Strength and Endurance Circuit A		Cardiovascular Circuit B	
Station	Exercise	Station	Exercise
1	Bench press	1	Running (440 yd)
2	Bent-knee sit-ups	2	Push-ups or pull-ups
3	Knee (leg) extension	3	Bent-knee sit-ups
4	Pulldown-lateral machine	4	Vertical jumps
5	Back hyperextension	5	Standing (overhead) press
6	Standing (overhead) press	6	Bicycling (3 min)
7	Dead lift	7	Hip stretch
8	Arm curl	8	Rope jumping (1 min)
9	Leg curl (knee flexion)	9	Bent-over rowing
10	Upright rowing	10	Hamstring stretch
		11	Upright rowing
		12	Running (660 yd)

Source: *Sports Psychology,* by Edward L. Fox. Copyright © 1979 by Saunders College Publishing/Holt Rinehart and Winston. Reprinted by permission of CBS College Publishing.

CIRCUIT TRAINING

Circuit training involves a combination of strength and endurance exercises performed in sequence at various exercise stations. This extremely efficient technique can be specifically designed for a variety of different sports activities. For example, the circuit can emphasize strength, muscular endurance, cardiovascular activities, or a combination of all three. Table 12.5 presents an example of a muscular strength, muscular endurance, and cardiovascular circuit-training program. See appendix C for the Universal super circuit.

PRE-EXERCISE SCREENING

For many years in the United States, physicians adopted a somewhat restricted approach to exercise prescription, suggesting that a stress electrocardiogram was needed in all men over the age of thirty-five years who wanted to increase their habitual physical activity. This requirement has now largely been discredited. The need for extensive

Table 12.6

		Suggested Lab Activity—Revised Physical Activity Readiness Questionnaire (rPAR-Q)
Yes	**No**	
____	____	1. Has a doctor said that you have a heart condition and recommended only medically supervised activity?
____	____	2. Do you have chest pain brought on by physical activity?
____	____	3. Have you developed chest pain in the past month?
____	____	4. Do you tend to lose consciousness or fall over as a result of dizziness?
____	____	5. Do you have a bone or joint that could be aggravated by the proposed physical activity?
____	____	6. Has a doctor ever recommended medication for your blood pressure or a heart condition?
____	____	7. Are you aware through your own experience, or a doctor's advice, of any other physical reason against your exercising without medical supervision?

NOTE: If you have a temporary illness, such as a common cold, or are not feeling well at this time—POSTPONE.

Produced by the British Columbia Ministry of Health and the Department of National Health and Welfare.

preliminary screening is particularly questionable given that modern exercise decreases rather than increases a person's overall risk of cardiac death.

The Canadian Physical Activity Readiness Questionnaire (rPAR-Q) (table 12.6) has proved to be a very safe screening and has shown remarkable success in detecting potential contraindications to exercise. The rPAR-Q is thus the currently recommended method of determining exercise readiness in symptom-free adults with no more than one major cardiac risk factor. A yes answer on one or more of the seven questions indicates the need for medical screening prior to beginning an exercise program.

EXERCISE PRESCRIPTION

The American College of Sports Medicine makes the following recommendations for the quantity and quality of training for developing and maintaining cardiorespiratory fitness and body composition in the healthy adult:

1. Frequency of training: three to five days per week.
2. Intensity of training: 60 percent to 90 percent of maximum heart rate.
3. Duration of training: fifteen to sixty minutes of continuous aerobic activity. Duration is dependent on the intensity of the activity; thus lower intensity activity should be conducted over a longer period of time. Because of the importance of the total-fitness effect and the fact that it is more readily attained in longer duration programs, and because of the potential hazards and compliance problems associated with high intensity activity, lower to moderate intensity activity of longer duration is recommended for the nonathletic adult.
4. Mode of activity: Any activity that uses large muscle groups, that can be maintained continuously, and is rhythmical and aerobic in nature: for example, running, jogging, walking, hiking, swimming, skating, bicycling, rowing, cross-country skiing, rope skipping, and various endurance game activities. See also figures 17.2–17.9 for cardiorespiratory machines.

EXERCISE PRECAUTIONS

Be familiar with the following exercise precautions before beginning your cardiorespiratory endurance program:

1. Get a thorough physical examination before starting your conditioning program.
2. If fatigue lasts two hours or more following an exercise session, the program is too rigorous. Reduce your level of exercise.
3. Alcohol and exercise do not mix. Alcohol constricts the coronary vessels of the heart muscle.
4. Cigarette smoking limits oxygen exchange in the lungs, thus preventing a high level of fitness attainment.
5. Always warm up before exercise and cool down after the activity.
6. Remember to use your heart rate as a guide to the intensity of the exercise.
7. Sporadic exercise may be detrimental to your health. Three to five exercise sessions a week are minimal for optimum benefit.

If any of the following symptoms occur while you are exercising, stop exercising and consult a physician before continuing your exercise program:

1. Fluttering, palpitating, missed, or extra heartbeats, sudden bursts of rapid heartbeats, or a sudden slowing of rapid pulse
2. Pressure or pain in the center of the chest, left arm, fingers, or throat
3. Dizziness, fainting, nausea, cold sweat, or light-headedness
4. Shortness of breath or inability to attain sufficient oxygen

Glossary

Aerobic   Continuous vigorous exercise of long duration, such as jogging, long-distance swimming, and cycling that utilizes large amounts of oxygen.

Anaerobic   All-out exercise lasting one to two minutes or less, such as weight lifting, sprinting, handball, and squash, performed in the absence of oxygen.

Cooling Down   Continuation of exercise at a low intensity following a vigorous workout, which allows the body to adjust to a resting state.

Duration   Amount of time utilized for each exercise bout.

Frequency   Number of exercise bouts per week.

Intensity   The level of physiological stress on the body during exercise.

Target Heart Rate   The proper intensity level of an endurance training program, approximately 70 to 85 percent of maximum heart rate.

Solutions to Critical Thinking

12-1. In order to develop and maintain cardiorespiratory fitness, it is necessary to exercise a minimum of three days a week for twenty to sixty minutes in addition to ten to fifteen minutes each for warm-up and cooldown. A rigorous once a week run will not increase fitness and in some cases may be dangerous to this person's health. Brisk walking once a week is a safer exercise and will burn up a few calories.

12-2. A cold shower could result in rapid vasoconstriction of peripheral blood vessels, further decreasing the venous return to the heart. This wrestler should cool down by light jogging, walking, and stretching for at least ten minutes after exercise. The shower taken after cooling down should not be ice-cold but near body temperature.

Review Questions

1. What is meant by the term maximum oxygen uptake?
2. Explain the method for calculating the proper training effect on the cardiorespiratory system.
3. Why is cooling down after exercise important?

References

American College of Sports Medicine. *Guidelines for graded exercise testing prescription.* 5th ed. Lea & Febiger, Philadelphia, PA, 1995.

Anspaugh, D. J., M. H. Hamrick, and F. D. Rosato. *Wellness: Concepts and applications.* 4th ed. McGraw-Hill, Dubuque, IA, 2000.

Arnheim, D. D., and W. E. Prentice. *Principles of athletic training.* 10th ed. McGraw-Hill, Dubuque, IA, 2000.

Bouchard, C., R. J. Shephard, T. Stevens, J. R. Sutton, and B. d. McPherson. *Exercise, fitness, and health.* Human Kinetics, Champaign, IL, 1990.

Brooks, G. 1985. Anaerobic threshold: Review of the concept and directions for future research. *Medicine and Science in Sports and Exercise* 17:22–23.

Corbin, C. B., R. Lindsey, and G. Welk. *Concepts of fitness and wellness.* 3rd ed. McGraw-Hill, Dubuque, IA, 2000.

Corbin, C. B., R. Lindsey, and G. Welk. *Concepts of physical fitness: Active lifestyles for wellness.* 10th ed. McGraw-Hill, Dubuque, IA, 2000.

Dishman, R. K. 1988. Exercise adherence research: Future directions. *American Journal of Health Promotion* 3(1):52–56.

Hickson, R. C., et al. 1985. Reduced training intensities and loss of aerobic power, endurance, and cardiac growth. *Journal of Applied Physiology* 58:492.

Hockey, R. *Physical fitness: The pathway to healthful living.* 8th ed. Mosby-Year Book, St. Louis, 1996.

Kaplan, N. M. *Clinical hypertension.* 4th ed. Williams & Wilkins, Baltimore, MD, 1986.

McGlynn, G. *Dynamics of fitness: A practical approach.* 5th ed. McGraw-Hill, Dubuque, IA, 1999.

Neiman, David C. *Fitness and sports medicine: An introduction.* 3rd ed. Bull Publishing, Palo Alto, CA, 1995.

Pollock, M. L., and J. H. Wilmore. *Exercise in health and disease.* 2d ed. W. B. Saunders, Philadelphia, 1990.

Powers, S., and E. Howley. *Exercise physiology: Theory and application to fitness and performance.* 2d ed. Wm. C. Brown, Dubuque, IA, 1994.

Prentice, W. E. *Fitness and wellness for life.* 6th ed. McGraw-Hill, Dubuque, IA, 1999.

Prentice, W. E. *Get fit, stay, fit.* Mosby-Year Book, St. Louis, 1996.

U.S. Department of Health and Human Services. *Healthy people 2000: National health promotion and disease prevention objectives.* U.S. Government Printing Office, Washington, DC, 1991.

Wenger, H. A., and G. J. Bell. 1986. The interactions of intensity, frequency and duration of exercise training in altering cardiorespiratory fitness. *Sports Medicine* 3:346–356.

chapter 13

flexibility

Objectives

After studying this chapter you should be able to

1. Describe the importance of flexibility.

2. Differentiate between static stretching and ballistic stretching.

3. Describe the importance of stretching.

4. Describe PNF stretching.

5. Describe and demonstrate basic stretching exercises.

FLEXIBILITY

The term *flexibility* encompasses the ability to move freely throughout a full, nonrestricted, pain-free range of motion about a joint or series of joints. Flexibility is not only an important component of physical fitness but also is an important aspect of your resistance-training program. There is a great deal of individual variation in joint looseness. Joint looseness may be the result of particular joint physical structure or unique individual characteristics.

Joint flexibility is controlled by a number of factors: the joint capsule contributes approximately 47 percent to the range of motion, the muscles contribute 41 percent, the tendons contribute 10 percent, and the skin contributes 2 percent. Because the joint capsule itself is rigid, the emphasis when attempting to increase or decrease flexibility is placed on the muscle and skin tissue. Stretching exercises enable these tissues to increase the range of the movement. Conversely, strengthening exercises may tighten up the muscles and tendons and can decrease the range of movement if not done correctly through the full range of motion.*

Women tend to have a greater range of movement in the joints than men primarily because men have generally larger and bulkier skeletal muscles, which tend to reduce joint movement. However, flexibility is one characteristic of well-developed muscles, regardless of gender.

All activities require varying degrees of flexibility. A competitive tennis player needs good shoulder flexibility. A laborer requires good lower-back flexibility. Even such everyday movements as walking and running require flexibility. Good flexibility reduces the possibility of the aches, pains, and inflammations associated with joints that are stressed through rigorous activity. Running for a long period of time without pre- and post stretching activities may lead to reduced flexibility in the legs and back and may result in lower-back problems.

There exists an erroneous concept that resistance training will result in a decrease of flexibility. Evidence indicates little support for this contention. Typically, heavy resistance training results in either an improvement or no change in flexibility Care should be taken to stress the full range of motion of both agonist and antagonist muscle groups and to choose exercises that stimulate both groups of muscles at each joint to insure adequate strength and balance between both sides of the joints.

Critical Thinking 13-1

A female basketball player is concerned that a strength-training program will be detrimental to her flexibility?

What can you tell her about the relationship between strength training and flexibility?

*Certain flexibility exercises have a greater potential for injury; therefore, caution should be observed when performing such exercises. Proper instruction by a certified professional in an exercise class is recommended if there is any doubt about a specific stretching exercise.

STATIC STRETCHING

Static stretching consists of stretching the muscle slowly and gradually for periods of ten to twenty seconds, followed by several seconds of relaxation. This method is a very effective stretching technique and does not impose unnecessary stress on the muscle. Stretching increases extensibility and reduces the resistance of the muscles. It also produces more efficient muscle contractions and reduces the chances of injury or soreness. In addition, an integral part of cooling down is static stretching of the muscles that have been used during exercise. The stretching will increase the exit of lactic acid from the muscles, prevent blood pooling in the muscles, and reduce muscle soreness.

BALLISTIC STRETCHING

Ballistic stretching, on the other hand, involves rapid bouncing, jerking movements, which have the potential for injuring soft muscle and joint tissue. The ballistic method of jerking and bouncing actually invokes what is called a stretch reflex, wherein the muscle senses that it is overextended and contracts as a means of protection. The purpose of stretching is to lengthen the muscle, not shorten it; therefore, ballistic stretching is counterproductive.

PROPRIOCEPTIVE NEUROMUSCULAR FACILITATION (PNF)

An alternative method of stretching is to precede a static stretch with an isometric contraction of the muscle group to be stretched. This stretching method is called **proprioceptive neuromuscular facilitation (PNF).** This method is effective in improving muscle relaxation and leads to increased flexibility. The procedure generally requires two people. A partner moves the limb passively through its range of motion. After reaching the end point of the range of motion, the muscle is isometrically contracted for six to ten seconds against the partner's resistance; the muscle then relaxes and is again stretched using static techniques. This method is also called contract-relax (c-R). It is vital that the partner is adequately trained in the technique so that injury will not result.

It is essential in sports activities that an extremity be capable of moving through a nonrestricted range of motion. All three methods of stretching have been shown to improve flexibility. Ballistic stretching is seldom utilized because of the increased chance of injury or soreness, even though many of our activities are ballistic in nature. Static stretching is the most widely utilized because it is easy to perform, safe, and does not require a partner. PNF stretching techniques have been shown to produce dramatic increases in range of motion in a very short time. The main disadvantage with PNF stretching is that it requires a trained partner.

STRETCHING AND WARM-UP PRINCIPLES

1. No matter what the nature of the exercise to come, a slow, gradual warm-up consisting of calisthenics, stretching, and slow jogging, should always precede exercise, even if you are highly trained.
2. Be ready to make minor adjustments to your stretching routine. You may be more flexible on some days than others.
3. Your warm-up should last ten to fifteen minutes.

4. Stretching following mild jogging should be slow but thorough.
5. Initial stretching should be gentle and specific to the muscles that will recieve the most stress.
6. The muscle must be stretched beyond its normal range, but not to the point of pain.
7. Stretch only to the point you feel tightness and resistance.
8. Avoid overstretching the ligaments and joint capsule.
9. Take caution with stretching exercises of the neck and lower back.
10. Always stretch slowly and in control.
11. Don't hold your breath while stretching.
12. Stretch at least three times a week for maximum results.
13. When utilizing PNF, make sure your partner is well trained in the technique.
14. Jogging should be conducted at an intensity and rate specific to your anticipated activity and level of fitness.
15. Only a few minutes should lapse between the completion of the warm-up and the activity.
16. Experiment with different types of warm-ups. Find the one that best fits your body. The warm-up should feel good.
17. A portion of the warm-up exercise should consist of skill drills and other skilled movements related to the anticipated activity to follow the warm-up.
18. Remember to stretch and cool down following the activity.

Figures 13.1 through 13.18 show a comprehensive group of stretching exercises that include the most commonly utilized muscles in the body and those that generally experience the most stress.

Figure 13.1 BEHIND THE NECK SHOULDER STRETCH.

Muscles Stretched:

Internal/External Rotators.

From a standing position, flex right arm and raise elbow above head. Right hand palm down behind back. Place left arm, elbow flexed, behind back and bring fingers together. You may use a stick if you cannot connect fingers. Repeat with left arm. Hold for fifteen seconds and repeat five times.

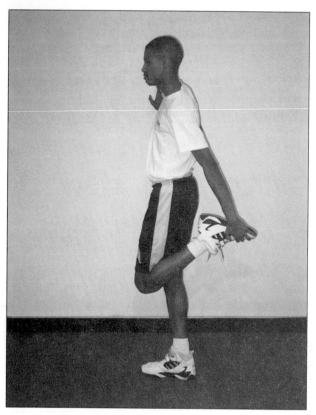

Figure 13.2 FRONT-LEG STRETCH.

Muscles Stretched:

Quadriceps.

Lean against a wall. Bring your left foot up behind you. Grasp the foot with your left hand. Hold for fifteen seconds. Repeat five times for each leg. Caution: Do not pull toward buttocks.

Figure 13.3 SHOULDER AND ARM STRETCH.

Muscles Stretched:

Shoulder Girdle.

Place both hands shoulder-width apart on a ledge or stationary bar. Bend knees slightly and let upper body drop down. Adjust height of hands and degree of knee bend to increase or decrease stretch. Hold for fifteen seconds. Repeat five times.

Figure 13.4 FORWARD-AND-BACK-ARM STRETCH.

Muscles Stretched:

Obliques, Back.

Stand with your feet shoulder-width apart. Bend forward about twenty degrees from the waist. Extend your left arm to the front and your right arm to the rear. Hold your arms shoulder high for fifteen seconds. Repeat five times. Then reverse arm positions and repeat five times.

Figure 13.5 HIGH-LOW ARM STRETCH.
Muscles Stretched:

Shoulder, Chest, Obliques.

Stand with your feet shoulder-width apart. Extend your right arm straight up from your body and extend your left arm straight down. Hold the stretch for fifteen seconds. Repeat five times. Then reverse arm positions and repeat five times.

Figure 13.6 ARM AND LEG STRETCH.
Muscles Stretched:

Trunk, Shoulder Girdle.

Stand with your feet shoulder-width apart. Raise your extended arms overhead. Place your weight on your toes and stretch to the sky. Hold for fifteen seconds. Repeat five times.

Figure 13.7 QUADRICEPS STRETCH.
Muscles Stretched:

Quadriceps.

While lying on your right side, flex the knee of your left leg and grab the ankle with your left hand. Gradually move your hip forward until a good stretch is felt on the thigh. Hold for fifteen seconds. Repeat five times. Repeat for the right leg while lying on your right side. Caution: Do not pull the ankle. Let the hip movement create the stretch.

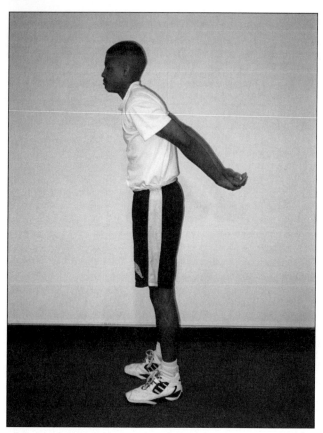

Figure 13.8 UPPER-CHEST STRETCH.

Muscles Stretched:

Anterior Shoulder, Rotators.

Stand with your feet slightly apart. Grasp your hands behind your back and raise your arms. Hold for fifteen seconds. Repeat five times.

Figure 13.9 NECK STRETCH.

Muscles Stretched:

Lateral Neck.

Stand with your hands on your hips. Flex your head toward your right shoulder. Hold for fifteen seconds. Then flex your head toward your left shoulder and hold for fifteen seconds. Repeat five times.

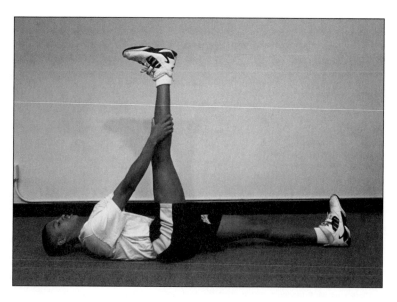

Figure 13.10 HAMSTRING STRETCH.

Muscles Stretched:

Hamstring.

Lie flat on back. Raise one leg straight up with knee extended and ankle flexed at 90 degrees. Grasp leg around calf and pull toward head. Repeat with opposite leg. Hold for fifteen seconds and repeat three times.

Figure 13.11 MODIFIED HURDLER STRETCH.

Muscles Stretched:

Hamstrings, Gastrocnemius, Lower Back.

Sit with your left leg extended and your right leg crossed in front with the heel near your crotch. Reach forward with your left arm as far as possible. Bend knee slightly. Hold for fifteen seconds. Repeat five times for each leg.

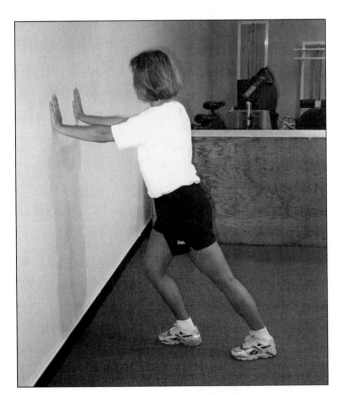

Figure 13.12 WALL LEAN AND HEEL STRETCH.

Muscles Stretched:

Hamstrings, Gastrocnemius.

Stand about three feet from the wall, with one foot in front of the other. Bend the front knee slightly, and keep the back leg fully extended. Keep heels on the ground. Hold for fifteen seconds. Repeat five times for each leg.

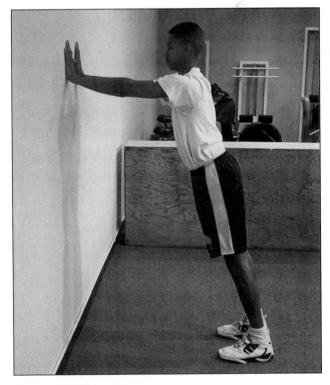

Figure 13.13 LOWER-LEG AND HEEL STRETCH.

Muscles Stretched:

Gastrocnemius.

(The Achilles tendon is a large tendon connecting the calf muscle to the heel.) Face a wall and stand approximately three feet in front of it with your feet several inches apart. Place your outstretched hands on the wall while keeping your feet flat on the floor. Gradually lean forward toward the wall. Hold the stretch for ten seconds. Repeat five times.

Figure 13.14 BACK STRETCH.

Muscles Stretched:

Lower Back, Gluteus, Hamstrings.

While lying on your back, bring both of your knees to your chest. Grasp both of your legs behind the knees and pull the knees toward your chest. Hold for ten seconds. Repeat ten times.

Figure 13.15 GROIN STRETCH.

Muscles Stretched:

Adductors.

Sit on the floor with the soles of your feet touching in front of you. Gradually push your knees down as far as possible. Hold the final stretched position for ten seconds. Repeat five times. Each day try to push your knees closer to the floor.

Figure 13.16 HIP FLEXOR.

Muscles Stretched:

Hamstrings, Gluteus.

Lie on your back on a bench with your legs over the edge of the bench. Bring your right knee to your chest. Use both of your hands on your kneecap to gradually press the knee toward your armpit. Hold for fifteen seconds. Repeat five times for each leg. Caution: Do not apply downward pressure with hand on knee joint.

Figure 13.17 LEG AND GROIN STRETCH.

Muscles Stretched:

Hip Flexors, Rectus Femoris, Iliopsoas.

Move one leg forward until the knee of the front leg is directly over the ankle. Rest the back knee on the floor. Without changing leg position, lower the front hip downward to create a stretch. Hold for fifteen seconds. Repeat five times. Change position and repeat for the other leg.

Figure 13.18 LOWER BACK AND HIP STRETCH.

Muscles Stretched:

Lower Back, Gluteus.

Get down on all fours by placing your hands and knees on the floor. Lean back onto your heels, extend your arms, and place your chest on the floor. Hold for fifteen seconds. Repeat five times.

Glossary

Achilles Tendon   A large tendon connecting the calf muscle to the heel.
Ballistic Stretching   Rapid bouncing, jerking types of muscle movements.
Flexibility   The range and the extent of the movement of a joint.
Hamstring   A group of three muscles in the upper leg that flex the leg at the knee.
Hyperextension   Extension beyond the normal range of the joint structure.
Proprioceptive Neuromuscular Facilitation (PNF)   A method of stretching where an isometric contraction of the muscle group to be stretched precedes a static stretch.
Static Stretching   A stretching method that consists of stretching the muscle slowly and gradually.
Warm-Up   Exercises performed immediately before physical activity to prepare the heart, lungs, and muscles to adequately meet the demands of rigorous exercise.

Solution to Critical Thinking

13-1.   Weight training will not have a negative effect on flexibility if lifting technique is done properly. Lifting the weight through the full range of motion will serve to improve strength and at the same time maintain range of flexibility.

Review Questions

1. What is the difference between static and ballistic stretching.?
2. What is the procedure utilized in PNF?
3. What are five important stretching and warm-up principles?

References

Etnyre, B. R., and E. J. Lee. 1988. Chronic and acute flexibility of men and women using three different stretching techniques. *Research Quarterly for Exercise and Sport* 589:222–228.

Etnyre, B. R., and E. J. Lee. 1987. Comments on proprioceptive neuromuscular facilitation stretching techniques. *Research Quarterly for Exercise and Sport* 58:184–188.

Fox, E., R. Bowers, and M. Foss. *The physiological basis for exercise and sports.* 5th ed. Brown & Benchmark, Dubuque, IA, 1993.

Osternig, L. R., R. H. Robertson, R. K. Troxel, and P. Hansen. 1990. Differential responses to proprioceptive neuromuscular facilitation (PNF) stretch techniques. *Medicine and Science in Sports and Exercise* 22:106–111.

Wilford, H. N., and J. F. Smith. 1985. A comparison of proprioceptive neuromuscular facilitation and static stretching techniques. *American Corrective Therapy Journal* 39(2):30.

Williams, P. E., T. Cantanese, E. G. Lucey, and G. Goldspink. 1988. The importance of stretch and contractile activity in the prevention of connective tissue accumulation in muscle. *Journal of Anatomy.* 158:109–114.

chapter 14

i n j u r i e s

Objectives

After studying this chapter you should be able to

1. Describe the major reasons for injury in strength training.

2. Define muscle balance and positioning.

3. Describe important safety procedures.

4. Describe common injuries, prevention, and treatment.

Many of the injuries that occur during strength training are avoidable. A number of individuals are injured because they take unnecessary risks such as trying to lift too much weight, use incorrect techniques, or ignore safety guidelines. They may be unaware of how easily they can injure themselves. An injury can force you to stop your program or cut back until you recover. The best way to insure steady progress is to avoid injury.

Weight training, because it places great stress on muscles, tendons, and ligaments, is an activity in which minor injuries may occur. Most, however, can be avoided if some simple rules are followed.

1. Lift Progressively.
   Start with a light weight and progressively add resistance with each set. Do not start with your heaviest set first, as the muscles and tendons are not prepared for such sudden exertion.
2. Insure Muscle Balance.
   You should exercise opposite muscle groups (prime mover and antagonist) in your workout to insure proper muscle balance.
3. Maintain Good Positioning.
   Proper positioning is important in maintaining the correct alignment of the skeletal system and in positioning the exercised muscles for maximum force development.
4. Lift Safely.
   Review chapter 3.
5. Always use the proper equipment.
   Review chapter 3.
6. Overtraining.
   The most common cause of injury to lifters is training error. For the beginner it is doing too much too soon, resulting in overfatiguing the muscle, with an inadequate rest and rehabilitation interval. The muscles respond fairly rapidly to the increased demand placed upon them with a lifting program. Tendons and ligaments, however, take significantly longer to adapt to the added stress and will require a more progressive adaptation period if injury is to be avoided.

The key to avoiding overtraining is to make sure you have adequate rest. The rest period is when the muscle recovers and when the gains in strength and endurance occur. You need to listen to your body and adapt the intensity and duration of your exercise program to the needs and ability of your body to recover. There will be times when the best workout you could have is a light workout or no workout at all.

One of the first signs of overtraining is mental staleness. If rest is insufficient in either quality or quantity, then often sickness such as colds or flu occurs.

A common progression is

1. staleness or slump
2. sickness
3. injury

If you learn to listen to your body, 2 and 3 can be avoided.

COMMON INJURIES

Injuries may also result from overuse and lack of rest for the muscles and tendons. The belly of the muscle contains the contractile elements and is where the work of the muscle is performed. The tendons are tough fibers that connect the muscle to the bones.

Lifting injuries can be classified into several groups:

1. tendinitis
2. runner's knee
3. strains and sprains
4. bursitis
5. dislocation and fractures

Tendinitis

Tendinitis is an inflammation of a tendon and is characterized by swelling and tenderness. It is usually caused by a repeated irritation to an area. This injury is most common when many repetitions of a lift are performed. Common sites for tendinitis are the Achilles tendon in the back of the heel, the patella tendon of the knee, tendons in the shoulder and elbows, and also tendons in the wrist and hand.

Runner's Knee

A number of people are now jogging for fitness. Of all the chronic knee injuries, the most common is runner's knee. It involves the degeneration of the shock-absorbing cartilage under the kneecap (patella) and covering the ends of the femur and tibia. The best way to protect against runner's knee is to strengthen the leg muscles, especially the quadriceps, the large muscle group on the front of the thigh that aid the power movements of the knee.

Strains and Sprains

A strain is a tear in the muscle and/or tendon. Strains can occur when the muscle is not warmed up properly, when a twisting or jerking occurs during the lift, when significant force is applied too rapidly (such as in raising or lowering the weight too quickly), or when a previously injured muscle is returned to heavy exercise without adequate rehabilitation.

A sprain is a tear in a ligament. Ligaments are structures that hold the bones together, such as those in the knee and ankle. The same circumstances that were listed as causing strains can also cause sprains.

Strains and sprains are classified by degrees:

First degree—tearing of a few fibers, resulting in mild tenderness and slight swelling.
Second degree—partial disruption of the involved tissues, causing more tenderness and swelling.
Third degree—complete tearing of the tissue, resulting in significant pain and swelling. The joint may be difficult to move and/or the torn muscle may exhibit a bulge.

Strains and sprains are the most common types of lifting injuries and occur most often in the following areas:

Strains

1. chest and back muscles (shoulder girdle)
2. arm muscles (shoulder girdle)
3. hamstrings
4. quadriceps

Sprains

1. knee
2. wrist
3. ankle

Bursitis

Another common injury in lifters is bursitis. Bursitis is an inflammation of a bursa, which is a sac that contains fluid. This sac is strategically located in or near joints to assist in the joint or tendon movement. Sometimes the sac becomes irritated from abrasion or gets pinched during a joint movement, resulting in inflammation, tenderness, and pain. The shoulder is the most common site of bursitis for lifters, with bursitis in the knees, hips, and elbows as the next most common sites.

Dislocation and Fractures

A dislocation is a separation of the joint surface, which can be either partial or complete. The shoulder, elbow, wrist, knee, and vertebrae are the most common sites for this injury. In other sports these usually occur by trauma, such as a collision in football or a fall in gymnastics. In weight training they can occur when incorrect alignment of a body part occurs during the lift, such as twisting the neck or back while lifting. Dislocation can also occur as a result of a severe sprain or strain that occurs during the lift. Some people, because of their joint structure, are susceptible to dislocation and should exercise caution. Have spotters and insure correct body position. Dislocation usually involves significant pain and lack of mobility as well as swelling and tissue damage.

Fractures are much less common in lifting than in other sports, but they do occur. The two most common sites are the wrist and feet. The overhead lifts such as the snatch and the clean-and-press place significant stress on the wrist joint and can cause a partial crack or complete break in the bones. This causes significant swelling and pain. The other lifting related fractures occur as hairline cracks in the bones of the feet. These are sometimes referred to as fatigue fractures, as they usually result from high levels of stress without adequate rest in between periods of exercise. These fatigue fractures exhibit tenderness and swelling.

Most athletes will sustain some injuries during their careers. Fortunately, most of these will be minor and with a little knowledge and care can be self-treated. The key is to learn what injuries you can treat and which ones need medical attention. Much of this awareness is developed by listening to your body.

The following guidelines are recommended in assessing whether or not to seek medical assistance. If the following conditions exist, you should seek assistance from an athletic trainer, nurse practitioner, physical therapist, and/or a physician.

1. pain that is severe or persists
2. inability to move the injured body part
3. the injury does not appear to be healing

The following procedures should be followed immediately after an injury such as strains, sprains, and/or tendinitis or bursitis.

> R. I. C. E.
> - Rest
> - Ice
> - Compression
> - Elevation

Using this regime will help relieve pain, control inflammation, and start the healing process. Let's examine each briefly.

HEALING

←──────────────────────────────────┐

Rest

In severe strains, sprains, bursitis, tendinitis, and in all fractures, rest is required, and prolonged rest may be essential to recovery. Your physician should be your guide.

In less severe cases, however, complete rest may not be required. Within a few days of an injury the tissues begin to repair themselves. Proper rehabilitation exercises can aid in the repair by flushing away the injury-produced by-products from the tissue and by bringing blood and nutrients to the area. Movement will help restore the functional ability of the muscle and allow for a quicker return to your sport. Allow the pain level and type of pain to be your guide. If the pain is sharp, throbbing, and/or very severe, then exercise or movement is not indicated. If, however, there is only minor pain, then movement may aid the healing process.

Compression

Wrapping the injured part with an elastic bandage will compress the area and limit swelling. Be careful not to wrap the part too tightly as the blood supply will be cut off. If the part becomes numb and/or turns blue, then the wrapping is too tight. The wrapping should remain on for twenty to thirty minutes, then released for fifteen minutes to insure adequate circulation. This process may be repeated.

Elevation

Elevating the body part helps drain excess fluid from the area and along with compression can help limit muscular bleeding and swelling. It may be advisable to elevate the part while sleeping.

Other Remedies

Aspirin and Ibuprofen

Aspirin is a powerful anti-inflammatory agent and can be effective in reducing swelling and relieving pain. If you experience stomach upset with aspirin, you can try buffered aspirin (such as Bufferin). Non-aspirin pain relievers that contain acetaminophen such as Tylenol can reduce pain but are not thought to diminish inflammation. Ibuprofen can be purchased over the counter under the names Advil and Pamprin.

Cortisone, Butazone

The anti-inflammatory agents cortisone and butazone are prescription drugs. They should be prescribed and administered only by a physician and are usually reserved for severe cases.

THE FAR SIDE By GARY LARSON

Unbeknownst to most historians, Einstein started down the road of professional basketball before an ankle injury diverted him into science.

> ### 🌀 Critical Thinking 14-1
>
> A nine-year-old boy sprained his ankle and his mother immediately applied hot packs to the injury.
>
> What is the danger in this procedure?

Heat and Cold

Both heat and cold are used for different conditions. In general, heat stimulates acute inflammation and cold acts as an inhibitor. In chronic conditions, heat, such as heat pads and hot baths, serves as a depressant and also reduces ischemia caused by muscle spasm. In acute injury, cold will cause vasoconstriction and prevent increased blood flow into the tissue. The cold (ice pack or pad) should be applied for twenty minutes and repeated every one and one-half hours throughout the day.

Rehabilitation

You should begin gently with range of motion exercises as soon as you can comfortably do so, unless your doctor recommends you not do so. The sooner you begin to use the muscles, the faster you will recover. Moderation is the key! Excessive pain means you are overdoing it!

If you have consulted a physician, athletic trainer, or physical therapist, ask him or her to recommend rehabilitation exercises.

Try to learn something from each injury. Some injuries are due to accidents, such as dropping a weight on your foot. In this case all you might learn is that you need to be more careful, pay better attention to detail, or refrain from lifting weights when you are not mentally involved in the activity.

For other injuries, however, you should try to determine

> ### 🌀 Critical Thinking 14-2
>
> A soccer player complained of a chronic swollen ankle that never resolved since spraining the ankle. He did not think it was a serious injury and avoided treatment, thinking that it would heal on its own. What is the reason for the swelling?

1. What is the injury? (medical personnel can help you if your anatomy background is weak).
2. What caused the injury?
3. How you can avoid such an injury?

If you answer these questions, you will be better able to prevent injuries in the future.

Glossary

Bursitis Inflammation of the bursae sac.
Dislocation Separation of a joint surface.
Muscle Balance Procedure where opposite muscle groups are exercised to insure proper muscle balance.

Sprain An injury to the ligament.
Strain An injury to the muscle or tendon.
Tendinitis Inflammation of the tendon.
Runner's Knee Degeneration of cartilage under knee cap (patella).

Solutions to Critical Thinking

14-1. Heat will increase the blood flow to the injury and also increase swelling and pain. Ice should be applied immediately for twenty minutes and repeated every one and one-half hours throughout the day. Also it would be important to have the ankle X rayed to determine if there was a break or epiphyseal plate tear and ligament tear.

14-2. In the acute phase of the injury, ice was not applied and the ankle was not allowed to heal properly. As a result lymphocytes and scar tissue accumulated in the area causing chronic swelling. In addition a ligament may have been torn, also causing swelling.

Review Questions

1. What is meant by the R.I.C.E. method in treating an injury?
2. When and how long should ice be applied to an injury?
3. What is the difference between a strain and a sprain?

References

Armstrong, R. B., G. L. Warren, and J. A. Warren. 1991. Mechanisms of exercise-induced muscle fiber injury. *Sports Medicine* 12:184–207.

Armstrong, R. B. 1986. Muscle damage and endurance events. *Sports Medicine* 3:370–381.

Arnheim, D. D., and W. E. Prentice. *Principles of athletic training.* 10th ed. McGraw-Hill, Dubuque, IA, 2000.

Cameron, M. *Physical agents in rehabilitation.* W. B. Saunders, Philadelphia, 1999.

Fine, P. G. The biology of pain. In J. Heil, ed. *Psychology of sport injury.* Human Kinetics, Champaign, IL, 1993.

Jones, B. H., J. M. Harris, T. N. Vinh, and C. Rubin. 1989. Exercise-induced stress fractures and stress reactions of bone: Epidemiology, etiology, and classification. *Exercise and Sports Sciences Review* 17:379–422.

Kellett, J. 1986. Acute soft tissue injuries—A review of the literature. *Medicine and Science in Sports and Exercise* 18:489–500.

Kibler, W. B., J. Chandler, and E. S. Stracener. 1992. Musculoskeletal adaptations and injuries due to overtraining. *Exercise and Sports Sciences Reviews* 20:99–126.

Kibler, W. B., T. J. Chandler, and E. S. Stracener. Musculoskeletal adaptations and injuries due to overtraining. In J. O. Holloszy, ed. *Exercise and sports sciences reviews.* Vol. 20. Williams & Wilkins, Baltimore, MD, 1992.

Knight, K. L. *Cryotherapy in sport injury management.* Human Kinetics, Champaign, IL, 1995.

Kreider, R. B. *Overtraining in sport.* Human Kinetics, Champaign, IL, 1998.

Meeusen, R., and P. Lievens. 1986. The use of cryotherapy in sports injuries. *Sports Medicine* 3:398–414.

Neiman, David C. *Fitness and sports medicine: An introduction.* 3rd ed. Bull Publishing, Palo Alto, CA, 1995.

Peacinn, M., and I. Bojanic. *Overuse injuries of musculoskeletal system.* CRC Press, Boca Raton, FL, 1993.

Prentice, W. E. *Rehabilitation techniques in sports medicine.* McGraw-Hill, Dubuque, IA, 1999.

Stone, M. H. 1990. Muscle conditioning and muscle injuries. *Medicine and Science in Sports and Exercise* 22:457–462.

Zachazewski, J., D. Magee, and W. Quillen. *Athletic injuries and rehabilitation.* Saunders, Philadelphia, 1996.

chapter 15

nutrition

Objectives

After studying this chapter you should be able to

1. Define and describe major nutritional constituents: carbohydrates, fats, proteins, vitamins, minerals, and water.

2. Describe the energy system for muscle contraction.

3. Describe criteria for diet rating.

4. Describe weight loss and weight gain procedures.

5. Describe the Food Guide Pyramid.

NUTRITIONAL CONCEPTS

Your dietary needs for strength training or other physically active programs are not very different from those recommended for all healthy individuals. Rigorous exercise programs, however, require more energy expenditure than a sedentary lifestyle. As a result you may need to consume additional calories; the exact amount will depend on the intensity of training, your age, sex, body composition, and your present fitness level. See table 15.1 for a general estimation of your caloric needs. A diet that is deficient in the basic nutritional requirements will interfere with your strength-training goals by producing early fatigue, reducing your performance level, and in some cases producing physical deterioration. On the other hand there is no evidence that taking additional dietary supplements (vitamins, protein, amino acids, etc.) will increase performance levels. In fact, large doses of some supplements, such as fat-soluble vitamins, may be detrimental to your health.

NUTRITIONAL REQUIREMENTS

The major nutritional requirements are carbohydrates, protein, fats, minerals, vitamins, and water.

Carbohydrates

Carbohydrates are chemical compounds containing carbon, hydrogen, and oxygen. Examples are starches, grain products, fruits, vegetables, sugars, and milk. Carbohydrates are the most efficient fuel for the body as they are most easily broken down. They should supply 55 to 60 percent of daily calories for the average person and 60 to 80 percent for endurance athletes. No more than 10 percent of your total calories

Table 15.1

Daily Caloric Needs (Determined by Multiplying Body Weight in Pounds with the Appropriate Number Relating to Activity Level)		
Physical Activity	**Women**	**Men**
Sedentary	14	16
Moderately active	18	21
Active	22	26

should come from simple carbohydrates (sugars). The remaining carbohydrates should be complex carbohydrates (starch). Carbohydrates can increase energy reserves (glycogen) in muscles and liver, thus prolonging the time before exhaustion during vigorous exercise.

Proteins

The main function of protein is the building and repair of tissue. It is an energy source only when fats and carbohydrates are not available. Excellent sources of protein are eggs, meat, fish, poultry, dried beans, peas, nuts, milk, and cheese. Protein needs of sedentary and most active people are about the same. The adult requirements are approximately 12 percent of total calories. The Food and Nutrition Board recommends 0.8 grams of protein per kilogram of body weight. Protein supplements are unnecessary and expensive. Excess protein will not build muscles, only exercise will. Extra protein is broken down and stored as fat.

Fats

Fats belong to a class of compounds called lipids and supply energy and promote absorption of fat-soluble vitamins. They provide the primary fuel for prolonged endurance type exercise. Less than 30 percent of your daily calories should come from fat and less than 10 percent from saturated fat. Avoid fatty foods before exercise as they require three to four hours to digest. Do not confuse body fat and dietary fat. Body fat is the stored form of excess caloric intake in either protein, carbohydrate, or fat.

Vitamins

Vitamins' main function is the metabolism of carbohydrates, proteins, and fats to produce energy. These organic compounds are needed in only small amounts by the body.

Individuals involved in vigorous physical activity do not require supplementary vitamins. If your caloric intake comes from a varied balanced diet high in complex carbohydrates, it should provide all the vitamins you need. Contrary to popular belief, vitamins do not provide energy or build muscle. There is no evidence of any vitamin improving physical performance. See appendix G for vitamin table.

Minerals

Minerals regulate body processes, maintain body tissue, and aid in metabolism. A varied diet generally provides enough minerals for active people, with the possible exception of iron for women. Women should also consume at least 1,000 milligrams of calcium per day to protect against the onset of osteoporosis. Losses of sodium and potassium through perspiration are minimal during exercise and are usually replenished by a normal diet. Salt tablets are not necessary and may be detrimental. Table 15.2 shows current and recommended nutritional allowances, as well as nutritional allowances recommended for the high-energy needs of vigorous physical exercise. See appendix G for mineral table.

WATER

Water is the most essential nutrient. One can exist for weeks without proteins, fats, vitamins, and minerals. Without water, however, one would perish in a few days. It is vital in the body because it dissolves substances, lubricates structures such as joints, and provides a way to transport nutrients and waste. Our body cells are mostly composed of water, which makes up approximately 60 percent of our total weight. In extremely hot weather, the body's ability to conserve water can be negatively affected. Water is a critical element for a physically active person in these circumstances. The bulk of our dietary needs comes from water (about ten cups a day from a combination of foods, fluids, and water itself).

Table 15.2

	Current	Recommended by American Heart Association	Recommended for High-Energy Needs
Current, Recommended, and High-Energy Nutritional Allowances			
Fats	42%	30%	10 to 20%
Protein	12%	12%	10 to 12%
Complex carbohydrates	22%	48%	60 to 80%
Sugar	24%	10%	5 to 10%

ENERGY FOR MUSCLE CONTRACTION

The basic energy sources for muscles, ATP (adenosine triphosphate) and PC (phosphocreatine), are produced by the body. A muscle will expend its entire store of these compounds in only a few seconds of exercise. Depending on the type and duration of exercise, the ATP in the muscles is resupplied either by carbohydrates (glucose in blood or glycogen in the muscle or liver) or stored fats. The duration and intensity of exercise will determine what type of fuel the muscle will use for energy. Exercises lasting one to two minutes are fueled by the anaerobic process (without oxygen) since little oxygen is available during this period of time. Sprinting, weight lifting, and jumping are examples of anaerobic activities. If the exercise continues past two minutes, the body is required to draw upon oxygen (aerobic). The oxygen system can utilize both glycogen and fats for fuel for the production of ATP. Activities that are low to moderate in intensity and of long duration, such as jogging, long-distance swimming, and cross-country skiing, use fat as their primary energy source.

DIETS

The world is full of various diets. However, no matter which diets are used (except for a specific medical problem), each diet should be judged by the following criteria:

Diet Rating

1. Does the diet provide a reasonable number of kcalories (kcal), enough to maintain weight but not an excess; and if a reduction diet, not fewer than 1,200 kcal for the average-size person?
2. Does it provide enough, but not too much, protein, at least the recommended intake or RDA (Recommended Daily Allowance), but not more than twice as much?
3. Does it provide enough fat for satiety, but not so much fat as to exceed current recommendations, between 20 and 35 percent of the kcal from fat?
4. Does it provide enough carbohydrates to spare protein and prevent ketosis, 100 grams of carbohydrate for the average-size person? Is it mostly complex carbohydrate, not more than twenty percent of the kcal as concentrated sugar?
5. Does it offer a balanced assortment of vitamins and minerals from whole food sources in all four food groups (milk and milk products; meat, fish, poultry, and eggs; legumes, fruits, and vegetables; and grains)?
6. Does it offer variety, in that different foods can be selected each day?
7. Does it consist of ordinary foods that are available locally and at prices people normally pay?

Table 15.3

How to Identify a Fraud
1. The use of anecdotes and testimonials to support claims.
2. Promises of quick, dramatic increases in strength and endurance.
3. Promotional literature devoid of reliable scientific research.
4. The claim that natural vitamins are better than synthetic ones.
5. The citing of so-called experts who may well be inexperienced and unknowledgeable.
6. An indication that their claims are suppressed by the medical community because they are controversial.
7. The advice that taking vitamin supplements will give you energy.
8. Literature suggests that people should take vitamin and mineral supplements just to be on the safe side.
9. The use of words like "natural" and "organic."
10. Warnings that you cannot get enough nutrients from your diet no matter how hard you try.

Fraudulent Claims

We are continually bombarded by unsound and unsubstantiated claims for various supplements and diet combinations that purport to increase muscle strength and endurance and boost energy. Slick advertising, along with personal and anecdotal evidence, persuade millions of individuals to use substances that are completely useless and in some cases physically harmful. Doses of dietary supplements exceeding minimum requirements have not been found to increase work performance. Most dietary claims are unfounded and not based on scientific evidence. Many of the so-called supplements commonly promoted and used have never been tested for efficacy or safety. Table 15.3 will give you some tips on how to spot the fraudulent.

If you follow the recommendations in figure 15.1, the Food Guide Pyramid, you will be on a sound basis for insuring that you are receiving a proper, nutritional diet.

"Super-Protein" Diets

Some athletes ingest large amounts of protein supplements, believing that doing so will help them build up their muscles and energy level, even though there is no scientific justification for the use of these supplements. Athletes generally do not need additional protein but additional calories in the form of complex carbohydrates to provide energy for muscle activity. Most athletes already consume twice as much protein as they can possibly use and probably are wasting about half as much as they eat.

It is impossible to force extra amounts of protein into the muscles just by eating more. For muscle cells to accept additional protein, additional demands have to be made upon the muscles. To make a muscle grow, you have to overload it. The muscle generally responds by taking in more nutrients and subsequently accelerating its growth.

The so-called "super-protein" diets are unnecessary, expensive, and in some cases harmful. For example, with large amounts of protein, the blood level of uric acid may increase and damage the kidneys and make the joints more susceptible to injuries. As for energy derived from protein, you burn up as much protein reading a book as running track at top speed. The body burns protein for energy only in starvation.

Vitamin and Mineral Supplemented Diets

Supplementing your diet with vitamins and minerals above the minimum daily requirement does not improve physical performance. In fact, excessive intake of

Critical Thinking 15-1

An individual beginning a weight training program was told that he would have to eat twice as much protein now; otherwise he would not gain any strength of increased muscle size.

What is the role of protein in resistance training?

Fats, oils, and sweets
Use sparingly.

● Fat (naturally occurring   ▼ Sugars
  and added)   (added)

These symbols show fats, oils, and
added sugars in foods.

Milk, yogurt,
and cheese
group
2–3 servings

Meat, poultry, fish,
dry beans, eggs,
and nuts group
2–3 servings

Vegetable
group
3–5 servings

Fruit
group
2–4 servings

Bread, cereal,
rice, and pasta
group
6–11
servings

What is the Food Guide Pyramid?

The Pyramid is an outline of what to eat each day. It's not a rigid prescription but a general guide that lets you choose a healthful diet that's right for you.

The Pyramid calls for eating a variety of foods to get the nutrients you need and at the same time the right amount of calories to maintain a healthy weight.

The Pyramid also focuses on fat because most American diets are too high in fat, especially saturated fat.

Fat

● In general, foods that come from animals (milk and meat groups) are naturally higher in fat than foods that come from plants. But there are many low-fat dairy and lean meat choices available, and these foods can be prepared in ways that lower fat.

Fruits, vegetables, and grain products are naturally low in fat. But many popular items are prepared with fat, such as french-fried potatoes or croissants, making them higher-fat choices.

Added sugars

▼ These symbols represent sugars added to foods in processing or at the table, not the sugars found naturally in fruits and milk. It's the added sugars that provide calories with few vitamins and minerals.

Most of the added sugars in the typical American diet come from foods in the Pyramid tip—soft drinks, candy, jams, jellies, syrups, and table sugar we add to foods such as coffee or cereal.

Added sugars in the food groups come from foods such as ice cream, sweetened yogurt, chocolate milk, canned or frozen fruit with heavy syrup, and sweetened bakery products such as cakes and cookies.

What counts as a serving?

Milk, yogurt, and cheese group (2–3 servings)	Meat, poultry, fish, dry beans, eggs, and nuts group (2–3 servings)	Vegetable group (3–5 servings)	Fruit group (2–4 servings)	Bread, cereal, rice, and pasta group (6–11 servings)
1 c. milk or yogurt 1 1/2 oz. natural cheese 2 oz. processed cheese 1 c. frozen yogurt 1 1/2 c. ice cream 2 c. cottage cheese	2–3 oz. cooked, lean meat, poultry, or fish 1/3 c. nuts (Count 1/2 c. cooked dry beans, 1 egg, or 2 Tbls. peanut butter as 1 oz. meat.)	1 c. raw leafy greens 1/2 c. other kinds of vegetables (raw or cooked) 3/4 c. vegetable juice	1 medium apple, banana, orange 1/2 c. chopped, cooked, canned fruit 3/4 c. juice	1 slice bread 1/2 bun or bagel 1 oz. dry cereal 1/2 c. cooked cereal, rice, or pasta 3–4 small, plain crackers

Figure 15.1   FOOD GUIDE PYRAMID: A GUIDE TO DAILY FOOD CHOICES.

Source: FDA Consumer, *June 1993.*

Adapted from E. N. Whitney, M. A. Boyle, Understanding Nutrition, *4th edition, West Publishing Co., St. Paul, MN, 1987.*

vitamins A, D, and K can cause toxic effects. Minimum daily vitamin and mineral requirements are met easily through a normal, well-balanced diet.

The only exception to this may be the iron requirement of females engaged in rigorous physical activity, particularly after menstrual blood loss. These women have been found to have significantly decreased levels of iron in their blood. Since overdoses of iron can be toxic, however, these women should take iron supplements only after consulting with a physician.

Fad Diets

A number of fad diets with varying combinations of nutrients unfortunately have found wide acceptance because of media misinformation and public ignorance. Be very wary of these diets because they may have a number of dangerous consequences. For example, individuals on diets that do not allow for protein or that are low in protein may suffer a loss of muscle tissue and severe weakness. A high-fat diet, sometimes advocated in combination with high protein and very little carbohydrates, may produce a loss of nutrients and electrolytes, very high cholesterol levels, and diarrhea. A high-protein and high-fat diet with low carbohydrates may produce kidney problems, dizziness, weakness, dehydration, irritability, and uric acid formation. Low-fat diets may lead to dry skin, constipation, irritability, stiff joints, and a number of other problems.

Other fad diets that have enjoyed unwarranted popularity include the low-carbohydrate diet, "super-protein" diets, and vitamin and mineral supplemental diets. "Diet foods" and using drugs to lose weight also are discussed in this section.

BASIC NUTRITIONAL RECOMMENDATIONS

1. Increase consumption of fruits and vegetables.
2. Decrease consumption of red and organ meats and increase consumption of poultry and fish. Remember, shrimp and lobster are higher in cholesterol than other fish.
3. Decrease consumption of foods high in fat and substitute polyunsaturated and monosaturated fat for saturated fat. Reduce saturated fat consumption to about 10 percent of total energy intake.
4. Substitute skim milk (nonfat milk) for whole milk.
5. Decrease consumption of butterfat, eggs, and other sources high in cholesterol. Reduce cholesterol intake to 300 milligrams a day (equivalent of one egg).
6. Decrease consumption of refined foods (cane and beet sugar) and processed foods (corn sugar, syrups, molasses, honey) that are high in sugar content.
7. Increase consumption of complex carbohydrates: grains, breads, cereals, potatoes, corn, and rice.
8. Decrease consumption of salt and foods with a high salt content.

How to Gain Weight

The best way to gain weight is to build muscle mass through careful and consistent physical training. Eat a well-balanced and nutritious diet with enough calories in the form of complex carbohydrates to support a weight gain.

How to Lose Weight

Exercise is an integral part of any weight-loss program. Approximately 3,500 kcalories are contained in one pound of stored fat. If, for example, your food intake for one day is equivalent to 2,200 kcalories and you burn up 2,200 kcalories in your daily activity, you will be in caloric balance; you will not gain or lose weight. However, if you burn

Critical Thinking 15-2

A student complained that she has been dieting by reducing her daily caloric intake by 500 calories for six weeks, yet has maintained her same body weight.

Why hasn't her body weight dropped significantly?

up an additional 100 kcalories a day through a vigorous exercise program, bringing your total daily expenditure to 2,300 and at the same time still taking in only 2,200 kcalories, you will incur a deficit of 100 kcalories a day. If you were to continue this regimen for thirty-five days you would accumulate a total caloric deficit of 3,500 kcalories, which should be equal to a loss of one pound of fat. A deficit of 200 kcalories a day would result in a loss of one pound of fat in one half that time. Maximum weight loss should not exceed two pounds a week or a deficit of 1,000 kcalories per day.

Glossary

Adenosine Triphosphate (ATP)   An energy-rich chemical compound stored in muscle cells; a source of immediate energy.

Carbohydrates   Chemical compounds containing carbon, hydrogen, and oxygen; examples are sugars and starches, major sources of energy.

Fats   Food stuffs containing glycerol and fatty acids.

Ketosis   The development of ketone bodies and acidosis (disruption of the acid/base balance) due to improper breakdown of fats.

Kilocalories   The amount of energy required to raise one kilogram of water one degree centigrade.

Minerals   Inorganic compounds, some of which are nutrients vital to body function. Examples include phosphorus, calcium, potassium, sodium, iron, and iodine.

Phosphocreatine   A chemical that can donate its phosphate to form ATP in the muscle.

Protein   Organic material that regulates body processes and builds and repairs body tissue.

Vitamins   Organic compounds that regulate a number of body processes and that are used in the metabolism of carbohydrates.

Solutions to Critical Thinking

15-1. Taking additional protein is unnecessary for a weight training program. The recommended amount is .8 grams per kilogram of body weight. Additional amounts will be stored as fat and place extra loads on the kidneys. Exercise builds muscle tissue, not excess protein.

15-2. Dieting without exercise is not an effective way to lose body fat. When an individual reduces her caloric intake, the brain's protective mechanism causes the basal metabolism to drop. For example, a drop of 800 calories can lower basal metabolism 5 to 10 percent. Even though she is eating fewer calories, they are burned less efficiently.

Review Questions

1. Discuss the method for losing body fat.
2. Why are super-protein diets unnecessary and may in fact lead to health problems?
3. Why is it important to limit the amount of saturated fat in your diet?

References

Atkinson, R. 1992. Treatment of obesity. *Nutritional Reviews* 50:338–345.

Boyle, M. A., and G. Zyla. *Personal nutrition*. 3rd ed. Wadsworth, Belmont, 1996.

Briggs, George M., and Doris H. Calloway. *Bogert's nutrition and physical fitness*. Saunders, Philadelphia, 1985.

Brody, Jane. *Jane Brody's nutrition book*. Norton, New York, 1988.

Brown, J. E. *Nutrition now*. 2nd ed. Wadsworth, Belmont, 1999.

Connor, S., and W. Connor. *New American diet systems*. Simon & Schuster, New York, 1992.

Guthrie, H. A., and M. F. Picciano. *Human nutrition*. Mosby-Year Book, St. Louis, 1994.

Katch, Frank I., and William D. McArdle. 3rd ed. *Nutrition, weight control and exercise*. Houghton Mifflin, Boston, 1988.

Lemon, P. W. R. 1987. Protein and exercise. *Medicine and Science in Sports and Exercise* 19 (Suppl.): 179–190.

Morgan, B. L. G. *The lifelong nutrition guide*. Prentice Hall, Englewood Cliffs, NJ, 1983.

National Institutes of Health technology assessment conference statement: Methods for voluntary weight loss and control. 1992. *Nutrition Reviews* 50:340–345.

Neiman, David C. *Fitness and sports medicine: An introduction*. 3rd ed. Bull Publishing, Palo Alto, CA, 1995.

Nutrition Action Healthletter. Washington, D. C. Center for Science in the Public Interest, 1501 16th St. NW, Washington, D.C. 20036.

Roitman, J. L. *Resource manual for guidelines for exercise testing and prescription* by American College of Sports Medicine. 3rd ed. Williams & Wilkins, Baltimore, 1998.

Sizer, F., and E. N. Whitney. *Nutrition: Concepts and controversies*. 8th ed. Wadsworth, Belmont, 2000.

Wadden, T., J. Sternberg, K. Letizia, A. Stunkard, and G. Foster. 1989. Treatment for obesity by very low calorie diet, behavior therapy, and their combination: A five year prospective. *International Journal of Obesity* 13(Suppl. 2):39–46.

Walberg, J. L. 1989. Aerobic exercise and resistance weight training during weight reduction. *Sports Medicine* 47:343–356.

Wardlaw, G. M. *Perspectives in nutrition*. 4th ed. McGraw-Hill, Dubuque, IA, 1999.

Whitney, E. N., C. G. Cataldo, and S. R. Rolfes. *Understanding normal and clinical nutrition*. 5th ed. Wadsworth, Belmont, 1998.

Whitney, E. N., and S. R. Rolfes. *Understanding nutrition*. 8th ed. Wadsworth, Belmont, 1999.

Williams, M. H. *Nutrition for health, fitness, and sport*. 5th ed. McGraw-Hill, Dubuque, IA, 1999.

chapter 16

drugs

Objectives

After studying this chapter you should be able to

1. Describe the present state of drug use in strength training programs.

2. Describe anabolic steroids and their physiological effect on the body.

3. Describe the American College of Sports Medicine position statement on anabolic-androgenic steroids in sport.

4. Describe the effects of amphetamines.

5. Describe the effects of growth hormones.

6. Describe the effects of cocaine.

7. Describe the effects of caffeine.

8. Describe the use of supplements.

The use of drugs by professional and amateur athletes to improve performance is prevalent at all competitive levels. Athletes have always looked for that "extra edge" that will give them the advantage over their opponent. With only hundredths of seconds, or a few inches, separating the winner from the also-ran, it is not surprising that drugs, thought to increase performance, find wide acceptance. Both male and female competitive athletes are presently using a wide range of pharmacological agents in the belief that it will increase their strength, endurance, speed, power, and skill. One of the most unfortunate aspects of the use of drugs is that many athletes appear to be willing to court major health risks in order to be competitive. They believe they must resort to the use of drugs.

ANABOLIC STEROIDS

Anabolic steroids are synthetic hormones and close relatives of testosterone, the male hormone. This hormone has had its chemical structure altered so that the androgenic or masculinizing effect has been reduced and its anabolic protein producing characteristics enhanced in order to promote muscle growth. There is also speculation that small residual androgenic effects increase performance by making the athletes more aggressive and competitive, resulting in an increased intensity of training motivation. Steroids have been used frequently in medical practice for malnutrition, infection, skeletal disorders, some cancers, and growth problems. Anabolic steroids promote anabolism (muscle growth) by increasing nitrogen retention. They may convert a mildly negative nitrogen balance to a positive one, depending on adequate protein and caloric intake. They may build lean body mass and increase strength in individuals who are intensively training in heavy resistance (weight lifting) activities. They do not directly improve performance in aerobic activities such as long-distance running, skiing, or swimming.

The real possibility of harmful side effects greatly outweighs the questionable increases in performance. Table 16.1 outlines the possible side effects of anabolic steroid use in males and females.

Anabolic-androgenic steroids have been associated with adverse effects on the liver, cardiovascular system, reproductive function, and psychological status. Steroids that are alkalated at the 17-carbon position (most all oral forms) are especially dangerous because of the strong link between this chemical structure and liver dysfunction. There are also additional side effects in women and children. Some are irreversible.

Table 16.1

Side Effects That Have Been Observed in Those Using Anabolic Steroids
Males
Liver damage
Impaired thyroid and pituitary function
Impaired cardiovascular function
Increased blood pressure
Prostate gland disorders
Acne, skin rash
Atrophied testes
Increased aggressiveness
Changes in libido
Gastro intestinal changes
Increased muscle cramps and spasms
Gynecomastia—development of breast-like tissue
Headaches, dizziness, nose bleeds
Females—These effects are in addition to those observed in males.
Deepening voice
Increase in facial/body hair
Acne
Clitoral enlargement
Menstrual irregulation
Increased fibrous (collagen) content of body

The use of anabolic steroids in adolescents may result in accelerated pubescence, precocious display of secondary sexual characteristics, and possible premature closure of the ends of the long bones, thus terminating bone growth. Injectable anabolic steroids are more potent than oral types because they do not require modification to protect from immediate metabolism by the liver. The increase in fat-free mass and possible reduction in fat mass may last for several months after the cessation of use. This fact is support for year-round random drug testing (Forbes et al. 1992). Although many claims are made for increases in performance and there is mounting anecdotal evidence, no studies have addressed whether or not steroids help or actually hinder performance. Another alarming aspect of anabolic steroid use by athletes is the potentially hazardous effect of increased aggressiveness (Pope and Katez 1988).

The American College of Sports Medicine Position Statement on Anabolic-Androgenic Steroids in Sports

It is the position of the American College of Sports Medicine that

1. Anabolic-androgenic steroids in the presence of an adequate diet can contribute to increases in body weight, often in the lean mass compartment.
2. The gains in muscular strength achieved through high-intensity exercise and proper diet can occur by the increased use of anabolic-androgenic steroids in some individuals.
3. Anabolic-androgenic steroids do not increase aerobic power or capacity for muscular exercise.

4. Anabolic-androgenic steroids have been associated with adverse effects on the liver, cardiovascular system, and psychologic status in therapeutic trials and in limited research on athletes. Until further research is completed, the potential hazards of the use of the anabolic-androgenic steroids in athletes must include those found in therapeutic trials.

5. The use of anabolic-androgenic steroids by athletes is contrary to the rules and ethical principles of athletic competition as set forth by many of the sports governing bodies. The American College of Sports Medicine supports these ethical principles and deplores the use of anabolic-androgenic steroids by athletes.

AMPHETAMINES

Amphetamines are a group of drugs that stimulate the central nervous system of the body. They generally cause a rise in blood pressure, cardiac output, blood sugar, breathing rate, and metabolism. Athletes take amphetamines in hopes that the increased arousal level and depression of the sensation of muscle fatigue will enable them to maintain higher performance levels for longer periods of time. There is very little scientific evidence that amphetamines improve speed, performance, or increase endurance. Most of the studies report that the drugs have very little effect. Some athletes use amphetamines to "get them up" for competition or psychologically ready to compete. This practice may require the athlete to resort to the use of barbiturates to enable them to come down from the amphetamine high in order to sleep. The result is a dangerous stimulant to depressant combination. One of the dangers of taking amphetamines during exercise is that the individual may overstress the body with possible damage to the heart. Other major risks are psychological dependence and the possibility of circulatory collapse.

CAFFEINE

There is some recent evidence that caffeine may in some circumstances increase endurance in moderately strenuous activity. Caffeine facilitates the use of fat as a fuel, and increases the permeability of the muscle cell to calcium, resulting in a more efficient contraction and the sparing of glycogen in the muscles. Caffeine may also have a psychostimulating effect, causing the athlete to feel that the exercise was easier. The adverse effects of using caffeine are that some individuals encounter an allergic response, cardiac arhythmias, headaches, insomnia, irritability, and a diuretic effect.

GROWTH HORMONES

There is a major concern that growth hormones (somatotrophic hormone) will replace anabolic steroids as the new high-tech drug. Growth hormone is produced by the pituitary gland in the brain. One of its functions is to stimulate and control the tissue building process of normal growth and development. It is used medically to treat children with retarded growth syndrome. With the advancement of bioengineering it will soon be possible to synthetically produce large amounts of this hormone inexpensively. Athletes are attracted to the drug because it increases protein synthesis and fat breakdown and decreases the amount of carbohydrates used by the body. However, its use in adults can lead to symptoms similar to those of acromegaly: enlarged bones of the face, hands, and feet, overgrowth of soft tissue, and a most dangerous abnormal enlargement of cardiac tissue. This hormone is most difficult to detect in screening tests because it occurs naturally in the body.

COCAINE

Cocaine is a central nervous system stimulant that produces similar effects to caffeine. Cocaine enhances alertness and masks fatigue. It produces a state of excitement and restlessness. Euphoria, heightened self-confidence, temporary relief of depression, and suppressed appetite all result from cocaine use. As these effects wear off, the user experiences a period of depression, confusion, and dizziness. Small doses slow the heart, but larger amounts stimulate the heart. Blood pressure increases as a result of constricted blood vessels, and respiration becomes shallow and rapid. Repeated use of large doses leads to weight loss, insomnia, anxiety, and paranoid delusion. Inhaling and snorting may also result in ulceration of the nasal tissue. Death may occur due to respiratory or cardiac failure.

ERYTHROPOIETIN

Erythropoietin has been used as an agent to stimulate increased numbers of red cells. This substance is normally secreted by the kidneys to maintain normal red cell count. The use of erythropoietin can be extremely hazardous, leading to blood clots and infection.

STEROID REPLACERS

There is no evidence that steroid replacers stimulate physiological functions in the muscles similar to those of anabolic steroids. The body lacks enzymes to synthesize them (diosgenin, smilogenin). Desiccated organs also have no physiological effect. Boran, which has been commonly promoted as an increaser of testosterone, actually decreases testosterone. -1- carnitine has been promoted as a substance that increases utilization of fat, but actually it has no effect at all on fat metabolism and may result in neuromuscular problems.

SUBSTANCES CURRENTLY BANNED BY THE INTERNATIONAL OLYMPIC COMMITTEE

Psychomotor Stimulants: Amphetamine, Cocaine, Methyphenidate.
Sympathomimetic Amines: Ephedrine, Isoprenaline.
Central Nervous System Stimulants: Caffeine, Doxaproam, and Strychnine.
Anabolic Steroids: Testosterone, Stanozolol, Nandrolone, Norethandrolone,
    Methandienone.
Hormones: Growth Hormone, Erythropoietin.
Narcotic Analgesics: Codeine, Heroin, Hydromorphone, Methadone,
    and Morphine.
Masking Agents and Diuretics: Probenecid, Furosemide.

SUPPLEMENTS

Unsound claims for supplements enter your world daily from radio, television, health clubs, books, magazines and newspapers. Separating facts from fiction is difficult even for professionals sometimes. A number of products purported to increase muscle growth, boost energy, increase strength, and reduce body fat are completely fraudulent. Over 2 billion dollars a year are spent on unnecessary supplements and vitamins. Seventy million Americans take vitamin supplements they don't need, and

14 billion dollars are spent on products that amount to pure quackery, from bee pollen to chromium. Many herbal remedies, mega doses of vitamins, and mineral therapies are not reliable or effective and may be dangerous to your health.

Many promoters of these ineffective and unproven remedies sincerely believe in the products themselves. In their naiveté and enthusiasm they unfortunately pass on this information.

With the increased use of dietary supplements such as HMB, DHEA, creatine, and androstenedione the American College of Sports Medicine has recently called for the Federal Food and Drug Administration (FDA) to revisit the Dietary Supplements Health and Education Act of 1994. Many of the so-called dietary supplements contain active ingredients and should be classified as drugs.

Some of the most commonly used dietary supplements are trace minerals such as chromium, single amino acids such as ornithine, plant sterols such as B sitosterol, vitamins, HMB (beta-hydroxy beta-methyl-butyrate), DHEA (dehydroepiandrosterone), creatine, and androstenedione.

The following is a list of supplements currently in wide use and questioned by the American College of Sports Medicine as to their effectiveness and efficacy.

A N D R O S T E N E D I O N E

Androstenedione is a very popular supplement taken supposedly to increase athletic performance. However, recent evidence indicates that it does not enhance muscle building or increase testosterone in the blood and may in fact produce adverse health effects. Researchers have found a lowering of good cholesterol, HDL, in the blood and increased estrogen levels, which could result in increased risk for cardiovascular disease. In addition, its use may cause breast enlargement and increased risk for pancreatic cancer.

D H E A

DHEA (dehydroepiandrosterone) is a hormone that occurs naturally in the body and diminishes with age. Exaggerated claims that DHEA slows down aging, burns fat and builds muscles, strengthens the immune system and wards off a variety of diseases are totally unfounded. None of these claims has stood the test of scientific examination. Most of the evidence is from limited animal studies. Present law unfortunately allows DHEA to be sold in health food stores because it is classified as a dietary supplement and does not have to prove its effectiveness or safety. However, large doses of DHEA could lead to menstrual irregularities in women and prostate enlargement in men.

C R E A T I N E

Creatine is a nitrogenous amino acid compound found naturally in skeletal muscle, brain, heart and other tissue. In skeletal muscle, one-fourth is free creatine and three-fourths phosphocreatine. During exercise, phosphorylated creatine is thought to be an immediate source for high-energy phosphate groups with which to replenish ATP (adenosinetriphosphate), which is the immediate source of energy in the skeletal muscle. There is some evidence that creatine may affect ATP replenishment for only the first few seconds of intense physical activity. The body also appears to have a target level for circulating creatine, and ingestion or supplementation may reduce the synthesis of creatine by the body. Some evidence indicates that creatine supplementation may slightly increase work done in the first few short duration, maximal effort trials. One study using a six gram daily amount found positive effects on short-term exercise included in aerobic endurance exercise. There are still questions to be asked about harmful long-term effects. Anecdotal reports have suggested an

Critical Thinking 16-1

A number of individuals are under the impression that because supplements are sold over-the-counter they are safe to take.

What would be your warning about over-the-counter supplements?

Critical Thinking 16-2

A student was told by his friends that if he didn't take creatine supplements he would not achieve his maximum strength potential.

What advice would you give him?

increase in muscle cramping, nausea, and elevated transaminases. It is recommended to avoid this substance until complete data are compiled.

BETA-ADRENERGIC AGONIST

These substances have been used in an attempt to desensitize nerve receptors to fatigue. They may cause increases in heart rate and other cardiac complications.

This substance is related to epinephrine hormone from the adrenal glands. There is no evidence that its use affects body composition or increases lean muscle.

HMB

There is limited evidence that HMB (beta-hydroxy beta-methyl-butyrate) may increase the cells oxidative capacity. Increased fat oxidation might lead to increase in muscle mass. Also it may have some effect on reducing cellular injury during strength training. However, long-term health effects are still not known.

CHROMIUM AND VANADIUM

Chromium and Vanadium both are proported to enhance glucose utilization; however they have no significant effect. Vanadium has been found to be effective only on diabetic rats.

Chromium picolinate has no effect on body fat or skeletal muscle and may cause chromosomal changes in body cells.

CARNITINE

Carnitine is produced in body cells and plays a part in activating fatty acids for energy. Supplements are not necessary.

Glossary

Amphetamines   Group of drugs that stimulate the central nervous system.
Anabolic Steroids   Synthetic hormone similar to male hormone testosterone that stimulates increases in muscle mass.
Anabolism   Constructive metabolism.
Androgenic   A substance that stimulates male characteristics.
Androstenedione   A relatively weak androgen.
Caffeine   Chemical found in coffee and tea that acts as a stimulant on the central nervous system.
Cocaine   Central nervous system stimulant derived from coca leaves.
Creatine   A naturally occurring compound synthesized by the kidneys, liver, and pancreas.
DHEA (dehydroepiandrosterone)   DHEA is a hormone that occurs naturally in the body.
Diuretic   A substance that increases kidney function, secretion of urine, and water loss.
HMB (beta-hydroxy beta-methyl-butyrate)   A leucine metabolite produced naturally in the body.

Solutions to Critical Thinking

16-1.   The American College of Sports Medicine has recently asked the Food and Drug Administration to revisit the Dietary Supplements Health and Education Act of 1994. Many of the dietary supplements have active ingredients and should be classified as drugs.

16-2.   The research on creatine is still not complete. There are a few studies indicating that it may enhance initial short bursts of muscle power. Many athletes have experienced muscle tetanus (muscle cramping) as a result of creatine supplements. However, there is little evidence on long-term health effects.

Review Questions

1. What are the dangers of taking over-the-counter supplements?
2. What are some of the health problems that may occur as a result of using anabolic steroids?
3. Discuss the American College of Sports Medicine Position Statement on Anabolic-Androgenic Steroids in Sports.

References

Carroll, C. *Drugs in modern society*. 5th ed. McGraw-Hill, Dubuque, IA, 2000.

Cheng, W., B. Phillips, and N. Abomrad. 1998. Effect of HMB on fuel utilization membrane stability and creatine kinase content of cultured muscle cells. *FASEP J.* 12.5:a 950.

Engelhardt, Martin, Georg, Neuman, Anneliese Berbalk, and Iris Reuter. 1998. Creatine supplementation in endurance sports. *Medicine and Science in Sports and Exercise* 30-7:1123–1129.

Forbes, G. B., C. R. Porta, B. E. Haerr, and R. C. Briggs. 1992. Sequence of changes in body composition induced by testosterone and reversal of changes after drug is stopped. *Journal of American Medical Association* 2676:397–99.

Greenhaff, P. L. 1995. Creatine and its application as an ergogenic aid. *International Journal of Sport Nutrition* 5:9100–9110.

Huie, M. J. 1994. An acute myocardial infraction occurring in an anabolic steroid user. *Medicine and Science in Sports and Exercise* 26:408–413.

King, Douglas, et al. 1999. Effect of oral androstenedione on serum testosterone and adaptation to resistance training in young men. *JAMA* 281:2020–2028.

Lamb, D. R. 1987. Anabolic steroids in athletics: How well do they work and how dangerous are they? *American Journal of Sports Medicine* 12:31–38.

Pope, H. G., and D. L. Katz. 1988. Affective disorders and psychotic symptoms associated with anabolic steroids. *American Journal of Psychiatry* 145:487–490.

Pope, H. J., and D. L. Katz. 1988. Effective and psychotic symptoms associated with anabolic steroid use. *American Journal of Psychiatry* 145:487–90.

Ray, O. S., and C. Ksir. *Drugs, society and human behavior*. 8th ed. McGraw-Hill, Dubuque, IA, 1999.

Stone, M. H. *Position statement on anabolic-androgenic steroid use by athletes*. National Strength and Conditioning Association, Colorado Springs, 1993.

Tennant, F., D. L. Black, and R. O. Voy. 1988. Anabolic steroid dependence with opioid features. *New Engineer Journal of Medicine*. 319:578.

Torgan, C. E., G. J. Etgen, J. T. Brozinick, R. E. Wilcos, and J. L. Ivy. 1993. Interaction of aerobic exercise training and clenbuterol: Effects on insulin-resistant muscle. *Journal of Applied Physiology* 75:1471–1476.

Williams, M. H. 1994. The use of nutritional ergogenic aids in sports: Is it an ethical issue? *International Journal of Sports Nutrition*. 4:120–131.

chapter 17

equipment

Objectives

After studying this chapter you should be able to

1. Describe the use of free weights and barbells in strength-training programs.

2. Describe free weights, Cybex Knee Extension, Mini-Gym, Biodex, Cybex 600, Kin-Com 500H, Kin-Com 125E, Lido, Merac, Universal Machine, Nautilus, CAM II, Hydra Fitness, Polaris, power exercise equipment, and cardiorespiratory equipment.

EQUIPMENT

The following are the major categories of resistive exercise equipment used to train muscles:

1. Free weights and barbells. This equipment cannot control speed or resistance through the full range of movement yet produces different levels of muscle stress at different points in the range of movement. There is a place in the range of movement, the sticking point, at which the mechanical factors are least favorable and the greatest amount of muscle force is required. In very heavy loads (1 RM) the exercise produces maximum stress at only one point in the range of movement. The advantage is that this type of equipment most closely mimics the action found in ballistic sport skills such as kicking and throwing.

2. Equipment that provides controlled or constant speed and variable resistance (true isokinetic equipment controls speed). This type of equipment, including categories 3 and 4, closely mimics sport skills that require tension movements through the range of movement, such as swimming and cycling.

3. Equipment that controls a constant and variable resistance by means of a hydraulic device.

4. Equipment where speed is variable and resistance is constant (some CAM devices and concentric-eccentric devices).

5. There is currently no machine whereby muscles contract under conditions of true constant speed and true constant resistance.

RESISTANCE MACHINES

There is no question that the unique design and rapid development of resistance machines has revolutionized resistance training. Thousands of individuals, in particular women, who would not go near free weights in the past, have been attracted to resistance programs as a result of the attractiveness, comfort, novelty, and challenge provided by resistance machines.

Most resistance machines provide a forced or guided two-dimensional movement pattern for the exercise. This results in limited variation of the resistance movement because of differences in individual body size. Also, most machines support the user, resulting in reduced demands for stability and balance of the user and the load. In particular, isokinetic machines allow the muscle to be exercised to its maximum potential throughout the joint's entire range of motion. They also prove a safer alternative during rehabilitation because the resistance mechanism essentially disengages when pain or discomfort is felt. Other machines allow rehabilitation when the use of the whole body is prohibited because of weakness or injury.

There are a number of different types of resistance-training machines. The most common are those machines that use a movable external resistance such as a weight stack or plate-loaded apparatus. These machines are somewhat like free weights in that the external resistance (weight stacks, plates, etc.) is constant.

FREE WEIGHTS

Free weights require greater motor coordination than do weight machines. Free weights also involve both concentric and eccentric activity. Eccentric muscle activity is not possible on some training machines such as hydraulic machines and certain isokinetic (controlled constant velocity) dynamometers.

STRENGTH AND MUSCLE ENDURANCE EQUIPMENT

Isokinetic Machines

Isokinetic machines have specially constructed dynamometers that control the velocities of the dynamometers' lever arm movements, therefore keeping velocity constant. Some isokinetic machines now allow for eccentric contraction.

Cybex Knee Extension

These are extension test machines that use electric servo-breaking to provide nearly complete accommodating resistance so that muscles shorten at a constant speed and can be maximally loaded throughout the full range of motion. They are used mainly in strength testing, rehabilitation, and research.

Mini-Gym

As a greater muscle force is applied, greater frictional forces are produced, resulting in a proportional increase in resistance and a steady movement speed. Eccentric contractions, however, cannot be performed with this equipment.

Biodex

Isokinetic, concentric and eccentric, isotonic, isometric, passive.

Cybex 600

Isokinetic, powered eccentric and concentric, continuous passive motion.

Kin-Com 500H

Isokinetic, concentric and eccentric, isotonic-concentric and eccentric, isometric, passive.

Kin-Com 125E

Isokinetic, concentric and eccentric, isotonic, concentric and eccentric, isometric, passive.

Lido

Isokinetic, concentric and eccentric, continuous passive motion, isometric, isotonic, concentric.

Merac

Isokinetic, concentric, isotonic, concentric, isometric, dynamic variable.

Universal Machine

This multi-station apparatus may use a sliding fulcrum to alter the resistance of weight blocks. It duplicates most free weight exercises.

Nautilus

A cam compensates for the variations in muscular force at different joint angles by changing the lever arm. As a result, the muscles exert maximal or near maximal force throughout the full range of motion in both positive and negative phases of muscle contraction.

CAM II

The apparatus uses pneumatic, or air, resistance by means of compressed air and pneumatic cylinders.

Hydra Fitness

This machine offers accommodating resistance that controls the speed of movement by restricting the speed of movement of hydraulic fluid through a hydraulic cylinder.

Polaris

With the Polaris device the weight to be moved is drawn over an oval-shaped plate. The muscles can move through a full range of movement in both positive and negative phases of muscle contraction.

POWER EXERCISE EQUIPMENT

Power exercise devices are computerized and use artificial intelligence. They coach the individual through his or her workout, giving verbal encouragement and stating when an increase in resistance is needed.

As long as you follow the basic principles of strength training as explained in chapter 3, you may accomplish your goals with any type of equipment. Whatever you enjoy and find gives satisfaction, security, and confidence is appropriate.

Figure 17.1 PLYOMETRIC EXERCISE FOR LOWER EXTREMITY.

Figure 17.2 ARM ERGOMETER.

Figure 17.3 COMPUTERIZED EXERCISE BICYCLE.

Figure 17.4 TREADMILL.

Figure 17.5 STAIR-CLIMBING MACHINE.

Figure 17.6 CROSS-COUNTRY SKIING MACHINE.

Figure 17.7 EXERCISE BICYCLE.

Figure 17.8 RECUMBANT EXERCISE BICYCLE.

Figure 17.9 VERSA-CLIMBER.

Review Questions

1. What is the difference between an isokinetic machine and a hydraulic plate machine?
2. What are the some of the advantages and disadvantages of resistance machines and free weights?
3. What are some of the safety concerns when using free weights?

References

Baechle, T. R. *Essentials of strength training and conditioning.* Human Kinetics, Champaign, IL, 1994.

Baechle, T. R., and R. Earle. *Weight training: A text written for the college student.* Creighton University, Omaha, NE, 1989.

Baechle, T. R., and B. R. Groves. *Weight training instruction: Steps to success.* Human Kinetics, Champaign, IL, 1994.

Baechle, T. R., and B. R. Groves. *Weight training steps to success.* Human Kinetics, Champaign, IL, 1993.

Fleck, Steven J., and William J. Kraemer. *Designing resistance training programs.* Human Kinetics, Champaign, IL, 1997.

Garhammer, J. *Sports illustrated strength training.* Harper & Row, New York, 1986.

Getchell, B. *Physical fitness: A way of life.* Prentice Hall, Englewood Cliffs, NJ, 1998.

Hoeger, W. K. *Life time fitness, physical fitness and wellness.* 2nd ed. Morton, Inglewood, CO, 1989.

Holloway, J., and T. R. Baechle. 1990. Strength training for female athletes. *Sports Medicine* 9(4):216–228.

Lombardi, V. P. *Beginning weight training: The safe and effective way.* Wm. C. Brown, Dubuque, IA, 1989.

McGlynn, George H. *Dynamics of fitness, a practical approach.* McGraw-Hill, Dubuque, IA, 1999.

Stone, M., and H. O'Bryant. *Weight training: A scientific approach.* Burgess International, Minneapolis, MN, 1987.

Weight Training Activities for Various Sports

Movement	Neck flexion and extension	Shoulder shrug	Military or overhead press	Behind the neck press	Upright rowing	Bent rowing	Lat machine	Triceps extension	Lateral arm raise	Bent-arm pullover	Biceps curl	Dumbbell curl	Bench press	Incline press	Parallel bar dip	Back hyperextension	Trunk extension	Weighted sit-ups	Hip flexion	Stiff-leg dead lift	Knee flexion	Knee extension	Squat	Hack squat	Toe raise
Baseball					×			×		×			×				×	×					×		
Basketball					×		×	×	×		×	×						×				×	×		×
Golf					×						×	×	×	×				×		×			×	×	
Gymnastics			×		×			×	×	×			×		×	×	×								
Football	×	×	×		×								×	×			×				×		×	×	
Soccer	×					×					×	×	×	×			×				×		×	×	
Rowing					×		×			×			×	×	×	×	×						×	×	
Tennis		×	×		×			×	×				×		×						×		×		
Wrestling	×		×				×	×					×	×	×	×	×						×	×	
Skiing		×			×			×	×				×		×	×	×						×	×	×
Hockey	×	×	×			×		×	×						×		×	×	×				×		
Backstroke		×		×	×		×	×							×			×				×		×	
Breaststroke		×					×	×		×			×			×		×		×				×	
Butterfly				×			×	×		×			×					×		×				×	
Freestyle		×			×	×		×		×			×		×	×		×						×	
Sprinting													×			×	×					×	×	×	×
Hurdling						×	×				×			×				×			×	×		×	×
Javelin		×	×					×		×			×					×			×	×		×	×
Long jump								×	×				×							×			×	×	
Distance running					×			×					×	×				×		×				×	×
Pole vault		×			×				×	×	×	×			×			×					×		
High jump									×	×			×	×				×					×	×	×
Discus and shot put		×						×			×	×	×				×	×					×	×	

Adapted from J. P. O'Shea, *Scientific Principles and Methods of Strength Fitness.* 1976. 2d. ed. McGraw-Hill Publishing Company.

appendix b

The far right column indicates the percentile ranking of each weight lifted. For example, a bench press of 125 pounds for an individual who weighs between 130 and 139 pounds would correspond to the 50 percentile. In other words, 50 percent of the individuals in the weight category pressed over 125 lbs and the remaining 50 percent pressed less than 125 lbs. The standard is based on 2,500 male college students.

Body Weight Class 120–129 lbs.

Sit-Up	Curl	Upright Rowing	Over-Head Press	Bench Press	Squat	Bent-Over Rowing	%
70	107.5	120	155	170	255	185	100
65	105	117.5	150	165	245	182.5	99.9
62.5	102.5	115	145	160	235	180	99.8
60	100	112.5	140	155	225	170	99.4
57.5	97.5	110	135	150	220	165	98.4
55	95	107.5	130	145	210	157.5	96.2
52.5	92.5	105	125	140	200	150	90.3
50	90	102.5	120	135	190	140	84.2
45	85	100	115	130	180	135	75.8
42.5	82.5	95	110	125	170	127.5	64.0
40	80	90	105	120	160	120	50.0
37.5	77.5	85	100	115	150	112.5	36.0
35	75	80	95	110	140	105	24.2
30	70	77.5	90	105	130	100	15.8
27.5	67.5	75	85	100	120	90	11.6
25	65	72.5	80	95	110	95	9.7
22.5	62.5	70	75	90	100	80	3.8
20	60	68.5	70	85	95	75	1.6
17.5	57.5	65	65	80	85	70	.2
15	55	62.5	60	75	75	65	.1
12.5	52.5	60	55	70	65	60	0

Body Weight Class 130–139 lbs.

Sit-Up	Curl	Upright Rowing	Over-Head Press	Bench Press	Squat	Bent-Over Rowing	%
70	112.5	125	165	175	265	150	100
65	110	122.5	160	170	255	145	99.9
62.5	107.5	120	155	165	245	142.5	99.8
60	105	117.5	150	160	235	140	99.4
57.5	102.5	115	145	155	230	135	98.4
55	100	112.5	140	150	220	130	96.2
52.5	97.5	110	135	145	210	125	90.3
50	95	107.5	130	140	200	120	84.2
45	90	105	125	135	190	117.5	75.8
42.5	87.5	100	120	130	180	115	64.0
40	85	95	115	125	170	110	50.0
37.5	82.5	92.5	110	120	160	105	36.0
35	80	90	105	115	150	102.5	24.2
30	75	85	100	110	140	100	15.8
27.5	72.5	80	95	105	130	95	11.6
25	70	77.5	90	100	120	90	9.7
22.5	67.5	75	85	95	110	85	3.8
20	65	72.5	80	90	105	80	1.6
17.5	60	70	75	85	95	75	.2
15	57.5	67.5	70	80	85	70	.1
12.5	55	65	65	75	80	65	0

Body Weight Class 140–149 lbs.

Sit-Up	Curl	Upright Rowing	Over-Head Press	Bench Press	Squat	Bent-Over Rowing	%
70	117.5	130	170	185	275	205	100
65	115	127.5	165	180	270	197.5	99.9
62.5	112.5	125	160	175	260	190	99.8
60	110	122.5	155	170	250	180	99.4
57.5	107.5	120	150	165	240	175	98.4
55	105	117.5	145	160	230	167.5	96.2
52.5	102.5	115	140	155	220	160	90.3
50	100	112.5	135	150	210	150	84.2
45	95	110	130	145	200	145	75.8
42.5	92.5	107.5	125	140	190	137.5	64.0
40	90	105	120	135	180	130	50.0
37.5	87.5	102.5	115	130	170	122.5	36.0
35	85	100	110	125	160	115	24.2
30	82.5	95	105	120	150	110	15.8
27.5	80	90	100	115	140	100	11.6
25	77.5	87.5	95	110	130	95	9.7
22.5	75	85	90	105	120	90	3.8
20	72.5	82.5	85	100	115	85	1.6
17.5	70	80	80	95	105	80	.2
15	67.5	77.5	75	90	100	75	.1
12.5	65	75	70	85	95	70	0

Body Weight Class 150–159 lbs.

Sit-Up	Curl	Upright Rowing	Over-Head Press	Bench Press	Squat	Bent-Over Rowing	%
75	122.5	135	175	195	290	210	100
72.5	120	132.5	170	190	285	202.5	99.9
70	117.5	130	165	185	275	195	99.8
65	115	127.5	160	180	267	185	99.4
62.5	112.5	125	155	175	255	180	98.4
60	110	122.5	150	170	245	172.5	96.2
57.5	107.5	120	145	165	235	165	90.3
55	105	117.5	140	160	225	155	84.2
50	100	115	135	155	215	150	75.8
47.5	97.5	112.5	130	150	205	142.5	64.0
45	95	110	125	145	195	135	50.0
42.5	92.5	107.5	120	140	185	127.5	36.0
40	90	105	115	135	175	120	24.2
35	85	102.5	110	130	165	115	15.8
32.5	82.5	100	105	125	155	105	11.6
30	80.5	97.5	100	120	145	100	9.7
27.5	77.5	95	92.5	115	135	95	3.8
25	75	92.5	90	110	125	90	1.6
20	72.5	90	85	105	120	85	.2
17.5	70	87.5	80	100	115	80	.1
15	67.5	85	75	95	110	75	0

Body Weight Class 160–169 lbs.

Sit-Up	Curl	Upright Rowing	Over-Head Press	Bench Press	Squat	Bent-Over Rowing	%
75	125	140	180	205	305	215	100
72.5	122.5	137.5	175	200	300	207.5	99.9
70	120	135	170	195	290	200	99.8
65	117.5	132.5	165	190	280	190	99.4
62.5	115	130	160	185	270	185	98.4
60	112.5	127.5	155	180	260	177.5	96.2
57.5	110	125	150	175	250	170	90.3
55	107.5	122.5	145	170	240	160	84.2
50	105	120	140	165	230	155	75.8
47.5	102.5	117.5	135	160	220	147.5	64.0
45	100	115	130	155	210	140	50.0
42.5	97.5	112.5	125	150	200	132.5	36.0
40	95	110	120	145	190	125	24.2
35	92.5	107.5	115	140	180	120	15.8
32.5	90	105	110	135	170	110	11.6
30	87.5	102.5	105	130	160	105	9.7
27.5	85	100	100	125	150	100	3.8
25	82.5	97.5	95	120	140	95	1.6
20	80	95	90	115	135	90	.2
17.5	77.5	92.5	85	110	130	85	.1
15	75	90	80	105	125	80	0

Body Weight Class 170–179 lbs.

Sit-Up	Curl	Upright Rowing	Over-Head Press	Bench Press	Squat	Bent-Over Rowing	%
75	124	145	185	215	315	220	100
72.5	122.5	142.5	180	210	310	212.5	99.9
70	120	140	175	205	300	205	99.8
65	117.5	137.5	170	200	290	195	99.4
62.5	115	135	165	195	280	190	98.4
60	112.5	132.5	160	190	270	182.5	96.2
57.5	110	130	155	185	260	175	90.3
55	107.5	127.5	150	180	250	165	84.2
50	105	125	145	175	240	160	75.8
47.5	102.5	122.5	140	170	235	152.5	64.0
45	100	120	135	165	225	145	50.0
42.5	97.5	117.5	130	160	215	137.5	36.0
40	95	115	125	155	205	130	24.2
35	92.5	112.5	120	150	195	125	15.8
30.5	90.5	110	115	145	185	115	11.6
30	87.5	107.5	110	140	175	110	9.7
27.5	85	105	105	135	165	105	3.8
25	82.5	102.5	100	130	155	100	1.6
20	80	100	95	125	150	95	.2
17.5	77.5	97.5	90	120	145	90	.1
15	75	95	85	115	140	85	0

Body Weight Class 180–189 lbs.

Sit-Up	Curl	Upright Rowing	Over-Head Press	Bench Press	Squat	Bent-Over Rowing	%
75	130	150	190	225	325	225	100
72.5	127.5	147.5	185	220	320	217.5	99.9
70	125	145	180	215	310	210	99.8
65	122.5	142.5	175	210	305	200	99.4
62.5	120	140	170	205	295	195	98.4
60	117.5	137.5	165	200	285	187.5	96.2
57.5	115	135	160	195	275	180	90.3
55	112.5	132.5	155	190	265	170	84.2
50	110	130	150	185	255	165	75.8
47.5	107.5	127.5	145	180	250	157.5	64.0
45	105	125	140	175	240	150	50.0
42.5	102.5	122.5	135	170	230	142.5	36.0
40	100	120	130	165	220	135	24.2
35	97.5	117.5	125	160	210	130	15.8
32.5	95	115	120	155	200	120	11.6
30	92.5	112.5	115	150	190	115	9.7
27.5	90	110	110	145	180	110	3.8
25	87.5	107.5	105	140	170	105	1.6
20	85	105	100	135	165	100	.2
17.5	82.5	102.5	95	130	155	95	.1
15	80	100	90	125	150	90	0

Body Weight Class 190 lbs.+

Sit-Up	Curl	Upright Rowing	Over-Head Press	Bench Press	Squat	Bent-Over Rowing	%
75	135	155	195	235	335	230	100
72.5	132.5	152.5	190	230	330	222.5	99.9
70	130	150	185	225	320	215	99.8
65	127.5	147.5	180	220	315	205	99.4
62.5	125	145	175	215	305	200	98.4
60	122.5	142.5	170	210	295	192.5	96.2
57.5	120	140	165	205	285	180	90.3
55	117.5	137.5	160	200	275	175	84.2
50	115	135	155	195	265	170	75.8
47.5	112.5	132.5	150	190	260	162.5	64.0
45	110	130	145	185	250	155	50.0
42.5	107.5	127.5	140	180	240	147.5	36.0
40	105	125	135	175	230	140	24.2
35	102.5	122.5	130	170	220	135	15.8
32.5	100	120	125	165	210	125	11.6
30	97.5	117.5	120	160	200	120	9.7
27.5	95	115	115	155	190	115	3.8
25	92.5	112.5	110	150	180	110	1.6
20	90	110	105	145	175	105	.2
17.5	87.5	107.5	100	140	165	100	.1
15	85	105	95	135	155	95	0

Source: Berger, R. A., *Weight Training Standards for Adult Males* (unpublished), Biokinetics Research Laboratory, Temple University, Philadelphia, PA.

appendix c

Universal Super Circuit

On the following two pages is a new high intensity program for athletes. It is designed to develop all four elements of fitness: strength, muscular endurance, cardiorespiratory endurance, and flexibility. It can be used for pre-season conditioning and is a quick way to get a thorough and balanced workout.

Important Notes

Be sure to consult your physician and obtain prior approval before engaging in this or any other strenuous training program.

Be sure to begin each exercise period by warming up and stretching to warm up the heart as well as the muscles.

The program shown on the following pages is meant to be performed on twelve Universal single-station machines, but can also be performed on a multi-station machine.

This program consists of alternating upper and lower body exercises: the aim is to reach target heart rate. See chapter 12.

Key to program: You do thirty seconds of aerobic conditioning (running in place, exercycle, jump rope, etc.) between each exercise station.

Procedures

1. How many reps? Fifteen to twenty
2. How many sets? One at each station
3. How many circuits? Three to five
4. How long at each station? Maximum thirty seconds
5. Intervals between stations. Thirty seconds of aerobic conditioning (run in place, jump rope, exercycle, etc.)
6. How much weight? Forty to 50 percent maximum for average person, 50 to 70 percent for conditioned athlete
7. How to determine working weight? Find out your maximum for one lift, take percent of that for working weight. Reevaluate every six to eight weeks.
8. Breathing: Exhale as weight goes up, inhale as weight comes down.
9. Intensity: Make your muscles contract explosively throughout the full range of motion to simulate natural resistance of athletic events.
10. Cooldown: Don't head for the showers until pulse, breathing, and perspiration are back to normal. Gradually decrease body movement, reversing the way you warmed up.

At each of the numbered stations do one set of fifteen to twenty reps. Maximum thirty seconds at each station. *In between* each station, do thirty seconds of aerobic conditioning. Do the circuit three to five times.

appendix d

Walking/Jogging Program for Cardiorespiratory Fitness

Fitness category	Starting level
"Very poor" to "poor"	1 to 2
"Average" to "good"	2 to 3
"Very good" to "excellent"	4 to 5
"Superior"	5 to 7

Level Exercise	Heart rate training effect level (intensity)	Frequency	Duration
1 Walk for 10 to 20 minutes	60%	3 days	2 to 4 weeks
2 Walk fast for 15 to 20 minutes	60%	3 days	2 to 4 weeks
3 Jog 100 yards and then walk 300 yards. Repeat four times. Add one repetition for each succeeding exercise session. When you reach eight repetitions, move to level 4. (approximately 30 minutes)	60%	3 days	2 to 3 weeks
4 Jog 200 yards and then walk 200 yards. Repeat four times. Add one repetition for each succeeding exercise session. When you reach eight repetitions, move to level 5. (approximately 28 minutes)	60%	3 to 4 days	2 to 3 weeks
5 Jog 400 yards and then walk 400 yards. Repeat four times. Add one repetition for each succeeding exercise session. When you reach eight repetitions, move to level 6. (approximately 26 minutes)	70%	3 to 4 days	2 to 3 weeks
6 Jog 800 yards and then walk 400 yards. Repeat four times. Add one repetition for every other exercise session. When you reach six repetitions, move to level 7. (approximately 22 minutes)	70%	3 to 5 days	2 to 3 weeks

Level Exercise	Heart rate training effect level (intensity)	Frequency	Duration
7 Jog 1,200 yards and then walk 600 yards. Repeat two times. Add one repetition for every other exercise session. When you reach four repetitions, move to level 8. (approximately 22 minutes)	70%	3 to 5 days	2 to 3 weeks
8 Jog 1 mile in 10 minutes and then walk 3 minutes. Then jog 1 mile again in 10 to 12 minutes.	70%	3 to 5 days	2 to 3 weeks
9 Jog 1 1/2 miles in 15 minutes and then walk 6 to 8 minutes. Then jog again 1 1/2 miles in 15 to 18 minutes.	70%	3 to 5 days	2 to 3 weeks
10 Jog 2 miles in 20 minutes.	70%	3 to 5 days	2 to 3 weeks
11 Jog 2 miles in 18 minutes.	70%	3 to 5 days	2 to 3 weeks
12 Jog 2 miles in 16 minutes.	70%	3 to 5 days	2 to 3 weeks
13 Jog 2 miles in 14 minutes.	70%	3 to 5 days	2 to 3 weeks
14 Continue at level 13 to maintain lifetime fitness.			

Source: From *Dynamics of Fitness: A Practical Approach* by George H. McGlynn. Copyright © 1987. Wm. C. Brown Publishers, Dubuque, Iowa.

appendix e

POST-SEASON	
Heavy training	3 weeks
Basic strength	2 weeks
Hypertrophy	2 weeks
Basic strength	3 weeks
Active Rest	2 weeks
OFF-SEASON	
Hypertrophy	2 weeks
Basic strength	5 weeks
Strength and power	3 weeks
Peaking	2 weeks
Active Rest	2 weeks
Sports Training Skills	10 weeks
Active Rest	1 week
IN-SEASON	
Maintenance	8–10 weeks
Active Rest	3 weeks

appendix f

Major Vitamins and Minerals

Vitamin	Major Function	Most Reliable Sources	Deficiency	Excess (Toxicity)
A	Maintains skin and other cells that line the inside of the body; bone and tooth development; growth; vision in dim light	Liver, milk, egg yolk, deep green and yellow fruits and vegetables	Night blindness; dry skin; growth failure	Headaches, nausea, loss of hair, dry skin, diarrhea
D	Normal bone growth and development	Exposure to sunlight; fortified dairy products; eggs and fish liver oils	"Rickets" in children—defective bone formation leading to deformed bones	Appetite loss, weight loss, failure to grow
E	Prevents destruction of polyunsaturated fats caused by exposure to oxidizing agents; protects cell membranes from destruction	Vegetable oils, some in fruits and vegetables, whole grains	Breakage of red blood cells leading to anemia	Nausea and diarrhea; interferes with vitamin K if vitamin D is also deficient. Not as toxic as other fat-soluble vitamins
K	Production of blood clotting substances	Green leafy vegetables; normal bacteria that live in intestines produce K that is absorbed	Increased bleeding time	
B–1 (Thiamin)	Needed for release of energy from carbohydrates, fats, and proteins	Cereal products, pork, peas, and dried beans	Lack of energy, nerve problems	
B–2 (Riboflavin)	Energy from carbohydrates, fats, and proteins	Milk, liver, fruits and vegetables, enriched breads and cereals	Dry skin, cracked lips	
B–3 (Niacin)	Energy from carbohydrates, fats, and proteins	Liver, meat, poultry, peanut butter, legumes, enriched breads and cereals	Skin problems, diarrhea, mental depression, and eventually death (rarely occurs in U.S.)	Skin flushing, intestinal upset, nervousness, intestinal ulcers
B–6	Metabolism of protein; production of hemoglobin	White meats, whole grains, liver, egg yolk, bananas	Poor growth, anemia	Severe loss of coordination from nerve damage
B–12	Production of genetic material; maintains central nervous system	Foods of animal origin	Neurological problems, anemia	

Vitamin	Major Function	Most Reliable Sources	Deficiency	Excess (Toxicity)
Folate (Folic acid)	Production of genetic material	Wheat germ, liver, yeast, mushrooms, green leafy vegetables, fruits	Anemia	
C (Ascorbic Acid)	Formation and maintenance of connective tissue; tooth and bone formation; immune function	Fruits and vegetables	"Scurvy" (rare); swollen joints, bleeding gums, fatigue, bruising	Kidney stones, diarrhea
Pantothenic acid	Energy from carbohydrates, fats, proteins	Widely found in foods	Not observed in humans under normal conditions	
Biotin	Use of fats	Widely found in foods	Rare under normal conditions	

Minerals of Major Concern

Mineral	Major Role	Most Reliable Sources	Deficiency	Excess
Calcium	Bone and tooth formation; blood clotting; muscle contraction; nerve function	Dairy products	May lead to osteoporosis	Calcium deposits in soft tissues
Phosphorus	Skeletal development; tooth formation	Meats, dairy products, and other protein-rich foods	Rarely seen	
Sodium	Maintenance of fluid balance	Salt (sodium chloride) added to foods and sodium containing preservatives		May contribute to the development of hypertension
Iron	Formation of hemoglobin; energy from carbohydrates, fats, and proteins	Liver and red meats, enriched breads and cereals	Iron-deficiency anemia	Can cause death in children from supplement overdose
Copper	Formation of hemoglobin	Liver, nuts, shellfish, cherries, mushrooms, whole grain breads and cereals	Anemia	Nausea and vomiting
Zinc	Normal growth and development	Seafood and meats	Skin problems, delayed development, growth problems	Interferes with copper use; may decrease HDL levels
Iodine	Production of the hormone thyroxin	Iodized salt, seafood	Mental growth and retardation; lack of energy	
Fluorine	Strengthens bones and teeth	Fluoridated water	Teeth are less resistant to decay	Damage to tooth enamel

appendix g

1. Transitional 4 weeks

No formal or structured workouts. Activity consists of recreational sports and low-volume, low-intensity fitness activities such as swimming, jogging, tennis, basketball.

2. Preparatory Period 16–18 weeks

    a. Weeks 1 through 6

Strength Training

Mon.	3–5 sets	at	8–12 RM
Wed.	3–5 sets	at	8–12 repetitions at 75–80% of RM
Fri.	3–5 sets	at	8–12 repetitions at 75–80% of RM

Endurance   swimming, jogging, rowing, cycling, etc.

Tues.	25–30 min. aerobic activity
Thurs.	25–30 min. aerobic activity

    b. Week 7 Unloading Week

Reduce volume and load from previous week by at least 25% in order to prepare for the next phase.

    c. Weeks 8 through 12 Strength Phase

Should participate in flexibility training before and after workout as part of warm-up and cooldown.

Strength Training

Mon.	3–5 sets	5 RM
Wed.	3–5 sets	5–6 repetitions at 80–95% RM
Fri.	3–5 sets	5–6 repetitions at 80–95% RM
Tues.	20–30 min. skilled drills, sprinting, and plyometrics	
Thurs.	20–30 min. skilled drills, sprinting, and plyometrics	

    d. Week 13 Unloading

Reduce volume at least 25% from previous week; prepare for next phase.

    e. Week 14 through 16 Power Phase

Flexibility training same as 8th through 12th week

Strength Training

Mon.	3–5 sets	2 RM to 4 RM
Wed.	3–5 sets	2 repetitions at 70–90% of 2–4 RM
Fri.	3–5 sets	2 repetitions at 70–90% of 2–4 RM
Tues.	Practice skills	
Thurs.	Practice skills	

Week 17   Unloading

Recover from intense training; light activities.

Week 18   5–10% increase

Transitional Phase 2 weeks, no formal workout

Preparatory Phase

Weeks 19 through 28

19th and 20th week

Flexibility Training Before and after workout as part of warm-up and cooldown.

Strength Training

Mon.	3–5 sets	8–12 repetitions at 70% of 1 RM
Wed.	3–5 sets	8–12 repetitions at 60% of 1 RM
Fri.	3–5 sets	8–12 repetitions at 50% of 1 RM

Weeks 21 through 22

Mon.	3–5 sets	8–12 repetitions at 85% of 1 RM
Wed.	3–5 sets	8–12 repetitions at 80% of 1 RM
Fri.	3–5 sets	8–12 repetitions at 70% of 1 RM
Tues.	20–25 min. anaerobic or aerobics depending on activity	
Thurs.	20–25 min. anaerobic or aerobics depending on activity	

Week 23   Unloading

Strength Training

Mon.	1–3 sets	2–4 repetitions at 80% of 1 RM
Wed.	1–3 sets	2–4 repetitions at 70% of 1 RM
Fri.	1–3 sets	2–4 repetitions at 60% of 1 RM

Week 24 through 27

Mon.	3–5 sets	2–4 repetitions at 95% of 1 RM
Wed.	3–5 sets	2–4 repetitions at 80% of 1 RM
Fri.	3–5 sets	2–4 repetitions at 70% of 1 RM

Week 28

Mon.	1–2 sets	1 RM
Wed.	1–2 sets	1 RM
Fri.	1–2 sets	1 repetition at 70% of 1 RM

Pre-Season

Transition Weeks 29 through 30

Preparatory Phase   Weeks 31 through 37

Week 31 through 32

| Mon. | 1–3 sets | 8–10 repetitions at 70% of 1 RM |
| Thurs. | 1–3 sets | 8–10 repetitions at 75% of 1 RM |

Week 33

Mon.	1–3 sets	5–6 repetitions at 85% of 1 RM
Thurs.	1–3 sets	5–6 repetitions at 80% of 1 RM

Week 34

Mon.	1–3 sets	2–4 repetitions at 90% of 1 RM
Thurs.	1–3 sets	2–4 repetitions at 80% of 1 RM

Week 35

Mon.	1–3 sets	2–4 repetitions at 95% of 1 RM
Thurs.	1–3 sets	2–4 repetitions at 80% of 1 RM

Week 36

Mon.	1–3 sets	1 RM
Thurs.	1–3 sets	1 RM

Competition

Week 37 to End of Competition

Week 37

1 set	10 repetitions at 75% of 1 RM

Week 38

1 set	5–6 repetitions at 80% of 1 RM

Week 39

1 set	5–6 repetitions at 85% of 1 RM

Week 40

1 set	2–4 repetitions at 90% of 1 RM

Week 41

1 set	2–4 repetitions at 95% of 1 RM

Week 42

1 set	2–4 repetitions at 95% of 1 RM

Week 43

1 set	2–4 repetitions at 95% of 1 RM

Week 44

1 set	2–4 repetitions at 95% of 1 RM

Week 45

1 set	2–4 repetitions at 100% of 1 RM

Adapted from Dan Wathen, Periodization, concepts and applications, in *Essentials of Strength Training and Conditioning*, ed. Thomas R. Baechle. (Champaign, IL: Human Kinetics, 1994).

appendix h

Web Sites

Chapter 1   The American College of Sports Medicine: *http://www.acsm.org/*
American Sports Medicine Institute: *http://www.nata.org*

Chapter 3   National Fitness Leaders Association: *http://wellness.uwsp.edu/nfla*

Chapter 4   IDEA, Health and Fitness Council: *http://www.ideafit.com/*

Chapter 5   Exercise and Sport Psychology: *http://www.psyc.unt.edu/apadiv47*

Chapter 6   Health and Fitness World Guide Forum: *http://www.worldguide.com/ fitness/nf.html*

Chapter 7   American Society of Exercise Physiologists:
http://www.css.edu/users/tboone2/asep/toc.htm
University of California Muscle Physiology Home Page:
http://www.neuromus.ucsd.edu/home.htm

Chapter 8   National Association of Strength Training: *http://www.nsca-cc.org/*

Chapter 9   American Council on Exercise: *http://www.acefitness.org/*
World National Sports Organization: *http://www.worldnationalsports.com/*

Chapter 11   Women's Sports Foundation: *http://www.lifetimetv.com/wosport/index.htm*

Chapter 12   American Heart Association: *http://www.amhrt.org*
The Physician and Sports Medicine: *http://www.physsportsmed.com*
Aerobic and Fitness Association of America: *http://webs.coolsite.com/afaa/*

Chapter 13   Stretching and Flexibility: Everything You Wanted to Know:
http://www.cs.huji.ac.il/papers/rma/stretching_toc.ntml

Chapter 14   Athletic Trainer.com: *http://athletictrainer.com/*

Chapter 15   Food and Nutrition Information Center: *http://www.nalusda.gov/fnic*
American Dietetic Association: *http://www.eatright.org*

Chapter 16   Online Pharmacology: *http://www.pharmacology.com/phatyme.htm*

appendix i

The Recommended Quantity and Quality of Exercise for Developing and Maintaining Cardiorespiratory and Muscular Fitness, and Flexibility in Healthy Adults

Cardiorespiratory Fitness and Body Composition

1. Frequency of training: 3–5 d·wk^{-1}.

2. Intensity of training: 55/65%–90% of maximum heart rate (HR$_{max}$), or 40/50%–85% of maximum oxygen uptake reserve ($\dot{V}O_2R$) or HR$_{max}$ reserve (HRR).[1] The lower intensity values, i.e., 40–49% of $\dot{V}O_2R$ or HRR and 55–64% of HR$_{max}$, are most applicable to individuals who are quite unfit.

3. Duration of training: 20–60 min of continuous or intermittent (minimum of 10-min bouts accumulated throughout the day) aerobic activity. Duration is dependent on the intensity of the activity; thus, lower-intensity activity should be conducted over a longer period of time (30 min or more), and, conversely, individuals training at higher levels of intensity should train at least 20 min or longer. Because of the importance of "total fitness" and that it is more readily attained with exercise sessions of longer duration and because of the potential hazards and adherence problems associated with high-intensity activity, moderate-intensity activity of longer duration is recommended for adults not training for athletic competition.

---

[1]Maximum heart rate reserve (HRR) and maximum $\dot{V}O_2$ reserve ($\dot{V}O_2R$) are calculated from the difference between resting and maximum heart rate and resting and maximum $\dot{V}O_2$, respectively. To estimate training intensity, a percentage of this value is added to the resting heart rate and/or resting $\dot{V}O_2$ and is expressed as a percentage of HRR (127) of $\dot{V}O_2R$ (236)

4. Mode of activity: any activity that uses large muscle groups, which can be maintained continuously, and is rhythmical and aerobic in nature, e.g., walking-hiking, running-jogging, cycling-bicycling, cross-country skiing, aerobic dance/group exercise[2] (213), rope skipping, rowing, stair climbing, swimming, skating, and various endurance game activities or some combination thereof.

Muscular Strength and Endurance, Body Composition, and Flexibility

1. Resistance training: Resistance training should be an integral part of an adult fitness program and of a sufficient intensity to enhance strength, muscular endurance, and maintain fat-free mass (FFM). Resistance training should be progressive in nature, individualized, and provide a stimulus to all the major muscle groups. One set of 8–10 exercises that conditions the major muscle groups 2–3 d·wk^{-1} is recommended. Multiple-set regimens may provide greater benefits if time allows. Most persons should complete 8–12 repetitions of each exercise; however, for older and more frail persons (approximately 50–60 yr of age and above), 10–15 repetitions may be more appropriate.

2. Flexibility training: Flexibility exercises should be incorporated into the overall fitness program sufficient to develop and maintain range of motion (ROM). These exercises should stretch the major muscle groups and be performed a minimum of 2–3 d·wk^{-1}. Stretching should include appropriate static and/or dynamic techniques.

From Feigenbaum, Matthew S., and Pollock, Michael L.: Prescription of Resistance Training for Health and Disease, *Medicine and Science in Sports and Exercise*, Jan.–June 31, 1999, p. 39. Used with permission.

credits

Photographs

George H. McGlynn and Gary T. Moran

Photo Reproduction

Agfa Gevaert

Models

Barbara Gaenslen, George C. McGlynn, Pernella Alser, and Bacari Harris

Locations

Mariner Square Athletic Club
Alameda, CA
University of San Francisco
San Francisco, CA

Artwork

Chapter 7

Shier, D., et al.: Hole's Human Anatomy and Physiology. *8th ed. St. Louis: McGraw-Hill, 1999.*

Chapter 10

Thompson, C.W., and Floyd, R.T.: Manual of Structural Kinesiology. *13th ed. St. Louis: McGraw-Hill, 1998.*

Arnheim, D.D., and Prentice, W.E.: Principles of Athletic Training. *10th ed. St. Louis: McGraw-Hill, 2000.*

index

Note: Page numbers in *italics* refer to figures; page numbers followed by *t* refer to tables.

A

A-bands, 56
Abdomen skinfold measurement, *51*
Abdominals
    exercises for, *61t, 93–96*
    location of, *92*
Acetaminophen, 136
Actin, *57*
Activities, energy cost of, 116*t*
Acute adaptations, 4
Adaptations, 4
Adductor brevis
    exercises for, *101*
    location of, *97*
    stretching, *130*
Adductor longus
    exercises for, *101*
    location of, *57, 97*
    stretching, *130*
Adductor magnus
    exercises for, *101*
    location of, *58, 97*
    stretching, *130*
Adolescents, 6, 23
Advanced training programs, 71–77
Aerobic exercise
    alternating with strength
        training, 29, 30
    cardiorespiratory endurance
        and, 10, 114
    fuel for, 115, 141
    running program for, 171–72
Age
    exercise and, 5–6, 22–23
    heart rate and, 49–50
Agonists, 58–59
All-or-none principle, 16
Amenorrhea, 109, 110
American College of Sports
    Medicine

exercise prescriptions, 120, 180
    position on steroids, 148–49
Amphetamines, 149
Anabolic steroids, 108, 147–49
Anaerobic exercise, 114, 115, 141
Androstenedione, 151
Antagonists, 23–24, 58–59
Anti-inflammatories, 136
Application of force, 22
Arm ergometers, *157*
Arms
    exercises for, *89–91*
    stretching, *125, 126, 127*
Aspirin, 136
ATP
    as energy source, 115
    role in contraction, 56–58
    sources of, 141
ATPase, 56
Atrophy, 59
Attention, 38

B

Back
    exercises for, 26, *93–96*
    stretching, *126, 129,*
        130, 131
Back hyperextensions, 26, *96*
Back positioning, 25
Balance, of muscle
    development, 23–24
Ballistic stretching, 124
Banned substances, 150
Barbells, 155
Behavior change, 36–37
Belts, 26
Bench press
    cheating on, 26–27
    one-RM test for, *42,* 43*t*
    procedure for, *83, 84*

Bent rowing, *85*
Beta-adrenergic agonists, 152
Biceps brachii
    exercises for, 61*t, 89*
    location of, *57, 88*
Biceps curl
    cheating on, 27
    one-RM test for, 43*t, 44*
    procedure for, *89*
Biceps femoris
    exercises for, *103*
    location of, *58, 98*
Biodex, 156
Bodybuilding
    benefits of, 3
    defined, 2
    programs for, 17, 30–32, 72
Body composition
    evaluating, 51–54
    obesity and, 11
    in women *versus*
        men, 107, 108–9
Body mass index, *53,* 54
Body weight
    gain and loss of, 144–45
    weight training standards
        for, 161–68
Bones
    effects of strength training
        on, 108
    loss with age, 5, 108, 110
Boran, 150
Bounds, 75
Brachialis
    exercises for, 61*t, 89*
    location of, *57, 58, 88*
Brachioradialis, *57, 58*
Breathing, 23, 24
Burnouts, 72
Bursitis, 135
Butazone, 136

C

Caffeine, 149
Calcaneal tendon, *58*
Calcium, 175
Calcium supplements, 110
Caloric needs, 139*t*
CAM II, 157
Carbohydrates, 139–40, 144
Cardiorespiratory endurance
    fitness and, 10, 113–21
    tests for, 48–51
    training programs for, 118,
      119*t*, 171–72
Carnitine, 152
1–carnitine, 150
Cheating, 26–27, 66
Chest
    exercises for, *83–84*
    stretching, *127*
Chest skinfold measurement, *51*
Childbirth, 109
Chromium, 152
Chronic adaptations, 4
Chronic hypertrophy, 59
Circuit training, 119
Cocaine, 150
Cold packs, 137
Commitment, 36
Compression, 136
Concentration, 38
Conditioning, defined, 2. *See also*
    Fitness; Strength training
Contractions
    all-or-none principle, 16
    cellular processes, 56–58
    energy for, 115, 141
    types of, 65–66
Contract-relax, 124
Cooldowns, 24, 118
Copper, 175
Cortisone, 136
Creatine, 151–52
Cross-country skiing machines, *158*
Cross sectional area, 65
Crunches, *94*
Curls, 61*t*, *89, 90, 91*
Cybex 600, 156
Cybex Knee Extension
    machines, 156
Cycling, 76*t*, 77, 176–78

D

Dead lifts, 26
Declined bench press, *84*

Deltoid

    exercises for, 61*t*, *86, 87*
    location of, *57, 58, 82*
DHEA, 151
Dietary guidelines, 139–45
Dietary supplements,
    142–44, 150–51
Diets, 141–44
Dislocations, 135
Dropping out, 35–36
Drugs, 108, 147–52
Duration
    cardiorespiratory fitness and,
      117, 120, 180
    defined, 18
Dynamic flexibility, 10

E

Eating disorders, 110–11
Eccentric loading, 65, 67, 73
Elderly people, 5–6, 22–23
Elevation, 136
Endomysium, 55
Endurance (cardiorespiratory). *See*
    Cardiorespiratory endurance
Endurance (muscular)
    defined, 2, 10
    fitness and, 10
    importance of, 15
    programs for, 30, 31*t*
    tests for, 43*t*, 45–46, 47*t*
    training programs for, 18*t*, 20
Energy systems, 115, 141
Epimysium, 55
Equipment, 26, 155–57, *158*
Erector spinae
    exercises for, 61*t*, *96*
    location of, *93*
Ergometers, *157, 158*
Erythropoietin, 150
Evaluation
    body composition, 51–54
    cardiorespiratory
      endurance, 48–51
    flexibility, 47–48
    muscular endurance,
      43*t*, 45–46, 47*t*
    strength, 41–45
Exercise amenorrhea, 109
Exercise bicycles, *157, 158*
Exercise dependence, 35–36
Exercise precautions, 121
Exercise prescription, 120, 180
Exhalation, 24
Extensor digitorum longus, *57*

External oblique

    exercises for, 61*t*
    location of, *57, 58, 92*

F

Fad diets, 144
Fasciculi, 55
Fast-twitch fibers, 59
Fat
    dietary, 140, 144
    tests for, 51–54
    in women *versus* men,
      107, 108–9
Fatigue fractures, 135
Female athlete triad, 110
Fitness
    cardiorespiratory, 10, 113–21
    elements of, 9–11
    programs for, 29–30, 171–72, 180
    training and, 4
Flexibility
    fitness and, 10–11
    importance of, 123
    misconceptions about, 1
    range of motion and, 24
    tests for, 47–48
Flexor carpi
    exercises for, 61*t*, *91*
    location of, *88*
Fluorine, 175
Focus, 38
Food Guide Pyramid, *143*
Foot positioning, 24–25
Forced repetition, 72
Forearm curls, *91*
Four-way hip extension, *101*
Fractures, 135
Fraudulent claims, 142, 150–51
Free weights, 155, 156
Frequency
    cardiorespiratory fitness and,
      117–18, 120, 180
    defined, 18
    of weight training, 21
Frontalis, *57*
Fuels, 115, 141
Full squats, 26

G

Gastrocnemius
    exercises for, 61*t*, *103, 105*
    location of, *57, 58, 98*
    stretching, *129*
Gemelli, *96*
Gender differences, 107–9

General adaptation syndrome, 75
Gloves, 26
Gluteus maximus
    exercises for, 61*t*, *99*, *101*
    location of, *58*, *96*
    stretching, *130*, *131*
Gluteus medius
    exercises for, *99*, *101*, *102*
    location of, *58*, *96*
    stretching, *130*, *131*
Gluteus minimus
    exercises for, *99*, *101*, *102*
    location of, *96*
    stretching, *130*, *131*
Glycogen, 115
Goal-setting, 36–37
Gracilis
    exercises for, *101*
    location of, *57*, *58*, *97*
Growth hormones, 149
Growth spurts, 6

H

Half squats, 26, *99*
Hamstrings
    exercises for, 61*t*, *99*, *103*
    location of, *98*
    stretching, *128*, *129*, *130*
Head-and-shoulder raise, 46, 47*t*
Head positioning, 25
Heart rate, 49–50, 115–16
Heat baths, 137
Hip abduction, *102*
Hip flexion, *100*
Hip flexors, stretching, *131*
HMB, 152
Hops, 75
Hormones, 108, 149
Hydra Fitness, 157
Hyperplasia, 60
Hypertrophy, 59–60, 108
Hypertrophy phase, 75, 76

I

Ibuprofen, 136
Ice packs, 137
Iliac crest, *92*
Iliac crest skinfold
    measurement, *51*
Iliacus, *96*
Iliopsoas
    exercises for, *100*
    location of, *97*
    stretching, *131*
Imagery, 38

Inclined dumbbell fly, *83*
Individuality principle, 16
Infraspinatus, *58*
Inguinal canal, *92*
Inhalation, 24
Injuries, 133–37. *See also* Safety
    rules
In-season training, 76*t*, 77, 173
Intensity
    cardiorespiratory fitness and,
        115, 120, 180
    classifying, 117*t*
    defined, 18
    establishing, 19
Internal oblique, *92*
IOC banned substances, 150
Iodine, 175
Iron, 144, 175
Isokinetic exercise
    advantages and disadvantages,
        67–68
    equipment for, 155, 156–57
    overview of, 66
Isometric exercise, 65–66, 67
Isotonic exercise, 65, 67

J

Jogging/walking program, 171–72
Joints, flexibility of.
    See Flexibility
Jumping exercises, 73–74

K

Kin-Com 125E, 156
Kin-Com 500H, 156
Kinesthetic feedback, 63
Knee problems, 108, 134

L

Lactic acid, 115
Lateral pull down, *86*
Latissimus dorsi
    exercises for, 61*t*, *86*
    location of, *57*, *58*, *81*, *92*
Leg extensions, *102*
Leg flexion, *103*
Leg press, *42*, 43*t*, *100*
Length, strength and, 65
Lido, 156
Lifting speed, 22
Ligaments, 59, 134–35
Linea alba, *92*
Long-term goals, 37
Lower back exercises, 26, *93–96*

M

Macrocycles, 75
Masseter, *57*
Maximum oxygen uptake, 113–14
Maximum strength, 9
Menstruation, 109
Mental preparation, 37
Merac, 156
Mesocycles, 75, 76*t*, 173
Microcycles, 75
1.5 mile run, 48, 49*t*
Milo of Greece, 22
Minerals, 140, 142–44, 175
Mini-Gyms, 156
Modified sit-and-reach test, 47–48
Motivation, 35–39
Motor units, 64
Multi-poundage system, 72
Muscle(s)
    agonists and antagonists,
        23–24, 58–59
    exercise-induced changes, 59–61
    injuries to, 133–37
    loss with age, 5
    structure of, 55–58
Muscle-boundness, 1
Muscle endurance. *See* Endurance
    (muscular)
Muscle fibers, 16, 55–58, 59–60
Muscle groups, 23
Muscle soreness, 60–61
Muscle strength. *See* Strength;
    Strength development;
    Strength training
Myofibrils, 56
Myosin, *57*
Myosin cross bridges, 56–58

N

Nautilus, 157
Neck muscles, stretching, *128*
Negative work, 73
Nerve impulses, 64–65
Nervous system, effects of strength
    training on, 22
Neuromuscular facilitation, 64
Neurons, 64
Nomograms, *52*, *53*
Nutrition guidelines, 139–45

O

Obesity, 11
Obliques, stretching, *126*, *127*
Obturators, *96*

Occipitalis, *58*
Off-season training, 76*t*, 77, 173
One-repetition maximum
    tests, 41–45
Orbicularis oculi, *57*
Orbicularis oris, *57*
Osteoporosis, 110
Overload principle
    defined, 16, 21–22
    strength development and, 64, 65
Overtraining, 118, 133
Oxygen, 115, 141. *See also* Aerobic
    exercise

P

Partial repetitions, 72
Peaking phase, 75, 76
Pec deck machine, *84*
Pectineus, *97, 101*
Pectoralis major
    exercises for, 61*t*, *83–84, 87*
    location of, *57, 79, 92*
Perimysium, 55
Periodization, 75
Peroneus longus, *57, 58*
Phosphocreatine, 115, 151
Phosphorus, 175
Physical Activity Readiness
    Questionnaire (rPAR-Q), 120*t*
Piriformis, *96*
Plyometrics, 73–75, *157*
Polaris, 157
Positive self-thoughts, 38*t*, 39
Power
    defined, 2, 11, 63, 73
    speed and, 63, 73
Power exercise equipment, 157
Power lifting, 2, 18*t*
Power phase, 75, 76
Pre-exercise screening, 119–20
Pregnancy, 109
Preseason training, 76*t*, 77
Press, *86*
Prime movers, 23–24, 58–59
Principles of strength training, 16
Progressive resistance exercise, 22
Proprioceptive neuromuscular
    facilitation (PNF), 124
Proteins, 140, 142, 144
Psoas major, *96*
Psoas minor, *96*
Puberty, 6
Pumping, 17
Push-ups, 45, 46*t*
Pyramid system, 71

Q

Quadriceps
    exercises for, 61*t*, *99, 100, 102*
    location of, *97*
    stretching, *126, 127*

R

Racquet sports mesocycle, 173
Range of motion, 24
Recharging, of myosin cross
    bridges, 58
Rectus abdominis
    exercises for, *93*
    location of, *57, 92*
Rectus femoris
    location of, *57, 97*
    stretching, *131*
Recumbent exercise bicycles, *158*
Red fibers, 59
Rehabilitation, 2, 137, 155
Repetition maximum test, 20–21
Repetitions, 19, 20
Resistance machines, 155–56
Resistance training. *See* Strength
    training
Rest, 117–18, 133, 136
Revised Physical Activity Readiness
    Questionnaire (rPAR-Q), 120*t*
Rhomboids
    exercises for, 61*t*, *85*
    location of, *58, 79*
R.I.C.E., 136
Rotators, stretching, *125, 128*
Runner's knee, 134
Running program, 171–72

S

Safety rules, 25–27. *See also* Injuries
SAID principle, 4
Sarcomeres, 56
Sarcoplasm, 56
Sarcoplasmic reticulum, 56
Sartorius, *57, 58*
Sciatic nerve, *96*
Screening, 119–20
Seated alternate dumbbell
    curls, *89*
Seated bar twists, *95*
Seated pulley rows, *85*
Seated triceps dumbbell curls, *90*
Self-assessment. *See* Evaluation
Semimembranosus
    exercises for, *103*
    location of, *58, 98*

Semitendinosus
    exercises for, *103*
    location of, *58, 98*
Serratus anterior
    exercises for, 61*t*
    location of, *57, 92*
Sets
    guidelines for, 19, 20, 21
    single *versus* multiple, 72
    strength increases and, *17*
Sex differences, 107–9
Shocks, 75
Shoes, 26
Short-term goals, 37
Shoulder dips, *87*
Shoulder girdle, stretching,
    126, 127, 128
Shoulder press, 43*t*, *44*
Side bend with dumbbell, *95*
Side effects, 148*t*
Single set systems, 72
Sit-ups
    procedure for, *93, 94*
    safety rules for, 26
Size training programs, 18*t*
Skeletal muscle. *See* Muscle(s)
Skinfold tests, 51–53
Slow-twitch fibers, 59
Sodium, 175
Soleus
    exercises for, 61*t*, *103, 105*
    location of, *57, 58, 99*
Soreness, 60–61
Specificity principle, 16, 22
Speed
    guidelines for, 22
    importance of, 63
    power and, 63, 73
Split-routine, 73
Sports, energy cost of, 116*t*
Sports training. *See also* Training
    programs
    aerobic *versus* anaerobic
      requirements, *114*
    programs for, 17–18, 29–30, 160,
      173, 176–78
Sprains, 134–35
Squats, 26
Stair-climbing machines, *158*
Staleness, 133–34
Standing jumps, 75
Static flexibility, 11, 124
Static stretching, 124
Sternocleidomastoid, *57, 58*
Steroid replacers, 150
Steroids, 108, 147–49

Strains, 134–35
Strength
　defined, 2, 9, 63
　effect of overload on, 64
　nerves' role in, 64–65
　size and, 65
　women *versus* men, 107
Strength development
　benefits of, 2
　fitness and, 9
　tests for, 41–45
　training programs for, 18*t*, 20, 30,
　　31*t*, 119*t*
Strength phase, 75, 76
Strength training. *See also* Weight
　　training
　advanced techniques, 71–77
　aging and, 5–6
　benefits of, 2, 3*t*, 4–5
　equipment for, 26, 155–57, *158*
　general guidelines for, 16,
　　23–26, 39
　misconceptions about, 1
　motivation and, 35–39
　program goals, 16–18
　safety and, 25–26
　for specific sports, 160 (*see also*
　　Sports training)
　for youth, 6, 23
Stretching
　benefits of, 11
　principles of, 124–25
　techniques for, *125–31*
Stretch-shortening cycle, 73
Stroke volume, 113–14
Super circuit, 169–70
Super-protein diets, 142
Super pump system, 72
Super sets, 30, 72
Supplements, 142–44, 150–51

T

Target heart rate, 115–16
Temporalis, *58*
Tendinitis, 134
Tendons
　function of, 55, 59
　injuries to, 134–35
Tensor fasciae latae, *57*

Teres major
　exercises for, *85*
　location of, *58, 80*
Teres minor
　exercises for, *85*
　location of, *58, 80*
Testosterone, 108
Tests. *See* Evaluation
Thigh skinfold measurement, *51*
Threshold effect, 115
Tibialis anterior, *57*
Toe raise, *103, 104*
Training concepts, 63–68
Training effects, 115–16
Training programs
　ACSM prescription, 120, 180
　advanced, 71–77
　basic types, 65–68
　by body weight, 161–68
　for elderly people and youth,
　　22–23
　goals of, 16–18
　guidelines for, 19–22
　racquet sports, 173
　by sport, 160
　volleyball example, 176–78
Transient hypertrophy, 59
Transversus abdominis, *92, 95*
Trapezius
　exercises for, 61*t*, *86, 87*
　location of, *57, 58, 82*
Treadmills, *158*
Tricep pulldowns, *91*
Tricep pullovers, *90*
Triceps brachii
　exercises for, 61*t*, *90, 91*
　location of, *58, 88*
Triceps skinfold
　　measurement, *51*
Trisets, 72
Tropomyosin, 56, *57*
Troponin, 56, *57*

U

Umbilicus, *92*
Universal machines, 157,
　　169–70
Upright rowing, *87*
Use and disuse principle, 16

V

Valsalva maneuver, 24
Vanadium, 152
Vastus intermedius, *97*
Vastus lateralis, *57, 58, 97*
Vastus medialis, *57, 97*
Versa-Climbers, *158*
Visualization, 38
Vitamins, 140, 142–44,
　　174–75
Volleyball training
　　cycle, 176–78

W

Walking/jogging
　　program, 171–72
Walking test, 48, 49*t*
Warm-ups, 24, 124–25
Water, 140
Web sites, 179
Weight gain and loss, 144–45
Weight lifting, 2
Weight rack, *86*
Weight training. *See also* Strength
　　training
　benefits of, 2, 3*t*
　defined, 2
　equipment for, 26, 155–57, *158*
　general guidelines for, 23–26
　initial settings for, 19–20
　methods summarized, 18*t*
　recommended frequency, 21
　safety and, 25–26
　for specific sports, 160
　standards for college-age
　　males, 161–68
White fibers, 59
Women, 107–9

Y

Youth, 6, 23

Z

Zinc, 175
Z-lines, 56
Zygomaticus, *57*

Weight Training Record Card

Before

Name _____

Class _____

Weight	
Weight	
Right Bicep	
Left Bicep	
Chest Inf.	
Chest Def.	
Abdominal Girth	
Right Thigh	
Left Thigh	
Hip	

Dates																	
Exercises		R	W	R	W	R	W	R	W	R	W	R	W	R	W	R	W
	1																
	2																
	3																
	1																
	2																
	3																
	1																
	2																
	3																
	1																
	2																
	3																
	1																
	2																
	3																
	1																
	2																
	3																
	1																
	2																
	3																

Weight Training Record Card

Name _____

Class _____

After

Weight	
Right Bicep	
Left Bicep	
Chest Inf.	
Chest Def.	
Abdominal Girth	
Right Thigh	
Left Thigh	
Hip	

Dates			R	W	R	W	R	W	R	W	R	W	R	W	R	W	R	W
Exercises																		
	1																	
	2																	
	3																	
	1																	
	2																	
	3																	
	1																	
	2																	
	3																	
	1																	
	2																	
	3																	
	1																	
	2																	
	3																	
	1																	
	2																	
	3																	
	1																	
	2																	
	3																	